BERTIE

Power and Money

BERTIE

Power and Money

COLM KEENA

Gill & Macmillan

Gill & Macmillan
Hume Avenue, Park West, Dublin 12
with associated companies throughout the world
www.gillmacmillan.ie

© Colm Keena 2011
978 0 7171 5069 4

Index compiled by Kate Murphy
Typography design by Make Communication
Print origination by Síofra Murphy
Printed by ScandBook AB, Sweden

This book is typeset in Minion 11.25/14 pt.

The paper used in this book comes from the wood pulp
of managed forests. For every tree felled, at least one
tree is planted, thereby renewing natural resources.

A CIP catalogue record for this book is available from
the British Library.

5 4 3 2 1

For Bernie, Seamus, Breda, Caitriona and Declan

CONTENTS

PART ONE

2006

Chapter 1 ∿

| SCOOP

A newspaper reporter's work is like that of a firefighter, in that there are periods when the reporter has to be there, just in case. During such dull periods the newspaper still has to be filled, and reporters can be assigned to write up reports about matters that are of little general interest. A way of escaping from the more tedious aspects of the job is to generate your own news, or scoops, since reporters who can do so win a little freedom from the line editors to whom they report, and with a bit of luck they can make their lives more interesting.

On the morning of 19 September 2006 I arrived at work on what looked as if it was going to be a quiet news day. The *Irish Times* was still in D'Olier Street, in a terrace of old buildings that had been connected to each other over time by the knocking of holes in their walls, creating a complex whole whose full details were known only to a select few. If you were going to the canteen and strayed from your normal route you could get lost in a warren of linoleum-covered staircases and bizarrely connected hallways.

I entered by the so-called works entrance in Fleet Street, climbed to the newsroom on the second floor and walked through it to a smaller room at the back that had once been the men's toilets but was now the business and finance section. It looked onto the dull brick wall of the building opposite, through the broken windows of which pigeons flew in and out. There was little by way of natural light.

At that period much of my section's work consisted of reporting on the phenomenal and seemingly never-ending growth of the Irish economy, and on the astonishing wealth that had been accumulated by business owners and investors over the previous decade or more. Every week there was yet another startling story about a killing made through the sale of assets, or about the latest purchase made by the Irish leviathans who were busy buying the choicest properties in the Western world. There was an air of unreality about the stories which created their interest while at the same time robbing them of any depth. Unfortunately, too few of us paused to reflect on what that might mean.

I sat at my desk with my takeaway cup of coffee, an almond croissant and a copy of that morning's edition. My to-do list was empty. Then the phone rang.

A short time later I had in my hands a number of documents that I read carefully so as to estimate their journalistic value. It was immediately clear that I had not only a scoop but one that concerned the Taoiseach, Bertie Ahern. Anything about Ahern was of journalistic interest. He had been in power for nine years and was the most popular politician in Ireland—possibly the most popular since the foundation of the state. He was at one and the same time the country's most powerful politician, one of its biggest celebrities and someone whose place in history was secure. Everything about him was news.

The documents concerned the workings of the Mahon Tribunal, the planning inquiry that had been set up by Ahern's first Government soon after it had come to power in June 1997. Scoops based on leaks about tribunals had become so frequent that they were something of a debased currency. The country was suffering from tribunal-allegation fatigue. The saving grace, however, was that this leak involved Ahern.

The information I had showed that the tribunal had written to a man called David McKenna informing him it had been told that he paid money to Ahern in or around December 1993. McKenna was a successful businessman who was friendly with Ahern and had on occasion brought him on a private jet to watch soccer matches in Manchester. The tribunal told McKenna that it was investigating a number of payments to Ahern. Furthermore, the information indicated that McKenna had replied to the tribunal saying that he had indeed paid money to Ahern. So what was at issue wasn't another allegation of a payment: it was a confirmed payment.

A tribunal can investigate only matters that are covered by its terms of reference, and the Mahon Tribunal was charged, in the main, with investigating allegations of corruption in planning. Allegations of corruption in different planning decisions over the years had been arranged by the tribunal into discrete sets of planned hearings, or modules, and I had to explain to my readers which module or planning decision the inquiry being made of McKenna, who ran a successful employment agency, belonged to.

Making my way across the newsroom, I stopped at the news desk and told the news editor, Miriam Donohue, that I had some material revealing that the Mahon Tribunal was investigating payments to Bertie Ahern in 1993.

'Oh, that sounds good. You'd better go up and talk to Geraldine,' she said.

Miriam was referring to the then editor of the *Irish Times*, Geraldine Kennedy. I walked across the newsroom and through a doorway that led to the editor's office, which was in fact a number of rooms. In the first were the desks of the editor's secretary and five or six more desks belonging to senior editors. On the right was the editor's office, while on the left, up a step, was the conference room, where the section heads met at scheduled hours every day to discuss what was going into coming editions and the progress of the items being worked on. This room, with its wall maps and set of tables arranged in a square, was used for less frequent meetings in which the organisers of the different elements of the paper's content would meet and apprise the editor or duty editor of their plans and progress. It also served as an important stage for all the gossip and office manoeuvring that exists in any organisation of substance and supposed power.

On the day I went up to the editor's office Geraldine was just finishing her weekly meeting with the political reporters who covered the goings-on in Leinster House. We sat at the conference-room table, and I told her what had happened and gave her the material I had to read through. Geraldine, a former political editor and a long-time political journalist, was immediately interested. She was cognisant of the fact that it was a controversial matter affecting the reputation of the most powerful person in the land. We discussed what I had and how I should go about preparing my report for publication. Any mistaken allegation about such a figure would be a huge embarrassment. Ahern would have to be given an opportunity to respond to anything that was going to be written. It was agreed that I would work closely with her on the story.

By the next evening the story was ready to run. I got in contact with people who acted as spokespersons for Ahern. The Government spokesperson said it was a matter for the party spokesperson, who said it was a tribunal matter and therefore confidential. I contacted McKenna and, on his instructions, his solicitor. The story was ready to roll. I sat at my computer in the messy business section and wrote the few paragraphs that were going to appear on the next day's front page. Geraldine came up and looked at it on the screen and suggested a few changes.

It is important to say that the report the *Irish Times* was about to publish was, we believed, more than just another tribunal leak of something that would in time have come to the attention of the public. The information we had belonged to what is called the private phase of the tribunal's inquiries, and it concerned a matter that, depending on how it panned out, might never come to be mentioned in the course of one of the tribunal's public hearings. The tribunal, naturally, investigated much more than it disclosed publicly, largely because a great deal of what it investigated turned out to be untrue or to be unconnected with the terms of reference that laid down its powers and duties. We were reporting something that might otherwise never be disclosed—the best sort of scoop. The payments might be of no interest to the tribunal in the context of its terms of reference, but they were of legitimate public interest.

The report was published on the front page on 21 September 2006, with the headline 'Tribunal examines payments to Taoiseach.' The first few paragraphs read:

A wealthy businessman David McKenna has been contacted by the Mahon Tribunal about payments to the Taoiseach, Bertie Ahern.

The tribunal is investigating a number of payments to Mr Ahern in and around December 1993, including cash payments, *The Irish Times* has learned.

Mr McKenna is one of three or four persons contacted by the tribunal concerning payments to Mr Ahern totalling between €50,000 and €100,000. The tribunal has been told that the money was used to pay legal bills incurred by Mr Ahern around this time. In a letter to Mr McKenna in June of this year and seen by *The Irish Times*, he was told the 'tribunal has been informed that you made payment of money to Mr Bertie Ahern TD, or for his benefit, in or about December 1993. The tribunal seeks your assistance in reconciling certain receipts of funds by Mr Ahern during this period.'

The tribunal requested a detailed statement from Mr McKenna. He was asked to name the person who requested the payment and his understanding as to why it was required. He was also asked who the payment was given to, and whether it was in cash or another form.

It is understood a solicitor who was an associate and personal friend of Mr Ahern's, the late Gerry Brennan, may have played a role in the matters being inquired into. Mr Brennan, a former director of Telecom Éireann, died in 1997.

Mr McKenna, a friend of Mr Ahern's and a known supporter of both him and his party, was estimated to be worth more than €60 million a number of years ago. However his publicly quoted recruitment firm, Marlborough Recruitment, collapsed in 2002.

Mr McKenna is also a friend and business associate of Des Richardson, the businessman appointed by Mr Ahern in 1993 as full-time fundraiser for Fianna Fáil and who also fundraises for Mr Ahern's constituency operation. The tribunal was told in private that Mr McKenna was one of the people who made a payment to Mr Ahern.

The report was printed across the top of the front page. What happened next is well captured in the diary kept by the then deputy political editor of the *Irish Independent*, Senan Maloney. The diary is also useful in providing a flavour of the political coverage of the time. I am grateful for his permission to use these excerpts.

Chapter 2 ∾

A POLITICAL REPORTER'S DIARY

September 2006

September is when the TDs pretend to be back, but aren't really. The Fianna Fáilers went to some hotel in Mayo for their annual think-in. A Deputy balanced a jug of water on his head in the bar at 4 a.m.

Bertie was interviewed by 'Morning Ireland' at breakfast in the hotel. He had a cut at Enda Kenny [Fine Gael leader], noting the local fellow was 'around a long time', having entered the Dáil in 1975, two years before himself. So much for Enda's portraying himself as the poster-child of national vigour.

But the remark only allowed the Taoiseach to be asked if he was nearing the end of his own shelf life. He responded with a classic Bertieism—that he knew his own 'shelf-by date'. In America a year ago, when Bertie spoke on the issue of the illegal Irish, he said that if support dried up in Congress we would have to 'fight our own canoe'.

In the afternoon Brian Cowen [Minister for Finance] promised that FF would have the 'bottle for the battle' when the election came around.

7 September

Mary Harney resigns after no fewer than thirteen years at the helm of the Progressive Democrats (PDs). She will be remembered for banning smoky coal in Dublin and for not being Charlie Haughey. She also blocked the Bertie Bowl [the proposed football stadium for west Dublin]. Her popularity has been dropping like a stone since she became Minister for Health.

'Why, I am not worthy,' says Michael McDowell [Minister for Justice and Harney's successor as head of the PDs].

12 September

Fine Gael hold their parliamentary party gathering in Sligo, and claim they will be able to pick up an extra 26 seats next time out. That's *twenty-six*. It sounds preposterous.

Pat Rabbitte [Labour Party leader] shows up to signal that Labour is willing. Later on, in the early hours, he leaves the north-west to return home. As it happens, his car is almost out of fuel—but there are no petrol stations between Sligo and Dublin open for custom in the early hours.

Pat drives on empty until the motor is spluttering. All the way through Leitrim he has fears of being stranded, having to sleep in his car. Eventually he passes a single old pump, relic of the 1950s, in the village of Newtownforbes.

He is reduced to banging on a Longford garage door at 1:30 a.m, miraculously raising a grizzled head from an upstairs window. 'Is it yourself?' asks the vest-clad rustic. 'It is,' replies Pat. The pump is opened, manages to dispense modern unleaded, and Pat makes it back to Dublin.

Five days later Mayo are crushed in the All-Ireland Final.

20 September

There's a court case today in which a lorry driver who consumed half a bottle of vodka (and some beer) before attempting to collect a skip 'made shit' of Michael McDowell's driveway.

That's what an angry Minister said to the driver, before noticing the latter was under the weather and calling the cops. McDowell was 'ranting and raving', the accused man managed to reveal in court before being fined and banned.

It was the week McDowell, new PD leader, announced it was party policy to send all trucks out of Dublin to a new port half way to Dundalk.

21 September

Yikes! A landmine this morning in the *Irish Times*. It reveals that the Mahon Tribunal is investigating payments to the Taoiseach.

The money is said to have come from businessman David McKenna in 1993 when Mr Ahern was Minister for Finance. Bertie, on a constituency visit to Clare, admits the reports are accurate, the source 'impeccable', and that whoever leaked it must have seen 'the full file'. But he also says the amounts quoted are 'off the wall' at €50,000–100,000.

The Taoiseach later suggests at a doorstep interview that some shadowy people have been out to discredit him over the last few days. The *Irish Times* says the money is connected to legal bills Mr Ahern had in 1993.

David McKenna is a millionaire who made his money out of Marlborough Recruitment, a firm that unfortunately went bankrupt. This is a peculiar story, and initially everyone seems to be adopting a wait-and-see attitude. There are some suggestions the money may be as little as £10,000 but whether the Minister for Finance should be taking even a few bob from businessmen, personal friends or not, is another question.

Bertie is furious. At a further impromptu press conference he denounces the leak as scurrilous, and says the money is a fraction of the amounts usually thrown around in tribunal stories. He says he's not going to answer questions about his 'Holy Communion and Confirmation money, or what I got for my birthday.' (He was 55 on 12 September.)

Mr Ahern, who in recent years flew to Manchester United matches with Mr McKenna in the latter's private jet, won't say the exact amount involved, or what it was used for. He mentions his separation. Meanwhile it is emerging that more people than McKenna may be involved.

The story is developing, and is already damaging.

Fine Gael quotes the Taoiseach in the Dáil from September 1997, speaking about the McCracken tribunal.

'The tribunal stresses a point I have repeatedly emphasised, that public representatives must not be under a personal financial obligation to anyone.'

Two days beforehand there was a BBC 'Panorama' broadcast about Premiership managers and claimed corruption. Now, with a week to go to the new Dáil session, Bertie is mixed up with alleged 'bungs'.

22 September

Swirling rumours in Leinster House and Government Buildings. The suggestions are that the total sum Bertie received was either £10,000 or £20,000, with four donors giving equal amounts. The pressure is on for the full list of names and amounts, so the public can judge the individuals and their possible links to Government.

Bertie makes a defensive prepared statement after a report launch in Government Buildings. He complains twice of the 'sinister' nature of the leak, and refuses to take questions, walking out past journalists who sit there in stony silence.

Yesterday the Taoiseach complained of reports (in *Village* magazine) that appeared to link him to bank accounts in Liechtenstein, Jersey and the Dutch

Antilles. Except Bertie called them the 'Dutch Anthills'. Trust the media to make a mountain out of an anthill.

Did he or didn't he pay tax on these payments? If they were loans, to get him out of a tight spot, no tax would be payable. Bertie didn't say they were loans, but instead that he 'dealt with them properly'. As Minister for Finance at the time, of course, he was responsible for clawing in the nation's tax, as well as being responsible for the tax authorities themselves, while also capable of re-writing tax law all by himself.

It is still all to play for in what the *Irish Daily Mail* is calling Bertie's biggest political crisis. His body language this morning was tight, testy and all bad. The latest rumour is that Miriam Ahern is due to give evidence to the Mahon Tribunal in October, which scarcely seems credible. Another is that the money raised was not for legal fees but intended as a 'golden handbag' in the marriage break-up.

The sooner the full truth is out the better. Everyone is waiting for the Sunday papers in 48 hours, but Ursula Halligan of TV3—which last night had lurid footage of tens and twenties in Euro banknotes filling the screen—dares to mention the phrase 'early general election'.

23 September

The *Irish Times* reports that the monies were loans, and were accepted on the basis that they would be repaid. It's suggested that at least some of the benefactors then wouldn't take the money back. Thirteen years on, some amounts remain outstanding. Does this make them gifts?

Couldn't Bertie, who signed blank cheques for Charlie after all, have sent his friends similar slips in the post if they were too shy to accept them in person? And what's with the shyness, anyway—what is Irish business coming to, if people won't allow their backs to be scratched in turn after they have seen to Bertie's seven-year itch?

He is truly blessed. His friends won't turn their backs on him. They are also maintaining mortared-up mouths when the media ring.

Michael McDowell goes to Finland to grapple with all these moral questions that the PDs used to pronounce upon with such penetrating rectitude. Silence from the moral mountaintop so far.

24 September

The Sunday papers are tamer than a dead goldfish. They haven't managed to find out anything new, but still editorialise a bit of outrage. Defence Minister Willie O'Dea goes on 'This Week' and blusters that it would be disloyal of the Taoiseach to reveal the names of his loyal friends.

He says he is sickened by talk of 'the public interest' when the case falls into the category of mere public curiosity. As if to confirm, a *Sunday Independent* telephone poll—the equivalent of asking your mates in the pub—says that 81 per cent of people want further details.

25 September

Bertie goes to Dublin Zoo to see the animals. Then he trots right past them, ignoring their microphones and tape recorders, greeting the zoo director instead—and both enter the Meerkat Restaurant to launch a five-year development plan.

Like an elephant in the living room, there is a great unspoken issue as the Taoiseach gazes past the massed ranks of predatory lenses and poised notebooks to tell all the zoo people what a great job they are doing.

Being the king of the political jungle, Bertie naturally has to do a walkabout in the gardens afterwards. He feigns not to hear questions as to whether he is going to make a statement. The colour writers are in the long grass, watching every ripple of his sleek tailored suit.

Snakes, vultures, monkeys who see no evil—if you can't muster a bit of a chuckle column out of an event like this, you should really jack in journalism. The rhinos are too far away to admire the thickness of Bertie's hide as he struts around, not even deigning to state that there will be no statement, with the odd squirrel perched quizzically, as if studying for tips on how to store stuff away.

Bertie is still shaking his head at questioners as he dives into a limo to be driven away. There are four plain-clothes detectives about, all packing weaponry, which is a doubling of his usual guard. It probably has to do with the fact that Ceann Comhairle Rory O'Hanlon was heckled and jostled today by hospital campaigners at the opening of the Monaghan bypass, which is likely the last bypass to be performed locally if A&E and surgery units are closed.

The wildebeest of the media dumbly follow Bertie next to Griffith College on the South Circular Road, where daughter Cecelia learned to write books like *PS, I Love You*. The Taoiseach promptly gets stuck in a lift with Cyprian Brady. The dour is stuck, and so is the door.

We know the Taoiseach is in a tight spot, but this is ridiculous. He, Cyp, a detective, and some Griffith College type are packed like sardines into a tiny, stationary cage. Workmen with hard-hats try to get the steel enclosure open. After five minutes they manage it, but then the occupants have to crouch from their platform and jump a few feet to the floor.

Not the Taoiseach's day.

26 September

Bertie gives a special interview to RTE television news in his St Luke's constituency office in which he admits accepting £39,000 (€50,000) from a dozen apostles in two tranches in 1993 and 1994. The doubt of the benefit is now gone; it remains to be seen if the public will give him the political benefit of the doubt.

The Taoiseach, in 25 minutes, is absolutely candid about his marriage break-up. He says the money he received was to help him over that 'very dark, very sad' period. Some of it went towards a £20,000 educational trust for his daughters—and at this point he closed his eyes and bowed his head, a father emotional at the recall of difficult times past. He had managed to save £50,000 up to the point of his legal separation, but after agreeing the final details in November 1993, after several dates in the High Court that year, he was left without a house, 'the £50,000 was gone' and he still had legal bills.

He took out a loan at the Allied Irish Banks branch in O'Connell St to meet the legal costs. The next month his friends organised a whip-round, even though he had previously refused a fund-raiser to assist him with his personal finances. He was presented with £22,500—seven people paying £2,500 each, and an eighth man paying £5,000.

'They gave me the £22,500, and I said that I would take this as a debt of honour, that I would repay it in full,' said Bertie, eyes as wide as sincerity would allow. He said that he assured his benefactors that he would pay interest on it. 'I know the tax law, I'm an accountant.'

But he added: 'I haven't repaid the money because they refused to take it.' In 13 years, he had never so much as paid interest, he disclosed—but an unrepayable loan is a gift, as the Opposition later point out. Bertie lamely offered that he thought his friends would accept repayment now, 'because they see the difficulty'.

The first bunch of bail-outs included Fianna Fáil fund-raiser Des Richardson, stockbroker Padraic O'Connor, former chairman of CERT (the hotel training agency) Jim Nugent, David McKenna, Fintan Gunne, personal friends Paddy Reilly and Mick Collins, and the publican Charlie Chawke, now one of the owners of Sunderland FC.

'Later on in 1994 another four friends gave me £16,500,' says Bertie. They were Joe Burke, Dermot Carew, Barry English and Paddy Reilly, 'known to my friends as Paddy the Plasterer'. Joe Burke had been appointed by Bertie as Chairman of the Dublin Port Authority. Dermot Carew owns the Beaumont House pub, and before that the Hill 16 premises. Barry English is a wealthy engineer, while Paddy the Plasterer has since moved on to become the landlord of a myriad rental properties in Dublin.

It was magnetic television:

I was not impoverished when I was going through the separation. It was a very dark period for me, and a very sad period for me. I didn't, I had taken out a loan like anyone else would, but colleagues knew what the situation was. From 1987 when I separated from Miriam until the end of 1993 was a long protracted period. That happens in family law cases. And delays and delay for one reason or another.

Miriam was, I had no account in my own name in that period. Miriam had joint accounts and I paid Miriam maintenance but also saved money during that period and I'd saved quite a substantial amount of money because it was from the time I was Lord Mayor in 1986. I'd saved in the order of £50,000.

The trouble was that in the separation I agreed to provide £20,000 for my children to an educational account as part of the agreement that I made. [*Lowers his eyes and composes himself.*] I don't like giving details of the children but, for completeness, I did that. I also had to pay off other bills, so the money I'd saved was gone. So, my friends knew that. I had no house, the house was gone, so they decided to try and help me.

On the crucial question of whether the favours were ever called in, Bertie offered this:

All I can say on that is they didn't, and never did they ask me. They were not people that ever tried to get me to do something. I might have appointed somebody [to a state board] but I appointed them because they were friends, not because of anything they had given me.

It is an admission of cronyism—appointing friends because of personal acquaintance, not considering the filling of State-funded offices on the merit of individual candidates. Des Richardson was appointed to the board of Aer Lingus. Jim Nugent was appointed to the board of the Central Bank. Three others were also elevated.

But Bertie insisted that there was a difference between 'somebody taking millions, somebody taking hundreds of thousands in exchange for contracts and other matters, and taking what is a relatively small contribution from friends who had a clear understanding they would be paid back.'

He maintained:

I've broken no law. I've broken no ethical code. I've broken no tax law. I've always paid my income tax. I paid capital gains tax, but I've never had much in my life to pay, and I paid my gift tax . . . I did point out to my friends a number of times that it was better that I clear these, and you know, they would sometimes laugh it off . . .

Nobody's laughing now.

27 September

The first day of the new Dáil session, and the Taoiseach faces Leader's Questions.

The Opposition knows the Taoiseach has milked public sympathy for all it's worth. They aren't going to run down the dead-ends of his marriage break-up, or the whip-around at the time he was in trouble. They daren't dabble in the human stuff with the most human of politicians.

So they go down the flanks. Enda Kenny effortlessly carves huge holes in the Taoiseach's rearguard, the ball at his feet, attacking what might be called 'Manchester Unidentified'.

What's this? Well, it's another issue, one that Bertie mentioned in his TV interview. It has absolutely nothing to do with his separation, so the Opposition need not court public disdain by addressing it. It's fair game.

Here's what Bertie said:

The only other thing, Bryan, totally separate and nothing to do with this, but I don't want anyone saying I didn't give the full picture. I did a function in Manchester with a business organisation, nothing to do with politics or whatever. I was talking about the Irish economy; I was explaining about Irish economy matters and I'd say there was about 25 people at that. I spent about four hours with them; dinner; I did question and answers; and all the time from 1977 up to current period I got eight thousand on that, which you know, whether it was a political donation . . .

This was the Taoiseach admitting to receiving £8,000 sterling in cash, in 1994, the year after his marital separation. He was Minister for Finance at the time, and the Green Book that provides guidelines to ministerial conduct at the time warns expressly against accepting anything of value in the course of one's office.

It's not good enough that Bertie might have been off-duty, among a few friends, possibly taking in a match at Old Trafford while he was at it. He was the Minister for Finance. He was talking about the Irish economy. They gave him money.

Bertie admitted on television:

I'd actually done the event a number of times, but I only once got a contribution. I've gone through them and given my personal accounts [to the Mahon Tribunal], that is the only other payment. It is nothing to do with this, but it was a payment that was in my accounts and I did give that to the tribunal as well.

This is an own-goal by the Taoiseach. The money went into his personal finances. He took it at a speaking engagement, at which the only reason he would be heard would be his standing as Minister for Finance.

Bertie presumably had to put through his own net because he knew the money was showing. The Mahon Tribunal has the detail, and he can't take the risk of keeping quiet and having it come out later. His television interview was his one-and-only chance to confess all.

Enda Kenny demands an answer on the Manchester payment. Bertie doesn't give him one, except to mumble incoherently.

Big Pat Rabbitte cuts in from the left, and lets fly. He can't believe that the Minister for Finance did not have a bank account of his own in the seven years he was Minister for Finance. The shot is true. Here's the replay of Bertie's TV commentary: 'I didn't have an account in my own name during the separation years [1987–93 inclusive]. I opened an account after the separation work was over.'

Now, on the opening day of the Dáil, Bertie confirms that he didn't have a personal bank account in those years. Rabbitte is pointed: 'Are you telling the House that during the period you were Minister for Finance, responsible for running the Exchequer, that you had no bank account in the jurisdiction? Did you have a bank account outside the jurisdiction?'

Ouch . . . one can already hear the Sunday papers ringing every Barclays branch and Lloyds-TSB in Lancashire. But if he had no account anywhere, what could he have been telling his eager-eared audience in Manchester: 'My advice, as Minister for Finance, is to have nothing whatever to do with banks . . .'

Mr Ahern is left clawing at the air:

I separated at the beginning of 1987 and it didn't conclude until the end of 1993 in the High Court. Over that period my accounts were in the joint names of my wife and myself. For obvious reasons, I did not use our joint account. I used cheques separately to deal with my issues and I did not open an account in my own name until afterwards.

The Taoiseach didn't have a bank account, yet he was able to use cheques—what, from an account in somebody else's name? This incredible stuff must be doing damage. Remember the Taoiseach said he had accumulated £50,000 in savings from the time he was Lord Mayor (1986) until the separation (concluded in November 1993).

If he had no bank account in that time, where was this money located? Was it thrown into a broom closet in St Luke's? If in a joint deposit account, how did Bertie 'use cheques separately' when he didn't open an account until afterwards?

Joe Higgins rises to speak. The Dublin West Socialist Party TD accuses Bertie of having cast Bryan Dobson in the role of agony aunt in order to divert attention from critical issues. 'Your personal circumstances are irrelevant, because you said last night that you had already got a bank loan to pay off pressing bills.'

It would have taken the Taoiseach two minutes to draft a letter to send back the money to his fans, says Joe. And he gives the example—'Ah, Jaysus, lads, you'll have me in huge trouble if you don't take back the fifty grand. My circumstances have improved, and I'll have fifty reporters traipsing after me for the rest of my life if this comes out. Bertie.'

He suggests a P.S.—'Tell Paddy the Plasterer to steer clear of Callely's house. He's in enough trouble with the painter already.'

That's a reference to Ivor Callely getting a free decorating job on his house in Clontarf from the builders Sisk. The firm had been given a lucrative contract with FÁS [the state training agency]—and Ivor was in charge of the State manpower agency at the time. The scandal-plagued junior minister resigned, but only after the Taoiseach himself said he was 'not impressed.'

Paddy the Plasterer, Sisk the Painter—and now it seems Bertie's own particular glasshouse, reduced to a house of shards, could do with Malcolm the Glazer.

Joe's P.S. is not the only one. The internet gags are already flying. There's a reworked version of Cecelia's book, with Bertie as the author, saying *PS, I Owe You.* Another of her books is called *Where Rainbows End.* Could this be where a Rainbow begins? [meaning the multi-party Government that included Fine Gael and the Labour Party]

There's a P.S. with the PDs.

Michael McDowell now finally breaks his silence—in order to blame Bertie's friends!

'The actions of a group of friends . . . in advancing to him monies . . . were ill-advised,' says the Tánaiste. 'It is reasonable to accept that the motive for the payments was benevolent and not intended to compromise, to corrupt, or to obtain improper influence or reward.'

He says the Taoiseach 'should probably have declined such help,' even in the difficult personal circumstances he faced in 1993. 'Accepting such help was an honest error of judgement . . .'

McDowell calls for the payments to now be fully refunded with interest. 'If the donors are reluctant to receive them, they can surrender them to charitable causes,' he adds, forgetting to warn them that any future charitable causes should not include high office holders in the politics of Ireland.

28 September

The *Irish Times* headlines: 'Pressure on Ahern eases as Tánaiste lends support.' It's premature, because the *Irish Independent* is highlighting the 'new questions' on the Manchester supporters, the prawn sandwich brigade who thought Bertie could do with some more bread.

The *Indo* reports that Irish business interests were behind the gathering and that some of Bertie's friends attended, which makes it different from his addressing a 'business organisation' in Britain and raises the ugly prospect of Irish interests shovelling it into Bertie's back pocket offshore.

The Taoiseach is today in Ballyjamesduff, leading to jokes among reporters present about the two Paddy Reillys named by the Taoiseach. That's because the Percy French song about Ballyjamesduff plaintively asks in each chorus: 'Come home, Paddy Reilly, to me.' To which the answer is presumably 'No, because I am too busy running my business here in Manchester and I cannot afford the time before a tribunal.'

Asked up in Cavan exactly who was at this Manchester function, Bertie muddies the water hopelessly: 'A group that was with me from Dublin,' he says, as well as local businessmen. He goes on to say that he had no official script, that he did not address the gathering in his capacity as Minister for Finance, that he paid his own airfare, and checked out the tax implications. But the damage is done.

There's war on the Order of Business in the Dáil, with attempts to raise Bertie's admission that the Manchester money came from the assembled folks, 'plus the group who were with me from Ireland.' He does not identify any of his Irish accompaniment. Government Chief Whip Tom Kitt, under pressure from Opposition parties, is forced to concede a special 35-minute debate next Tuesday.

Meanwhile Michael McDowell is reading the transcript of the doorstep in Ballyjamesduff, and frowning heavily. He goes outside to face the technology, and whatever journalists are still scribbling into notebooks these days. 'Having spoken to the Taoiseach and studied the transcript of his County Cavan comments, there are now very significant matters of concern,' he says. The Government moves to the brink.

These matters are 'not completely put at rest by the facts in the public domain.' He demands to know identities [of those who attended], the nature of the event, and what the money had ultimately been used for. 'All these issues have to be clarified now.'

The primary concern is in terms of standards. 'That's the crucial thing, and whether it can be defended. That's the issue.' It is a complete reversal of today's *Irish Times* lead.

On 'Prime Time' they are talking gravely about the possible end of the Ahern era. He just shouldn't take money at functions he attends while Minister for Finance. Brian Lenihan, Minister for Children, says doing so would be 'unthinkable'.

Brian was long passed over for promotion by Bertie, in a row that goes back to 1990 when Bertie was the messenger for Haughey in the shafting of Lenihan Senior during the Presidential election.

29 September

The *Daily Mail* has Bertie 'hanging by a thread.' It suggests that Bertie might have used Celia Larkin's bank accounts during the years he had none of his own. 'So where is Cowen?' asks another headline.

Brian Cowen can't afford to appear like some kind of Gordon Brown figure, smouldering with ambition while Bertie threatens to combust. So he goes on 'Morning Ireland' and gives an energetic performance, insisting that the Taoiseach did 'nothing incorrect'. An interesting focus on the letter of the law, backing up Fianna Fáil clucking that the Green Book of advice for Ministers amounted only to 'guidelines' with no force of law.

Geraldine Kennedy, Editor of the *Irish Times*, is summoned before the Mahon Tribunal with Colm Keena, the journalist who wrote the original story. Geraldine, a former PD TD, tells the Chairman cheerfully that she destroyed the leaked documents to protect her source.

So the sneaky leaker is safe, and only Bertie stands on the precipice. Meanwhile in the pubs after a torrid working week, people are asking themselves if they really want to lose the Taoiseach over a relatively trifling amount accepted a dozen years ago.

30 September

Michael McDowell has been having second thoughts too. In today's papers he is quoted as saying he has an 'abhorrence' of heads on plates. That might be news to Mary Harney, but it is decidedly good news for Bertie.

The Opposition immediately accuse the PDs of running the white flag up the pole. They predict a climbdown as soon as Bertie clears the air. They even suggest McDowell might be helping Bertie to write his script.

A fly in this soothing ointment is the emergence of a claim that one of the amounts given to Bertie in 1993, from Padraic O'Connor, was a cheque drawn on the corporate account of NCB Stockbrokers.

Rather puts a hole in the 'personal loans' story.

1 October

The Sundays again fail to break any new ground. But they do report that Bertie Ahern has repaid with interest the loans he received from his apostles. Mr Ahern sent out 12 cheques on Friday, totalling €90,867, to be personally delivered by courier.

The amount includes €40,000 in accumulated interest, reflecting an effective rate of 5 per cent compounded over the years. This is a huge step by the Taoiseach in his political rehabilitation. Most of the recipients redirect the money to charity.

The *Sunday Indo* says that by repaying the money 'with such apparent ease', Mr Ahern has left himself open to the accusation that he could have done so at any stage over the last few years, and is only doing so now to save his career.

But the most important material is the sampling of public opinion done by a couple of papers. Six out of ten think Bertie was wrong to accept money while in office. But nearly two-thirds (65%) do not believe he should resign.

There is a decided climate of forgiveness now, overriding detail, nuance and points of principle or moral ethics. Enda Kenny still makes the point that his party wouldn't stand for it, and that if the same material had come out about him, he would no longer be leader. Again, this needn't surprise, nor affect matters much.

It's a week since Willie O'Dea said that being lectured on morality by Fine Gael was akin to being called 'big, green and ugly' by the Incredible Hulk.

Even the little issue of the corporate cheque is being teased out into meaninglessness. It turns out it was a bank draft, not a company counterfoil, went to Bertie's solicitor anyway, and the Taoiseach needn't have known anything other than that it was a donation by an individual.

Meanwhile lots of old buffers with businesses in Britain are coming out and half remembering the Manchester gathering, held in the Four Seasons hotel, and they are vague and kindly and 'ah, sure God help us,' and it is all grist to Bertie's mill.

One of them tells Pat Kenny on the radio that he met Tim Kilroe of Aer Arann at the urinals in the hotel toilet and the latter happened to mention the whip-around for some fella from the Irish parliament who had 'woman problems'.

3 October

Bertie doesn't clarify a thing in his next Dáil appearance, despite expectations that he was going to copiously explain, beat his breast, and plead for mercy—leaving the other side so tactically surprised that they only manage to rehearse some of their old indignation, to little effect.

They may have been banking on some new hassle emerging, or the Taoiseach showing a few more chinks in his armour; but instead he stonewalls. The entire Cabinet sits alongside him as he proceeds to read a deadly dull speech outlining how he did nothing wrong.

He can't remember practically anyone who was at the Manchester meeting. Wouldn't trust his memory in any case. Some of his friends from Dublin were there, but 'all as I knows is' they didn't get the whip-round going.

'As I survey the events of the last two weeks, I realise that my judgement in accepting help from good and loyal friends and the gift in Manchester (albeit in the context of personal and family circumstances) was an error,' manages Bertie.

'It was a misjudgement although not in breach of any law or code of conduct at the time,' he adds. 'It was not illegal or impermissible to have done what I did. But I now regret the choices I made in those difficult and dark times.'

Here it comes, the big grass-roots appeal: 'The bewilderment caused to the public about recent revelations has been deeply upsetting for me and others near and dear to me. To them and to the Irish people, I offer my apologies.'

And that's it. Labour and Fine Gael are left flummoxed. The Taoiseach should have said what he did was wrong, sniffs Enda Kenny. Pat Rabbitte acidly comments that Bertie would have us believe he took gifts from strangers and loans from friends . . .

We should have known it was going to be boring when we saw the official description on the Dáil order paper: 'Statements on disclosures relating to the Mahon Tribunal.'

And then we remember that old footage of Bertie delivering the 1993 Budget, shown a lot in the last week. Yes, there's that sole black mark against him. Right on his forehead, in fact. An unmistakable smudge for Ash Wednesday.

It was indeed a dark time.

4 October

Who does Bertie do his banking with? Friends First. The apparent low-key public attitude to the political crisis—a lack of instant jokes for one thing—suggests the affair may be playing itself out.

Fine Gael spindoctor Ciaran Conlon is rueful at the popular perception that 'they're all the same,' as if it's not worth talking about standards any more. Fianna Fáil is cynical in stoking that attitude, he suggests. 'We say Charlie Haughey—they say Lowry. We say Ray Burke—they say Lowry. We say Liam Lawlor—they say Lowry. We say Beverley Flynn—they say Lowry. We say Pádraig Flynn—they say Lowry . . .'

Bertie closes down Leader's Questions today, saying he isn't going to stand up in the Dáil every day to re-hash his financial affairs. And the Opposition look like they've been well and truly scolded.

And then something happens.

It involves the man at the urinal.

His name is Michael Wall. He was at the Manchester dinner where Bertie got £8,000, and then three years later Bertie got his house off the very same chap. Mr Wall, a Manchester-based retired owner of a coach-hire firm, sold the Taoiseach the house he now lives in, at 44 Beresford Avenue, off Griffith Avenue in Dublin 9.

Mr Ahern only named two people in the Dáil who were at the dinner, one of them dead. He did not name Michael Wall, even though three years later he would buy his house from the man. This house revelation, on RTE radio's 'Drivetime' show, lusciously recounted by investigative reporter Philip Boucher-Hayes, is truly bizarre. Moreover, both Labour and Fine Gael explicitly say so. Michael McDowell, who had asked Bertie for a full list of attendees, didn't even get the one closest to home, as it were.

The PDs are said to be 'considering this information' overnight, no doubt wondering whether they have just had their noses rubbed in it again by Fianna Fáil.

5 October

A big row between McDowell and Bertie is all the talk of Government Buildings. Bertie has to come into the Dáil on a Thursday for the first time in this administration—to take an Order of Business that the Tánaiste and PD leader was originally scheduled for.

McDowell doesn't even sit in the chamber, fuelling talk of a deepening rift. But the Taoiseach is in confident, even buoyant, mood. He confirms that Michael Wall sold him his own four walls. He says he rented the house for two years—moving into it in 1995, just a year after the Manchester dinner.

He reveals he was talking to Michael Wall three times over the previous weekend in a bid to recollect who was in Manchester, but didn't mention him in the Dáil—despite the bizarre house link—because Mr Wall 'didn't eat the dinner.' He attended the function only in his official capacity as minibus driver to the Taoiseach and his mates . . . If he was in the bar ('eating a packet of peanuts,' as RTE political correspondent David McCullagh said straight-faced on air), then he wasn't officially in attendance. Bertie is off the hook.

Except he isn't. Michael McDowell is understandably feeling that he has been talking to the wall too. He demanded the Taoiseach identify those in attendance, and Bertie doesn't even mention that he had significant financial dealings with the bloke who drove the bus . . .

So here we are: Bertie called the original *Irish Times* story 'off the wall'. Now it turns out he bought his house 'off the Wall'—and that's only at the very fringes of an overall crisis in trust. The Taoiseach has been repeatedly offering distractionary material in his answers 'for completeness'—and sending the media diving down culs de sac—but he didn't mention his house in 'completeness.' Even though he now tells the Dáil that the Mahon Tribunal has been investigating his house, and that a file on his house has been sent to them . . .

Mr Ahern also says that he believes the former Tánaiste, Mary Harney, 'would have been aware that I got loans from friends.' Her spokesman instantly and categorically denies this. It is 'mistaken' and 'untrue'. The question arises now as to whether the PDs are going to seek humiliation for Bertie in asking him to correct the record of the House. Fianna Fáilers are saying they can go whistle. Bertie's not going back in.

The stand-off is eased in the afternoon when Harney does a doorstep and says the Taoiseach can't have meant what he actually said. She knew he was interacting with the tribunal, he told her during the summer about a forgery attempt to link him with a bank in Mauritius, but he certainly didn't say anything about loans from friends.

She rejects a claim by Caoimhghín Ó Caoláin, the Sinn Féin leader in the Dáil, that she decided to get out of the leadership because she had been told by *Irish Times* editor Geraldine Kennedy what was 'coming down the tracks'. It's not true, she says, ending a rumour that had been doing the rounds in Leinster House almost as soon as 'Bertiegate' erupted.

The rest of the PDs stay totally silent all day. Their spokespersons say 'no comment' when anything is asked of them. Speculation rises inevitably that they may be preparing to pull the plug. Fianna Fáil backbenchers and even Ministers are bullish, prepared to open the door for them if they want to walk. They think they can stay in power with Independents.

RTE notes that Bertie Ahern holds the record for being the shortest-serving Tánaiste in history, at 27 days. Michael McDowell has been Tánaiste for 22.

6 October

Former Labour leader Ruairí Quinn mocks Michael McDowell, his Dublin South-East constituency colleague, as 'erratic' on 'Morning Ireland'. Yesterday's events effectively mean that the Justice Minister has marched his Yorkists up to the top of the hill for the second time in a week. Either way of getting them off again literally involves 'downside' for the Tánaiste. It can either be further humiliation or departure from Government.

At lunchtime Mr McDowell says he is 'working to restore relations with Mr Ahern,' which is a small slice of a pie made without any pride ingredients. Bertie confirms in Limerick that he hasn't spoken to the Tánaiste since he appeared in the Dáil.

McDowell says the Government is safe if the damage that has recently been done is repaired. He plans to meet Bertie over the weekend. 'The two parties have been very careful not to say things to aggravate the situation,' he manages, while the damage has been caused by 'events'.

10 October

McDowell is putting up with the smell of putrefaction in Government, with Labour in particular taunting him that he's 'no Desmond O'Malley' [the founder of the PDs]. Fine Gael are meanwhile slapping up posters of

McDowell's face in Dublin South-East with a line about single party Government that says: 'Thanks to him, it's a reality.'

The PD leader responds with a sudden appearance alongside the Taoiseach on the red carpet inside Government Buildings, announcing they've just cobbled together a plan to strengthen the Ethics Acts by making people intending to take money from friends ask the Standards in Public Offices Commission first.

Brian Lenihan said taking a bag of dough would be 'unthinkable,' but Mac is making it thinkable—and all the important thinking about it will have to be done for a witless politician in that position by the SIPO, a many-headed quango. It's patently ridiculous.

The hacks and cameras are given 18 minutes to get to Merrion Street for this impromptu love-in between Bertie and his re-enamoured bride. Panting, brows beaded with perspiration, they are then lectured by McDowell.

> The Irish people have a far more intelligent grasp of the issues, their importance, their implications and the options flowing from them than the small minority of commentators who have called for the dissolution of this Government. It is reassuring to note that all the evidence suggests that the substantial majority of the public want the Progressive Democrats to remain part of that Government and that they back the Taoiseach to remain in office and me to continue as his Tánaiste at this important juncture. I want to take this opportunity to reject as completely untrue the suggestion that there were angry exchanges between myself and the Taoiseach . . . There have never been any angry words between myself and the Taoiseach in the last seven years—or indeed before. I want to put on the record the simple truth that the Taoiseach and I asked our respective parties to refrain from public comment for a short period to assist us in repairing the damage done to the Government by recent events.

Only the PDs complied with that one.

Next comes a major blooper. After the TV lights switch off, the Taoiseach and Tánaiste having taken only four questions—all directed at McDowell—the two men stage a handshake for photographers. But the mikes remain on, and they pick up Mac muttering to Bertie through gritted teeth: 'We survived it.'

Oops, that's embarrassing. Bertie, the doughty old performer, doesn't say anything, but just keeps grinning and gurning. He's not agreeing. This is McDowell's mistake.

A couple of hours later, in the Dáil, Pat Rabbitte flaunts the headlines of the past five or six days about the Coalition on the brink, the Tánaiste in hiding, and Independent TDs beginning to write out their shopping lists.

The Tánaiste says none of it ever happened, chides Rabbitte. It was all an invention by a small minority of commentators.

The House chortles as he wonders aloud if anyone had ever heard such patronising, vainglorious nonsense as McDowell's claim in his script that it would be 'an act of supreme moral and political folly to reward the wrongful actions of a leaker' by pulling out of Government.

The Tánaiste stated in black and white that he wanted to know the identity of the donors, the mysterious money men at Manchester. He stated he wanted to know the nature of the function. The Taoiseach told us it was an organised function, that he made a speech, and that they were his friends. He then told us it wasn't an organised function, he didn't make a speech and he doesn't know who was present, apart from two people.

And still McDowell had been given no names. And no answers.

13 October

Friday the thirteenth will haunt Pat and Enda for a long time to come. There's a Bertie hat-trick in the opinion polls.

Poll: Bertie's personal approval rating is actually up. *Poll*: Satisfaction with the Government is up. *Poll*: Fianna Fáil has its highest level of support in two years—up no fewer than eight percentage points!

The survey, carried out for the *Irish Times* by TNS/MRBI, shows that while two-thirds of the electorate think the Taoiseach was wrong to take unsolicited funds, they simply refuse to regard him as 'Dirty Bertie' and want him to stay in power.

It's as if the people realised he was in a spot of personal difficulty and organised a bit of a whip-round.

As soon as the poll comes out, Fianna Fáilers are joyously texting each other with messages like: 'Carlsberg don't do opinion polls, but . . .'

Taken at the conclusion of the payments affair, the poll offers a plague on the houses of Pat and Enda—with Labour down four points and Fine Gael down two.

Bertie is back on course for a General Election three-in-a-row. And they called Haughey a Houdini?

The Taoiseach has just gone over Niagara Falls in a barrel, and here he is, having bobbed to the bank, poking his head out while the crowd cheers.

18 October

A Swedish Cabinet Minister has resigned because she didn't pay her TV licence, which rather puts Irish politics into perspective. Actually she didn't pay her licence for 16 years and ended up being in charge of broadcasting . . .

19 October

The Dáil has been demonstrating its relevancy by debating a proposal to make it an offence to detonate a nuclear device in Ireland. Prosecutable in the courts, if there are any afterwards.

Minister Dick Roche admits it is slightly 'odd' that the transposition to Irish law of the United Nations Nuclear Test Ban Treaty would allow for a Dr Strangelove who makes a large hole in the national territory to be tried summarily in the District Court, should the DPP so decide.

22 October

The Fianna Fáil faithful troop out to Bodenstown for the annual Theobald Wolfe Tone commemoration. Last year they commemorated an entirely different person named 'Theobold' on the invitations, but this year they just call him Wolfe Tone.

A local apparatchik, addressing the throng, says that the Holy Trinity of Irish national heroes (Brian Boru, Red Hugh O'Donnell and Éamon de Valera, apparently) has now been joined by a fourth: Bartholomew Patrick Ahern.

29 October

Fianna Fáil support has zoomed for the third time in two weeks in the latest opinion poll, carried out by Red C for the *Sunday Business Post*. Party popularity is up six points. The Blueshirts are down two, while the Red Rose has wilted four.

It's been a Hallowe'en horror for the Opposition. Everything has blown up in their faces—or worse, as happened with a man in Sunderland who tried to launch a Black Cat Thunderbolt firework from an unusual angle and ended up with a 'scorched colon'.

PART TWO

Evidence

Chapter 3 ∾

| ST LUKE'S

Bertie Ahern's passionate care for his power base in Drumcondra and for the Dublin Central constituency was always a key element of his political character. He regularly came first in the country in the percentage of first-preference votes won in a poll and, apart from his initial general election campaign in 1977, was invariably elected on the first count in Dublin Central.

He had a dedicated team of workers supporting him and a canvassing operation that was probably unrivalled in the state. Even during his period as party leader (when it was party policy to manage the vote in the various constituencies so as to get as many Fianna Fáil TDs as possible returned, by spreading the party vote among its candidates), Ahern breached the rule and sought as many first-preference votes for himself as he could. In the 2007 general election campaign a leaflet was delivered to houses in the part of the constituency where the present writer lives seeking first-preference votes for Ahern, second-preference votes for Cyprian Brady and third-preference votes for Mary Fitzpatrick, daughter of the former constituency TD Dr Dermot Fitzpatrick. It said that this was what the party wanted supporters to do 'in your area', but the same leaflet was delivered throughout the constituency. In this way Ahern gathered the vast bulk of the votes. Brady, who received only 939 first-preference votes, swept past Fitzpatrick after Ahern's huge surplus was distributed and won the second seat. Brady was a member of Ahern's inner circle, a group that considered itself to be part and parcel of Ahern's electorally successful political career.

The former Taoiseach Charles Haughey once famously dubbed these people the Drumcondra Mafia, and the name stuck. They were fiercely loyal and driven supporters of Ahern who acted not out of party loyalty or because of any particular political beliefs but because of their friendship and association with Ahern, and because of a team spirit that, for many of them, went back to their younger days. Ahern would in time appoint some of them to state boards, and in these and other ways many benefited financially as a result of their involvement with him. Patronage has always been an essential part of Ahern's recipe for political success.

If the streets of Drumcondra and the constituency of Dublin Central were the stuff of Ahern's beginnings and the springboard for his political career, his constituency centre, St Luke's, was at the heart of his Tammany Hall, ward-boss operation. It is a detached red-brick building in Lower Drumcondra Road, close to the Tolka, along a stretch of a busy thoroughfare where most of the buildings are commercial. A former doctor's surgery, it was purchased for £56,000 in 1988 and renovated for use as a constituency centre with upstairs living accommodation. Apart from Sinn Féin representatives, most TDs tend to operate from rented or temporarily donated constituency offices. Ahern's permanent purchased base was unusual in Irish politics and was indicative of his commitment and drive, of the strength of his local organisation and of the ability of Ahern and his supporters to raise money. The Mahon Tribunal's inquiries into Ahern's personal finances led to a partial examination of where the money to buy St Luke's came from and who exactly owned the building. It should have been a straightforward, provable matter, though it proved to be anything but.

The property was bought from a Catherine Daly. A contract for the sale was signed on 19 November 1987 by Daly, as vendor, and by Des Richardson, Joseph Burke and Tim Collins, as purchasers. Richardson's name on the contract for sale was typed, as was Daly's, while those of Burke and Collins were handwritten. When asked about this in May 2008 at the tribunal, Richardson rejected any suggestion that he had initially signed the document as sole purchaser.

The deed of assignment—the document that records the actual transfer of the property—is filed in the Registry of Deeds. It is dated 18 May 1988 and signed by Daly as vendor and by five persons as purchasers: Richardson, Burke, Collins, James Keane and Patrick Reilly ('Paddy the Butcher'). The solicitor acting for the purchasers was Gerard Brennan, a supporter of Ahern. On its own, the document shows that the property belonged to these five men. The Registry of Deeds has no record of any mortgage taken out on the property at the time of the purchase, and no-one has suggested that there was one. The property was bought outright. In its intense examination of Ahern's finances, and of his and his constituency's various bank accounts, the Mahon Tribunal never managed to find an account from which the funds that were used to purchase the house originated. Nor were any of the witnesses who gave evidence able to point to an account where the money had resided before being passed to Daly.

All five of the trustees were close supporters of Ahern and minor business figures. Burke was a builder and renovator of pubs. Collins had a tiling business. Richardson, an engineer by training, was involved in recruitment services. Reilly had his own butcher's business in Stoneybatter and supplied meat to hospitals. Keane was involved in a DIY centre called Big J.

Before the purchase of St Luke's, Fianna Fáil in the North Dublin and Dublin Central constituencies used a building in Amiens Street, the ownership of which went back decades. During the mid-1980s it was decided that the building should be sold, and when it was, in 1989, the proceeds were distributed among a number of Fianna Fáil organisations. In 2008 a spokesperson for the party told the *Sunday Tribune*: 'The beneficiaries were three of the local constituency comhairles in Dublin. The proceeds of the sale were divided as agreed. The proceeds that accrued to Dublin Central are held in a constituency account.' In October 2006 Ahern mentioned the Amiens Street sale while being questioned in the Dáil about his personal finances. 'The house was sold by the trustees and officers of the party, and I probably was a trustee. The money is in the accounts.'

From the evidence heard by the tribunal it appears that the money received by Ahern and his operation in 1989 was still on deposit in 2008 in an investment account. It was not used to purchase St Luke's or to pay off any debts that had arisen from its purchase.

Since he was first elected to the Dáil in 1977 Ahern operated from a number of places. As well as his office in Leinster House and the use of Amiens Street, he had also kept an office in his mother's house near All Hallows College in Drumcondra. Later he rented offices above Fagan's pub in Drumcondra Road, almost opposite St Luke's.

St Luke's was very much seen as Ahern's constituency centre, not the party's, and it was a physical representation of his power in the constituency. The building was also a representation of his superior strength as a politician. In the period between the breaking up of his marriage in 1987 and his moving to a house in Beresford Avenue in 1995, Ahern made use of the apartment in the upstairs portion of St Luke's as his living quarters. His former supporter Royston Brady recalls that the upstairs bathroom was the first room he ever encountered with under-floor heating and that Ahern insisted that they take off their shoes to feel its warmth. No-one else used the apartment.

After Haughey's resignation as Taoiseach and party leader in 1992 there was speculation that Ahern might contest the leadership of the party, which would otherwise go to Albert Reynolds. As was so often the case when confronted with a sudden difficult decision, Ahern appeared to dither. If he went forward and won he would become leader; but if he lost, Reynolds might consider him a threat and seek to isolate him. If he held back and bided his time he could slip into the role of heir-apparent; but what if Reynolds held on to the job for a long period? His time might come and pass.

It appeared that Ahern didn't know what to do, and both his supporters and those of Reynolds grew increasingly frustrated. There were references by Reynolds supporters to Reynolds's family life and allusions to the people's right to know 'where their Taoiseach slept at night.' Ahern was nominally living at home with his mother but was also in a relationship with his partner, Celia Larkin. This was seen by some members as a political disadvantage for a party leader, and it appeared that if Ahern was to put his name forward his marital status would become an issue. According to *Bertie Ahern: Taoiseach and Peacemaker* (1998) by Ken Whelan and Eugene Masterson, Ahern and Reynolds met in the Berkeley Court Hotel in Dublin to discuss the matter. Ahern told the authors that he had informed Reynolds that he was not going to contest the leadership and that Reynolds made it clear that he 'wouldn't stay around very long.' Ahern held back, and Reynolds, when he took over, kept Ahern as Minister for Finance while sacking an unprecedented number of his Government colleagues. However, the use against Ahern of his marital situation had been noted by Ahern and his supporters.

During this period there was an editorial in the *Sunday Tribune* that read:

> In terms of age and style, Bertie Ahern would represent a break, but there are questions about his finances which are worrying. He is currently living in a house which 'supporters' bought for him and which cost over £120,000. What hostages to fortune have been given in that transaction?

Ahern, who did not have a practice of picking fights with the media, was sufficiently concerned by this to ask his solicitor, Gerry Brennan, to write a letter of complaint and seek an apology. He got his response in the following week's edition.

In the course of an editorial on the Fianna Fáil succession last Sunday, we stated that 'supporters' of Bertie Ahern TD had purchased for him a house costing over £120,000. We inquired what hostages to fortune had been given in that transaction. We have been contacted by a solicitor on behalf of Mr Ahern who informs us that while Mr Ahern has the use of an office and an upstairs apartment in the premises he has no interest whatsoever in the ownership of the house which is held in trust for the local Fianna Fáil organisation. We are glad to take this earliest opportunity of correcting any error in this regard and insofar as we have misrepresented the situation and insofar as our query concerning hostages to fortune is unfair to Mr Ahern, we apologise for any embarrassment or hurt this may have caused him.

The barrister David Byrne was appointed by Ahern as his first Attorney-General in 1997. Two years later Ahern appointed him to the European Commission. Byrne had become one of Ahern's advisers in November 1994, when he at last became leader of Fianna Fáil. In May 2008 Byrne was called to give evidence to the Mahon Tribunal about St Luke's after Ahern's solicitor wrote to the tribunal asking that the former commissioner be called. Some weeks earlier the tribunal had been given documents that, it was told, had been found in St Luke's among the voluminous files kept there. They concerned the purchase and ownership of St Luke's.

The tribunal was told that in April or early May 1997, when Ahern was preparing for the general election that would see him elected as Taoiseach, Byrne received a packet in the Law Library from Brennan. It was marked 'private and confidential', came with a compliments slip (but with no covering letter) and contained a number of documents concerning St Luke's, which included copies of the *Sunday Tribune* editorial, Brennan's letter in response and the paper's apology and clarification.

Also included were two letting agreements, dated 10 January 1992 and 21 January 1994, between the legal owners of the property and Ahern and concerning his occupation of the building, the deed of assignment for St Luke's, a 'Declaration of Trust' (in which the five men named in the Registry of Deeds in relation to St Luke's said they were holding the property in trust) and some other newspaper articles.

Byrne told the tribunal he could not recall receiving instructions from Brennan or Ahern in relation to the matter but presumed that he was contacted because the issue of St Luke's had arisen when Ahern was considering contesting the party leadership in 1992. In the period before the 1997 general election, when Ahern was hoping to become Taoiseach, Byrne said 'there was a desire to, as it were, draw all the features of this story together into one place and also to have an eye on the legal aspects of this.' He was to draft a document on St Luke's, and if there were new queries by the media about the matter during the campaign it could be referred to as part of Ahern's response.

Byrne met Ahern and Brennan twice to discuss the issue and produced a draft report that was never completed, because on 24 May 1997, twelve days after the second consultation, Brennan died unexpectedly. Des Richardson phoned Byrne to tell him of Brennan's death. Byrne spoke to a solicitor, David Anderson, who, with the approval of the Law Society, took over the management of Brennan's practice before its sale. Byrne also contacted another solicitor, Hugh O'Donnell, who subsequently, with the appropriate authority, took control of Ahern's files in the Brennan practice. Anderson later acted for Ahern in dealings relating to his home in Beresford Avenue.

Henry Murphy, senior counsel for the tribunal, pointed out that it had received a letter from Ahern's solicitor concerning the draft report after it had been found among the files in St Luke's. The letter said the document was

in fact prepared for and on behalf of the Fianna Fáil constituency organisation and various components thereof, including the trustees of St Luke's. As you know such entities are represented [at the tribunal] by Ivor Fitzpatrick & Co., solicitors, and I would suggest that you now seek their authority on their clients' behalf.

In other words, the tribunal was being told that the report belonged not to Ahern but to the trustees and to Fianna Fáil and that it had been prepared not for Ahern but for these bodies. As it transpired, this was the exact opposite of the impression created by evidence the tribunal heard later.

The draft report was dated 6 May 1997. The general election of that year was on 6 June. It was twenty-three paragraphs long and divided into seven sections. The title was 'Report on acquisition, legal ownership and financing of St Luke's 161 Lwr Drumcondra Road'. It dealt in brief with the decision to sell the Amiens Street building and said some of the proceeds of the sale were distributed among various cumainn, 'and the balance was put on the Fianna Fáil deposit account for the constituency.' It stated that the purchase price for St Luke's was £56,000 and that it was expected that renovations totalling £48,497.90 would be required. According to the report, when stamp duty was included the total amount estimated to be required for the building was £107,859.

To raise the funds necessary to purchase and renovate the premises, the St Luke's Club was informally established at a meeting held in the Gresham Hotel on 3 December 1987. This meeting was attended by over 20 people, most of them from the constituency, who resolved having regard to the funds required, that this sum could be raised over a period of four to five years by 25 people giving a commitment to provide £1,000 each per annum. It was also resolved that St Luke's should be purchased and that five of the members of the club should be appointed to act as trustees for the acquisition of the property. A resolution was also passed to the effect that the primary beneficiaries of the trust would be the local Fianna Fáil party and the ultimate beneficiary the Fianna Fáil national party.

The following paragraph said that the club—formed on 3 December 1987—had raised £16,000 by early 1988.

It was resolved that a further £50,000 would be raised by a bank loan should this be necessary. The fund continued to increase in value and by late 1989 the fund had accumulated £73,200. This left a shortfall of £34,657. This occurred because a number of commitments made were not fulfilled or only partly fulfilled. (Check this paragraph.)

In fact no bank loan was taken out. The note to check the contents of the paragraph for accuracy was, Byrne told the tribunal, indicative of the fact that the document was a work in progress that went no further after Brennan's death. Although the document introduced the whole St Luke's issue by dealing with the sale of the property in Amiens Street, none of the proceeds of its sale went to the purchase of St Luke's. That part of the proceeds associated with Ahern was placed in the investment account, where it was still sitting in 2008 when the tribunal was investigating these matters.

The two crucial issues for the report were the source of the funding and the ownership of the building. On the latter point the report stated:

The property was acquired by deed of assignment to the five trustees in mid-1988. A deed of trust was also executed by the club members as settlors [people who put assets into a trust], naming the five members of the club as trustees and specifying that the trustees held the trust property upon the following trusts.

The document then went on to list the use to which the building was to be put and the powers available to the trustees in furtherance of this use.

> It follows from this that the five legal trustees are the legal owners of the premises but specifically for the benefit of the Fianna Fáil party in Drumcondra electoral constituency with‘ the trustees having the discretion to apply the trust property for the ultimate benefit of the Fianna Fáil party itself.
>
> Accordingly, if the property is ever sold, the net proceeds of the sale must be applied for the benefit of the local Fianna Fáil constituency organisation or, at the discretion of the trustees, for the benefit of the Fianna Fáil party itself. Such proceeds cannot be handed over to any individual member of the party.

Byrne made it clear at the tribunal that all the information he put in the report came directly from Ahern and Brennan or from the documents Brennan had sent him. Brennan had acted as solicitor in all the dealings relating to St Luke's, including its funding, and therefore had an intimate knowledge of what had happened.

There was in fact no 'deed of trust . . . executed by the club members as settlors, naming the five members of the club as trustees and specifying that the trustees held the trust property, on the stated trusts'. Indeed, there was nothing in the documents seen by Byrne or by the tribunal that identified any settlors, members of the club or any contributor to the fund that was used to buy the property. At one point during his evidence Tim Collins, one of the people who signed the deed of assignment, gave the impression that he had never heard of the St Luke's Club. 'The first time I've come across that, St Luke's Club. Now, reading that now,' he said.

The tribunal did see a 'declaration of trust'. This was a document in which the persons named in the deed of assignment as having bought St Luke's declared that they were holding the property in trust. This was among the documents sent to Byrne in the Law Library ten years after the purchase of the property. Byrne told the tribunal he had never seen a deed of trust. He said the mention of a deed of trust executed by the settlors and the trustees, and the reasons for the trust, as appeared in his draft report, arose from his notes from his first meeting with Brennan and Ahern. The notes from his second meeting included the statement 'no formal deed of trust', so he believed that he must have raised the issue at the second meeting. The notes from the second meeting recorded that there was a declaration of trust in existence. (One difference between a declaration of trust and a deed of trust is that the former is a declaration by the trustees and does not name the settlors.) Byrne said that the earlier note about there being a deed of trust must have been a transcription of what Brennan had told him and that Brennan must have made a mistake.

Byrne agreed with Murphy that the declaration of trust made it obvious that the property was held in trust and that little else by way of documentary evidence was required. Furthermore, considering the simplicity of the matter, and that Brennan was not only a solicitor but the solicitor who had been involved in structuring the ownership, there seemed little need to get Byrne involved. 'So why were you consulted?' Murphy asked. Byrne said he was asked to apply his skills as a barrister to drawing together all 'the complex issues' into one document and to presenting his opinion on the legal status of St Luke's and Ahern's residence there, given the media interest in the matter during the 1992 leadership controversy, when it had been raised by the *Sunday Tribune*. Byrne said, 'There clearly was an apprehension that this issue may arise again. And if it does, we need to have this thing in writing so that we know what the situation is in relation to it.'

In other words, the document was to be something that Ahern could point to if he was questioned about St Luke's, its ownership and how it came to be purchased in the context of his bid to become Taoiseach. But the document, albeit in draft form, was full of inaccuracies about exactly the points it was created to clarify, and it was drafted by someone who had got all his information from Ahern and Brennan.

The net effect, then, if the media had asked questions of Ahern, would have been that Ahern, who knew about the matter, would have referred the reporters to Byrne's report; and Byrne's report, if it had not been radically altered, would have been wrong.

On 6 June 2008 Ahern was questioned about St Luke's at the Mahon Tribunal. He said:

Queries had been put to them [the trustees] a number of times, and they were anxious that we would pull one document together, and certainly one or two of them were very anxious that this would be done before there was a general election. And, as I recall, they asked Gerry Brennan if he would pull that together. He subsequently asked David Byrne and myself to work with him in drawing that document together. We had two or three meetings about that. Two or three meetings with Mr Byrne. There was two or three meetings with the trustees around about the same time.

When asked by Des O'Neill SC, counsel for the tribunal, Ahern agreed that Byrne did not attend the meetings with the trustees. He also agreed that Brennan had been a participant in every one of the items covered by Byrne's report and had access to the associated legal files.

The report was given to the tribunal in March 2008 after it was told that it and an associated memorandum had been found in a room in St Luke's called the library room. The memorandum was concerned with the funding of St Luke's and appeared to be addressed to Brennan and Byrne. Byrne said he had never seen the document before, but he thought that it had perhaps been drafted as a result of questions he had raised with Ahern and Brennan and that it was never sent to him because the whole question of the report was dropped after Brennan's unexpected death.

The memorandum set out information about a number of accounts that were linked to Ahern or St Luke's and had become the subject of public hearings in May and June 2008. 'As requested we checked the details on IV', the memorandum began, in a reference to the fourth section of Byrne's draft report, dealing with finance. The content of the memorandum was read into the record by Ahern's counsel, Conor Maguire SC. It said the trust was created and a bank account, the CODR (Cumann O'Donovan Rossa) account, opened in 1987.

Tim was secretary, Joe chairman and the donors paid into the account in 1987, 1988, 1989 and 1990. The loan was not required. The total figure was as per the list but there were some late payments.

This information was all incorrect.

The document also mentioned a £30,000 'loan we gave to the Minogue/O'Keeffe ladies through Celia.' This was a reference to a payment from an account called the B/T account, which became a significant matter in the erosion of Ahern's credibility during February 2008. The reference is incorrect in that the money was given to Larkin and not to 'the Minogue/O'Keeffe ladies', who were related to her. Larkin used the money to purchase the house in which her elderly relatives had been living as tenants. It was purchased in Celia Larkin's name, and there was no legal document in existence, as far as the tribunal could ascertain, stating that the payment to her was a loan. Nor was there any charge on the house. By the time the issue became public at the tribunal, the house was worth close to €1 million because of the property boom.

Under questioning by O'Neill, Ahern agreed that both Byrne's draft report and the associated memo contained inaccuracies. The draft report was not accurate in that it indicated that the money had been raised by twenty-five people contributing £1,000 each per year, £73,200 being accumulated by late 1989. Ahern agreed that the twenty-five people donating £1,000 a year had never happened. He said that at the time of the meeting in the Gresham Hotel, where, the tribunal had been told, a number of people committed themselves to paying £1,000 a year towards the purchase of St Luke's, some had suggested paying larger sums up front and being paid off as the others contributed over the years.

'What did in effect happen wasn't recorded by Mr Byrne [in the draft report] because it wasn't given to him, isn't that right?' O'Neill said.

'Obviously,' Ahern replied.

O'Neill said the background documents, including the contract between the vendor and the purchaser, showed that the property had in fact been acquired on 8 January 1988. The money was actually paid over on that date. The deed of assignment registered in the Registry of Deeds was dated May 1988, four months later. O'Neill said this contrasted with the statement in Byrne's draft report that the 'property was acquired by deed of assignment to the five trustees in mid-1988.' Ahern didn't take issue with O'Neill. However, Ahern's counsel argued that the report was factually correct, given the date on the deed of assignment. The Gresham Hotel meeting had taken place on 3 December 1987, the tribunal was told.

Ahern also agreed that the report was inaccurate in stating that by early 1988 the St Luke's Club had raised £16,000. This had to be wrong, since no bank loan was taken out that year, despite the reference in the draft report to there being a resolution to borrow £50,000. The house had been purchased in January 1988 for £56,000 plus stamp duty and other costs.

When O'Neill put it to Ahern that if the Byrne report had been given to the media it would have been misleading, Ahern countered that it would have been misleading in relation to the financing of St Luke's but accurate about other matters, such as the history of St Luke's and what cumainn and committees made use of it, that is, the sort of information the media would have no interest in, because it was not directly relevant.

O'Neill also raised the issue of the two letting agreements, copies of which were sent to Byrne in the Law Library in 1997. The documents were letting agreements dated 10 January 1992, the year Reynolds became party leader, and 21 January 1994, the year Ahern succeeded him. Neither document was stamped by the Revenue Commissioners. They both described the premises occupied by Ahern and the rent that was to be paid. Ahern said he thought there would have been a letting agreement for 1993. O'Neill pointed out that in Ahern's

submission to the Revenue Commissioners in January 2007, in the wake of
the disclosures concerning money he had received, his accountant, Des Peelo,
wrote:

> Mr Ahern did not make financial contributions during his circa
> intermittent two or three years stay at St Luke's, in Drumcondra. We are
> not clear as to the tax status of this latter benefit and accordingly make a
> voluntary disclosure of same pending clarification of this matter with the
> Revenue.

Ahern said the submission to the Revenue Commissioners, made on his
behalf and on his instructions, was incorrect.

O'Neill asked Ahern if the letting agreements might have been drafted
solely so that he would be in a position to use them if anyone ever asked him
a question about his use of the upstairs of St Luke's, 'whereas no such [letting]
arrangement existed at all? And these were merely documents which were
insurance to be produced in the event of somebody suggesting that your
occupation of the property was in circumstances other than as a tenant?'

Ahern's counsel interrupted O'Neill. The chairperson of the tribunal,
Judge Alan Mahon, asked Ahern if there was 'anything in the suggestion . . .
that these were anything but genuine?' Ahern replied:

> They were not prepared by me . . . They were prepared by the trustees.
> They were prepared by a member of the Law Society [Gerry Brennan]
> and put to me to sign. And they were, if the suggestion by Mr O'Neill is
> that a member of the Law Society would produce some kind of bogus
> documents—the answer to that is certainly no.

Ahern's counsel, Conor Maguire, intervened and said that, by raising the
issue, O'Neill had tried to trap and 'demean' Ahern. O'Neill said he rejected
the accusation, and Judge Mahon said he did not see the questioning as an
attempt to set a trap. When O'Neill had finished his questioning, Maguire
read out a letter from the tribunal to Ahern's solicitors confirming that it was
not investigating the ownership of St Luke's or how it was acquired.

Maguire then read into the record the contents of another document that
had been given to the tribunal in early 2008. The document was entitled
'Attendance for the file' and was signed by Gerry Brennan, with a date of
3 December 1987. It concerned the meeting that the tribunal was told was held
in the Gresham Hotel on that date. It wasn't among the documents Byrne

received in the Law Library in 1997, although he said the matters recorded in
the note would in effect have created a trust, since the meeting, as per the
note, recorded the intention of the donors (the settlors) that the property to
be bought with their money be held in trust. The document read:

> I attended at the above meeting when it was confirmed that the contract
> for the purchase of 161 Lower Drumcondra Road had been signed. [The
> contract had been signed on 19 November.] After some discussion
> regarding the property and its development [and] after my advice to the
> meeting regarding the holding of the property in trust it was proposed
> and seconded that the following would take place:
>
> No 1. That Joe Burke, Tim Collins, Paddy Reilly and Des Richardson
> and [Jimmy Keane, another Ahern associate] would be trustees if they so
> agreed to act.
>
> No 2. That the property, when completed, would be held in the names
> of the trustees for the benefit of Fianna Fáil party in Drumcondra
> electoral constituency as it presently stood, with the discretion for the
> trustees to apply the trust property for the benefit of the party ensuring
> that the ultimate beneficiary of the trust would be the party.
>
> It was also agreed and confirmed that the trustees would have the
> powers in relation to leasing, mortgaging, financing, development ... and
> that the trustees would have full discretion to use and develop the
> property once the ultimate beneficiary was the party. Finally it was agreed
> by the meeting that I would act as solicitor in connection with the
> completion of the purchase and also in connection with the completion
> of the appropriate declaration of trust in accordance with the wishes of
> the meeting. After some brief discussion of the matter the meeting
> concluded.

In May 2008 Liam Cooper, a member of the O'Donovan Rossa Cumann
since the 1980s and a former treasurer of the Dublin Central Comhairle Dáil
Ceantair (constituency council), said he had never heard of the Gresham
Hotel meeting until it was mentioned at the tribunal. He had raised the matter
with Ahern after it had been brought up at the tribunal, and Ahern told him
about it, he said. 'And I believe him.'

Some time after Ahern's and Byrne's appearances at the tribunal, a solicitor,
Sheena Beale, who had acted for St Luke's when a mortgage was applied for
in 1999, gave evidence. During Beale's evidence O'Neill pointed out that the
declaration that stated that the five men who had bought the house from Daly

were holding it in trust had been filed and stamped by the Revenue Commissioners four years after the house had been bought. He said that normally a declaration of trust would be filed and stamped on the same day a property was transferred to its new owner. Beale agreed. The declaration of trust in relation to St Luke's was dated 18 May 1988, the same date the property was assigned to the five Ahern supporters. However, it was not stamped by the Revenue Commissioners until four-and-a-half years later, by which time Ahern was Minister for Finance in the first Reynolds Government. By this time Ahern was also of the view that something would have to be done about St Luke's in the light of the *Sunday Tribune* article so that when the opportunity next came round to be party leader he would be able to answer questions about its ownership and put any potential controversy to rest.

Chapter 4 ～

| LOOT

In time, documents found in the archives of various banks used by
Bertie Ahern, and calculations made by the tribunal concerning exchange
rates on the day he made some of his deposits, served to challenge much
of his story about dig-outs in Dublin and donations in Manchester. But it was
an ancillary aspect of the evidence of the Dublin stockbroker Padraic O'Connor
that brought about Ahern's eventual downfall.

This evidence caused the tribunal to conduct a close examination of a
number of bank accounts, including ones that Ahern had not disclosed in his
original sworn affidavit of discovery (a list produced by the person making
the affidavit, who swears that it contains all the items it should contain). Ahern
was asked to list bank accounts held by him or into which money had been
lodged for his benefit. His disclosure in relation to the second part of that
order was incomplete.

The new evidence raised questions about whether or not Ahern had been
pocketing money ostensibly raised to fund his political operation.
Moreover—and this proved to be the killer blow—fresh and substantial
foreign currency was discovered in one of Ahern's personal accounts years
after he had given exhaustive evidence about the source of the funds in his
accounts (salary) and about any involvement he might have had with foreign
currencies (almost none).

Both Padraic O'Connor and Des Richardson agreed in their evidence that
the former was approached by the latter in late 1993 and asked for money and
that some time later that money was paid. Richardson said that he approached

O'Connor as part of his efforts in relation to the first dig-out for Ahern, which he said he had organised with Brennan, and that it was at all times clear to O'Connor that the money was for Ahern personally. He also said that at the end of the meeting he asked O'Connor if his firm, NCB Stockbrokers, would take out a table at a fund-raising dinner to be held in the Royal Hospital, Kilmainham, to raise funds for Ahern's O'Donovan Rossa Cumann.

O'Connor was the managing director of NCB Stockbrokers, and he said the money given to Richardson was a political donation from the firm, not a personal donation from him to Ahern. Richardson had told him, O'Connor said, that because Ahern had been appointed national treasurer of Fianna Fáil he had less time to raise funds for his constituency operation. Richardson, he added, told him he was approaching four or five parties with a view to collecting the annual running costs of St Luke's. The total figure, he recalled, was in the region of £20,000–25,000, and NCB was asked to give £5,000. O'Connor said that he was not a close friend of Ahern's in the sense presented by Ahern in his comments to the tribunal, the Dáil and the general public, and that he had no memory of being asked to attend the fund-raising dinner. Both men were forthright and clear in their evidence.

O'Connor's version of events was backed up by some of his colleagues in NCB with whom, the tribunal was told, he discussed the matter before deciding to make the payment, and who also gave evidence. An odd aspect of the payment was that the firm didn't simply make a political donation and record it in its books as such: instead a fake invoice was produced by a company called Euro Workforce Ltd, and a payment was issued by NCB on foot of the invoice. VAT was even paid, so that the £5,000 donation became £6,050 when VAT was included. Euro Workforce Ltd was a personnel company with an address at 25 Merrion Square, Dublin. It had formerly been owned by Richardson and Collins together with Des Maguire. The bogus invoice was found in the NCB files with O'Connor's signature on it, so he obviously knew about the bogus invoice. He told the tribunal that he had since forgotten about that aspect of the matter.

O'Connor was closely questioned on his evidence that he and the firm were anxious to conceal the fact that they were making a political donation to Ahern and that this explained the bogus invoice. It was pointed out that in 1994 and 1995 the firm had attended the annual fund-raising dinners in Kilmainham for Ahern's constituency operation and had written cheques to the O'Donovan Rossa Cumann and treated the matter in the NCB books as a normal political donation. O'Connor said the difference was the more private, focused nature of the Richardson fund-raising exercise, but Ahern said the way in which NCB had treated the £5,000 payment indicated that it was other than a normal political donation.

Interestingly, in the light of what will be shown later, Ahern told the tribunal that he had asked his constituency treasurer to check on this matter and find him copies of the NCB cheques made out to the cumann. The constituency people also went through the records of the annual dinners at Kilmainham and found references to NCB attending in 1994 and 1995. Ahern was given copies of these records, which he forwarded to the tribunal. They also found a letter from Joe Burke to NCB, dated November 1995, in which Burke, the chairperson of what was called the house committee (the house being St Luke's), wrote to NCB saying he was delighted that they would be attending the dinner. Ahern also forwarded this document to the tribunal.

The payment to Ahern of £5,000 was a bank draft made out to Richardson, which the tribunal was able to find in the bank's archives. According to Richardson he bought the draft with the money that had come from NCB. He said that, while he and Brennan dealt with many of the cash donors to the dig-out, he personally dealt with O'Connor and that the payment was, unusually, not in cash.

While O'Connor said he was not a personal friend of Ahern's, he had known him since they worked together during the currency crisis of the later months of 1992. The international markets were betting against the Irish pound, and Ahern, as Minister for Finance, was the person who had to decide when, or if, it would be devalued. Vast amounts of money were involved, and Ahern eventually devalued the currency. When O'Connor gave evidence he said that he presumed that when Richardson had called on him it was in connection with his work on the currency crisis.

O'Connor, who had worked on currency matters while employed as an economist, offered his services *gratis* to Ahern because his position with NCB gave him an insight into what the currency markets were thinking. O'Connor told the tribunal: 'I worked with him. I admired what he was doing. I liked him.' He also said he later had dealings with Ahern, who spoke at conferences and seminars at which NCB was trying to persuade overseas investors to buy Irish stocks.

'I am sure I would have assumed that NCB was approached because of the fairly regular contact I had with Mr Ahern over the previous year or eighteen months,' O'Connor said. Based on documents the tribunal showed him he agreed that he had met Ahern within weeks of the payment as part of his business dealings with him as Minister for Finance. O'Connor did not agree with Ahern's evidence that he had thanked O'Connor for the loan. He said he did not recall being thanked and that it could not have happened that he was thanked for a personal contribution to Ahern's personal finances.

This convoluted saga had the tribunal scratching its head, and an in-depth trawl of the matter was carried out to see if any definitive money trail could be established. The more the tribunal investigated it the less clear it became. In time it emerged that the £5,000 draft wasn't paid for with NCB money at all but with money that came from an account in the name of a company called Roevin Ireland Ltd, which had at one point owned Workforce (later Euro Workforce). Richardson told the tribunal that he had had an involvement with Roevin and that, as part of the arrangements made after the business closed, he was given the right to the money lodged in the account. It was, he said, his money. To add further murkiness to the whole affair, the company had in turn been owned at one time by a parent company, Doctus, which was based in, of all places, Manchester.

The Roevin account was opened on 12 October 1992 with a lodgement of £39,000. There was a later withdrawal of £2,000, but otherwise there were no transactions up to 22 December 1993, when it was used to buy the bank draft given to Ahern.

The tribunal was never able to establish where the NCB money went after it was paid to Euro Workforce Ltd. O'Connor was asked if, to accommodate NCB's desire for confidentiality, he had agreed with Richardson that a 'contra' arrangement (whereby one entity would pay money to Ahern, and NCB would pay a similar amount to another entity, but the two transactions would not be joined up or directly linked in any way) would be made. 'There was no such discussion,' said O'Connor.

O'Connor also said if he had been asked to make a personal charitable donation to Ahern he would have made it with his own funds. He said that, to his knowledge, no political donations had been made between his becoming managing director of NCB in 1991 and his being approached in December 1993 by Richardson.

The essential point was that the tribunal wasn't able to establish a money trail from NCB to Ahern's account. If Richardson had wanted to he could have said the draft was part of his contribution to the dig-out, and O'Connor would never have been dragged into the tribunal's inquiries in the first place. This would have saved Ahern a lot of trouble.

Richardson had contacted O'Connor in 2005, and they met in the Berkeley Court Hotel. This was before the tribunal had been told of any dig-out or of any contribution from O'Connor. O'Connor was told that the tribunal was inquiring into Ahern's finances and that Richardson was helping him track down various payments. Richardson asked O'Connor if he recalled a payment in the early 1990s; O'Connor said he did. Richardson put a date on the payment, December 1993, and asked O'Connor for his recollection. O'Connor said that he had no documents, that it was a matter for NCB and that he no longer worked for the firm. He told the tribunal that Richardson never mentioned the idea that the payment was part of any whip-around for Ahern personally. After the meeting O'Connor spoke on the phone to his former colleagues in NCB, Chris McHugh and Graham O'Brien. 'Their recollection was really precisely the same as mine,' the tribunal was told. At this time, he said, there was no indication that Richardson had in mind a different description of the payment to O'Connor.

The following summer the men met again. Richardson called O'Connor, and they met briefly in the Radisson Hotel, close to O'Connor's home. O'Connor said Richardson was

> very keen to get the documentation that would establish how the payment was made, because, as he explained it to me, efforts were being made to put together material to explain Ahern's finances . . . I think it was at that meeting that I got the first inkling that my recollection wasn't the only version of events, as it were. Because he did say to me, you know, 'That's your recollection, and presumably you will be asked and you will have to give them your recollection.' I wasn't told what the alternative version was about.

O'Connor told the tribunal he didn't think he was told anything about the payment being a loan to Ahern or about it being part of a dig-out. 'Because I think my surprise was total when I heard that first in the interview with Bryan Dobson.'

This differed from Richardson's evidence, which was to the effect that, at this second meeting, he made it clear to O'Connor that he believed the payment had been a personal donation to Ahern. When this was put to O'Connor he said he wasn't 'absolutely sure that there wasn't some suggestion that, well, we don't think it was NCB. I just don't recall that.'

In the wake of Ahern's interview with Dobson, and without notice, O'Connor got a short letter from Ahern thanking him for the loan he had 'kindly extended to me all those years ago.' Enclosed was a cheque from Ahern for €11,829 'in full and final settlement of the outstanding loan.' O'Connor took legal advice and sent a note to the Department of the Taoiseach thanking Ahern for the cheque and informing him that he was writing to Richardson about the matter. 'Best personal regards, Yours sincerely.' In his letter to Richardson, O'Connor said he had received the cheque from Ahern. 'As the Taoiseach says in his letter, this all took place a very long time ago. As I said to you when we spoke some time ago, the payment to which I believe the Taoiseach's letter and cheque relate was made by NCB rather than by me personally.' The payment was paid through Richardson, he wrote. 'I do not want to presume as to how you dealt with it.' He said he intended to hold Ahern's cheque uncashed.

The tribunal barrister Des O'Neill asked O'Connor why he had not informed Ahern of his version of how the payment came about. O'Connor said it was because of personal considerations.

> My primary instinct was, as far as was possible, given how public it was, to keep my head down and keep out of it. I didn't want to get drawn into what was going to be . . . a political issue . . . I didn't see that my personal interests or my privacy would be served by having that engagement with either Mr Ahern or Mr Richardson. I didn't see that that would improve my position in any way. And all I was interested in, frankly, was my own position and the position of my family.

O'Neill put it to O'Connor that the Taoiseach had made a statement to the public, on television, to explain 'an unusual set of circumstances', and it was apparent to O'Connor 'as a citizen that the explanation that was being given, insofar as you could test its veracity, was untrue.' A consequence of O'Connor adopting the position he did was that the Taoiseach's version of events went unchallenged, O'Neill said. O'Connor agreed. He said he didn't want to be drawn into a political issue. He also agreed that he had not known at the time that the issue would eventually feature in a public sitting of the tribunal. O'Connor said his solicitor had in fact argued in private correspondence with the tribunal that the matter did not fall within its terms of reference and so should not be investigated in public.

During one of his private interviews with the tribunal O'Connor said why he had chosen not to contact Richardson. 'I didn't see the point. I mean . . . this is politics, and I am not political . . . Whatever Bertie Ahern decides to say to try and save his political existence, that's politics.'

Ahern's counsel chose not to put any questions to O'Connor. Ahern later said this was because he considered O'Connor to be a friend. O'Connor's legal representative never questioned Richardson, and O'Connor said he saw this as a matter for the tribunal. Richardson's counsel, Jim O'Callaghan, did put questions to O'Connor, and O'Connor appeared at one point to become annoyed.

> I did not have that personal relationship [with Ahern] . . . I did not know of his marital issues. To this day I don't know how it can be even suggested that I might have been one of those people who might be approached . . . I would have been very surprised if I was approached. I did not know Gerry Brennan. Never met him. I had never heard of him. Mr Richardson knew me vaguely. How these two people could put my name on a list and then say that they came to me or one of them came to me with what I would have regarded as an extraordinary request—it didn't happen.

When O'Callaghan put it to O'Connor that the circumstances concerning the method of payment indicated that it was a personal donation to Ahern, using NCB money, O'Connor replied: 'That's offensive and it's absolute nonsense.'

The money lodged to Ahern's account, which the tribunal was told arose from the first of the two dig-outs, comprised £15,000 in cash, the £5,000 draft and a cheque for £2,500. The cheque came from a company called Willdover Ltd, which was controlled by Richardson and which he used to invoice Fianna Fáil for his services as a full-time fund-raiser for the party, appointed by Ahern. In other words, the money Richardson said he gave Ahern as his contribution to the dig-out originated with Fianna Fáil, though it had become Richardson's when paid to Willdover.

O'Connor's evidence concerning his motive for authorising an NCB payment contradicted Ahern's whole dig-out story; but it was his evidence concerning an aspect of his thinking when deciding to make the payment that would finish off Ahern. O'Connor was contacted by the tribunal in 2006, and on 16 October of that year he made a statement in which he said that Richardson had told him that he (Richardson) was 'approaching four or five companies to request a contribution of £5,000' from each of them. At a private interview with the tribunal nine days later O'Connor said he had a vague recollection that one of the companies mentioned might have been a competitor firm of stockbrokers. When giving evidence in November 2008 he amended this to say that Richardson might not have mentioned competitor firms being approached; rather, this may simply have been a worry on O'Connor's part. The worry was that NCB might be at a disadvantage if it did not make a payment and a rival firm did.

O'Connor's comments in the private interview prompted the tribunal to write to eleven other stockbroking firms asking them if they had received requests in or around December 1993 for donations for Ahern. All replied that they had not, or that, if they had, they could not recall being asked. However, Davy Stockbrokers told the tribunal that it had made a political donation to Ahern in November 1992. In time, a copy of the Davy cheque was retrieved from bank archives and forwarded to the tribunal. It was made out to Bertie Ahern and had been lodged on 28 January 1993. The details as to where it had been lodged were recorded on the back of the cheque and showed an account number in the Irish Permanent Building Society, Drumcondra. This was not one of the twenty-two accounts declared by Ahern when he had sworn his affidavit of discovery in February 2005, listing accounts into which money to be used for his benefit had been lodged.

The tribunal wrote to Ahern about the Davy payment and the account in the Irish Permanent on 30 November 2007, when he was already preparing for his next appearance at the tribunal to deal with the dig-out lodgements and other aspects of his personal finances. Everything indicates that he immediately realised that the inquiries were going in a direction that held great danger for his political survival.

In its letter of 30 November the tribunal asked for Ahern's knowledge of the Davy payment and the circumstances surrounding its lodgement to the identified account in the Irish Permanent as well as for any related documents in his possession. When he appeared before the tribunal on 21 and 22 December he had not yet responded to the letter. The subject was not raised during his evidence, and the tribunal broke for the Christmas period.

On 7 January 2008 Ahern's solicitors wrote to the tribunal. They said the Davy cheque had been sent to St Luke's and was

> handled in that office by the finance election committee as a political donation for the benefit of Fianna Fáil Dublin Central. The cheque was allocated to the building trust for the purpose for which that account was established. It was a fund for use in connection with St Luke's which is held for the benefit of Dublin Central Fianna Fáil.

The tribunal was told that a constituency committee called the house committee was in charge of the account into which the money was lodged.

On 14 January the tribunal wrote to Ahern with a lengthy list of questions and proposals for orders of discovery (ascertaining what documents existed or had existed that might be relevant and ordering their production). It asked him to identify the members of the house committee for the period concerned, to provide minutes of all decisions made by it, to produce documents relating to the account into which the Davy cheque was lodged, and to identify the members of the finance committee at the time of the 1992 general election.

Ahern was also asked to provide the records of receipts for the 1992 election campaign that would show the Davy cheque being received. The tribunal had by this time seen a copy of a statement on the account, and the £5,000 Davy cheque had been lodged with a second cheque of a similar amount, making for a £10,000 lodgement. Ahern was asked the identity of the donor of the second cheque. He was also asked about a number of other transactions on the account, including a withdrawal of £30,000 from the account on 30 March 1993, by way of a cheque to a Patrick O'Sullivan, solicitor.

Ahern was also asked about a series of sizeable lodgements from 1989 to 1995 and was told that the tribunal was considering making an order of discovery for documents belonging to the house committee of St Luke's concerning the receipt of funds between 1 January 1989 and 1 January 1995. The tribunal, by way of the Davy cheque, was travelling deep into the finances of Ahern's Drumcondra operation in the middle years of his political career.

Ahern's solicitor at the tribunal was Liam Guidera of Frank Ward and Company, solicitors to Fianna Fáil. The tribunal got its first response to its letter on 5 February, that is, three-and-a-half weeks later. Guidera said that the information and documents that had been requested 'relate to the activities of Fianna Fáil Dublin Central constituency organisation' and that the proposed orders of discovery were not properly directed at Ahern and ought to be directed at other persons. The requests, Guidera said, should go to the Fianna Fáil Dublin Central organisation. 'I understand that the organisation has sought its own legal advice and that the tribunal will be contacted in that regard in due course. However, my client wishes to make it clear that he objects to this line of inquiry.'

Notwithstanding the objections to the request for information, the solicitor said that, at the time of the 1992 general election, the usual practice was that the treasurers of the Dublin Central Comhairle Dáil Ceantair 'and a number of volunteer members of the Fianna Fáil Dublin Central organisation, including members of the House Committee, would have been involved in raising funds to finance the election campaign.'

The members of the committee dealing with finances for the November 1992 election were Joe Burke, Tim Collins, Paddy Reilly (Paddy the Butcher), deceased, Jimmy Keane, deceased, and Gerry Brennan, deceased. They were also the members of the house committee in the period 1989–95, the tribunal was told.

The letter from Guidera was the first time the tribunal heard that Ahern was adopting the position that he was not the proper person to answer questions about the affairs of his constituency organisation. Asked later by Des O'Neill if there was a divide between him and his constituency organisation that was such that he was incapable of acquiring constituency documents to assist the tribunal, Ahern said:

No, there is no difficulty with me getting assistance. But can I say, Mr O'Neill, what I have been dealing with in this tribunal, with the greatest of respect, has been my wife's accounts, my children's accounts, my accounts. I haven't been dealing with the Fianna Fáil accounts. The Fianna Fáil accounts for Dublin Central constituency are under the direction of the constituency, under the offices of the constituency. Of course I work with them. Of course they would co-operate with me. But they are Fianna Fáil constituency or Fianna Fáil business.

The statement is interesting, since what emerged from the evidence heard by the tribunal was that the Irish Permanent account into which the Davy cheque was lodged was not under the control of the officer board of Ahern's constituency. Rather, the account was under the sole control of Ahern's long-time supporter and associate Tim Collins, who wasn't even a member of Fianna Fáil, let alone an elected constituency officer. Furthermore, the officer board had no control of the account and, as the evidence would in time show, had not known how much was in it until it was told by the tribunal in 2008.

Bertie Ahern appeared before the tribunal on 21 and 22 February 2008. On 1 February, Ahern's solicitor wrote to the tribunal asking that the matters concerning the Irish Permanent account be looked at by way of private inquiry before becoming the subject of public evidence. He also said that, 'as far as our client is concerned, the constituency is properly under the control of the constituency organisation.' Nevertheless, the hearing went ahead.

O'Neill queried Ahern about O'Connor's evidence that he had been worried that, in December 1993, Richardson might have approached other rival stockbroking firms. He told him about the tribunal's decision to write to eleven other stockbroking firms and about the responses it had received. Ahern's counsel, Conor Maguire, intervened and said he was very concerned that he had not been told of their responses. He should have been, he argued, and he asked that the tribunal rise to allow him to consider the matter. He argued that Ahern should not be asked about the Davy cheque, because he had not been told that the other stockbroking firms were being written to; but the chairperson rejected the application. When Ahern replied that the Davy cheque would have been recorded by the constituency organisation when it had been received, O'Neill asked him if he had those records with him. Ahern said he didn't. O'Neill asked why not. 'Because I don't have constituency records. It's Fianna Fáil constituency accounts. And I do not have Fianna Fáil constituency accounts, but I know it's recorded.' This was the first the public heard of a division that had apparently emerged between Ahern and his famously supportive constituency organisation.

The Irish Permanent account into which the Davy cheque had been lodged was called simply 'B/T'. This had not been mentioned publicly until Ahern's appearance on 21 February, nor had the fact that Tim Collins had opened the account during the 1989 general election campaign. Collins was the sole signatory. When opening the account he had stipulated that the statements on the account be kept in the branch. He also signed a declaration stating that the funds belonged to him personally and that he was not holding them as nominee for any other party. The tribunal had ascertained all these facts by the time of Ahern's appearance, because it had been able to get certain documents from the Irish Permanent files. Neither Ahern nor his constituency organisation had provided the tribunal with anything at this point.

Ahern, during questioning from the chairperson, Judge Alan Mahon, said that there was a list available of the political donations received in 1992 and that the Davy contribution was on it. He said Davy had donated £5,000; some of it had gone into the 1992 election account and some into 'the building trust account, that is a call they [the officers of the constituency] make, where the money goes.' In other words, Ahern was saying that the initials on the Irish Permanent account stood for 'building trust' and that the decision about whether a political donation went into the election account or the B/T account was determined by the officers of the constituency.

When O'Neill asked Ahern for the whereabouts of the documents the tribunal had sought from him on 30 November, he said, 'In the hands of Fianna Fáil party Dublin Central . . . I am not here answering for Fianna Fáil Dublin Central. Fianna Fáil Dublin Central have their own system. I can co-operate and I can assist.'

When the chairperson said he would have assumed that the committee and the constituency would co-operate with Ahern and provide him with documents (even if, legally, he could not instruct them to do so), he appeared to agree. O'Neill suggested that the documents could be brought to Dublin Castle from St Luke's during the lunch break and produced at two o'clock. Ahern said it would not be possible, and O'Neill suggested that it be produced by 10 a.m. the next day.

Ahern was asked at one point if he would have a role in the decision to put money received into the 'election account' or the 'building trust account'. He said he would not. 'That is why we have a democratic organisation and we elect officers, and people work hard to do that.' O'Neill then asked him if this was a reference to the treasurers of the constituency organisation.

> The officers, well, normally. The officers of the Comhairle Dáil Ceantair are the elected officer board. In an election they normally would ask— somebody would take on the responsibility. Now it's an election agent. Then somebody would take on the responsibility of trying to gather funds and they would be the signatory of the account.

Ahern disclosed that, during the 1992 election, Tim Collins had opened an 'election account'. O'Neill asked if this was the only election account. Ahern replied, 'Yeah, well, the Comhairle Dáil Ceantair perhaps could have also a separate election account.'

In time it would emerge that the elected constituency officers had indeed opened an account for the 1992 general election. By the end of the campaign the account run by the officers was in the red, while the account run by Collins had a substantial balance.

Ahern said the accounts for the 1992 election were 'not necessarily' run by the treasurers. The election account was run by the finance committee. The secretary of that committee was Collins, and the account was in his name, he said. Ahern could not say if Collins was a member of a particular cumann. In fact Collins was never a member of Fianna Fáil.

Ahern said Collins was elected to the trust that was set up when money was being raised to buy St Luke's.

> The trust was set up by those who donated to the trust. And he was appointed by them to be secretary of the trust. The trust was run by the Cumann O'Donovan Rossa committee, which he was secretary of, and the finance committee at that time was linked to that, and he was secretary. He was effectively secretary of the trust when all the work was being done to set up the trust.

According to the Byrne memorandum, considered in the previous chapter, the persons who established the trust and who contributed the funds to St Luke's were part of a grouping called the St Luke's Club. As we have seen, Collins was asked about this term when he appeared before the tribunal, and he gave the impression that he had never heard of such a club.

Ahern was asked about the fact that the account name was simply the initials B/T. He said the constituency used a lot of initials. By way of example he mentioned CDC, for Comhairle Dáil Ceantair. O'Neill said he was specifically referring to initials being used for the names of bank accounts. Ahern said there was the CODR (Cumann O'Donovan Rossa) account, and O'Neill's reaction showed that this was another account he hadn't heard of before.

'You haven't discovered that to the tribunal,' he said.

'Because it's not my account,' Ahern replied.

The only accounts he had disclosed that were not personal accounts were accounts into which money was lodged to 'elect me', Ahern declared. The other constituency accounts did not hold money for his benefit.

O'Neill made the point that if Collins had died in the early 1990s the money in the B/T account would have formed part of his personal estate. Ahern said that Collins's family 'are not like that.' He said the officers of the constituency knew over the years that the money in the account was connected to St Luke's. If it had ended up in Collins's estate 'his wife would have been on to one of our officers in five minutes to give it back.'

No Comhairle Dáil Ceantair document was ever produced to the tribunal in which the constituency organisation recorded the existence of the B/T account in the 1990s. In 1995 the 'rainbow' Government, headed by John Bruton of Fine Gael, introduced legislation that established new controls over political fund-raising. One of the stipulations was that each constituency organisation had to nominate an account into which all political donations were deposited. It also had to nominate a party officer who would liaise with a newly established Standards in Public Office Commission in relation to the operation of the account. The lodgements to the B/T account ceased with the coming into effect of the new legislation in 1995, and the account remained untouched until 2008 and its discovery by the tribunal.

In 1995 the address on the B/T account was changed to Collins's home address in Malahide from the 'care of the branch' address that had previously been in use. Ahern said that in about 1995 or 1996 Collins began to suffer health problems and withdrew from much of his work connected with St Luke's. He said responsibility for the B/T account was taken over by a new

Comhairle Dáil Ceantair officer, Dominic Dillane, but he later amended this evidence when Dillane brought it to his attention that he had not joined Fianna Fáil until 1999. Ahern gave no evidence about who he believed was in charge of the B/T account on behalf of the constituency organisation from 1995 to 1999. Dillane told the tribunal that he had learnt of the account on being appointed Comhairle Dáil Ceantair treasurer a year or so after joining the party. He became active with the party after he had met Royston Brady when the latter was canvassing for it. Brady believes that Ahern selected Dillane to be constituency treasurer precisely because he had no personal knowledge of matters that occurred before his becoming involved with the party. Information discreetly disclosed by Brady to reporters during the Ahern payments crisis had come from Dillane to Brady years earlier, according to Brady, who sometimes socialised with Dillane. In 2003 Dillane was appointed a director of Fáilte Ireland, the state tourism board.

At the time of Ahern's appearance before the tribunal the balance in the B/T account, which had not been touched since 1995, was €47,803.52. Ahern said the purpose of the B/T account was to hold money so that it would be available if it was needed for work on St Luke's. In fact up to €200,000 had been spent on the renovation and maintenance of St Luke's since it was purchased in 1987, but none of it had come from the B/T account. Most of the lodgements were large, round-figure amounts, including lodgements of £5,000 every January between 1993 and 1995. Ahern was questioned about these during his February appearances.

As we have seen, the tribunal had sought a written explanation from Ahern on 30 November 2007 about the lodgements and withdrawals on the B/T account. As Judge Mahon explained to Ahern's counsel during the February sittings, because the tribunal had not received the answers it had sought by way of correspondence, it decided to seek them by the direct questioning of Ahern in the witness box. The chairperson said the tribunal had warned Ahern before his appearances in the witness box in late December that it might ask him about the B/T account.

Where information is not furnished to the tribunal in a timely fashion, it often necessitates the convening of a public sitting of the tribunal to obtain such information by way of sworn evidence before the tribunal.

As Mr Ahern was scheduled to give evidence on 20th and 21st December 2007, he was notified of the fact that the tribunal intended to take his sworn evidence in relation to this issue. Furthermore, Mr Ahern was notified of the fact that should his evidence fail to be completed, he would be questioned on this issue when he returned to give evidence to the tribunal.

It is now 22nd February 2008, almost three months since the tribunal's initial request for information concerning the then named BT account. Accordingly the tribunal does not believe that it is in any way premature to conduct public hearings for the purposes of taking Mr Ahern's sworn evidence in relation to this account.

Ahern was able to give explanations for most of the lodgements and withdrawals on the B/T account when O'Neill asked about them. He said the lodgements, bar one, were political donations or funds raised by golf classics. The withdrawals were expenses relating to his constituency operation. One withdrawal, of £20,000 in cash, arose from a decision to get some work done on St Luke's. Subsequently a decision was made not to go ahead with the work, he said, and a short time later the £20,000 in cash was relodged.

The cheque of 30 March 1993 to the solicitor Patrick O'Sullivan was a decision of the house committee, he said, to give a loan to a member of staff. Three elderly relatives of the staff member were afraid that the house in which they had been living for a long period was going to be sold. They had tenancy rights but were afraid that a new owner would move other tenants in to live with them. The loan was advanced to the staff member so that the house could be purchased. There was no charge on the house, Ahern said. Asked when the loan had to be repaid, he said, 'That was worked out with the officers, but in fact it hadn't got to be repaid for a period; but the individuals opted to pay it back, and they have.' Asked when, he said, 'In recent times, certainly not years. In the recent past. Weeks or months, but recently.' He agreed it was in the period since the tribunal had first queried the matter.

On the second of Ahern's February appearances O'Neill said it had been expected that he would produce certain documents by 10 a.m. but that this had not happened. Rather, a letter had been received from Ahern's solicitor, Liam Guidera, at 9:30 a.m. informing the tribunal that the documents were the property of the Fianna Fáil constituency organisation, not of Ahern. The letter also suggested that the matter of the B/T account should not be pursued in public hearings for the time being.

My client has passed on to the constituency officers his exhortation that the requests of the tribunal be complied with if possible. However I understand that the constituency officers wish to consult with their legal representatives in that regard. It is hoped that this will not delay matters unduly. However in the circumstances I must reiterate the observations by Mr Maguire senior counsel [for Ahern] that these are matters which are the subject of an ongoing and unfinished private inquiry. It would be far more sensible to attempt to address the tribunal's queries by way of correspondence and private interview in the first instance, rather than by way of what we consider will transpire to be an unnecessary public hearing.

When Ahern said he understood that the constituency officers would consult their solicitor, and in time make the documents available, O'Neill asked, 'On what basis is that understanding founded, Mr Ahern?'

Ahern said he had briefly met a number of the senior officers of the constituency the previous night and told them they should work to make the data being sought by the tribunal available as soon as possible. 'And they, as I understand it, they are meeting their own solicitor, and they are working to make that data available.'

Ahern said he had no new documents in his possession.

They have told me that they are going to give all of the information that we've gathered over the last few weeks. And they want to discuss that with their solicitor. And they are going to get it to the tribunal as quickly as they can. And that's what they are endeavouring to do . . . They are preparing those documents, but they have been advised that those documents must go to their own solicitor before they can come to the tribunal. That's what they informed me.

He said the constituency officers declined to give the documents to him for this reason. 'I don't think that they have any other difficulty,' he said.

The tribunal had received a letter from another solicitor, Hugh Millar, before the sitting. Millar also asked that matters relating to the B/T account not be aired in public that day, because the issue had still to be properly canvassed in private. Nevertheless, the hearing went ahead.

Ahern told O'Neill that when he got the letter of 30 November 2007 from the tribunal concerning the Davy cheque it had been immediately apparent that the Irish Permanent account, into which the £5,000 cheque had been lodged, was the B/T account. He said he had not been able to contact Tim Collins 'because he was in the United States.' Ahern got in touch with the Drumcondra branch of the Irish Permanent, seeking details on the account, but the manager—who called over to St Luke's, having been asked to do so by Ahern's secretary, Sandra Cullagh—said he would need formal instructions from the account-holder. Ahern said he then asked Joe Burke to take up the matter, because Burke was the 'chairman of the house committee'. He said he might not have told his solicitors about the B/T account, since he was getting ready for his appearances at the tribunal on 21 and 22 December.

When O'Neill put it to Ahern that the Irish Permanent manager would not give him details on the B/T account because it had 'none of the indices of being a Fianna Fáil account,' Ahern disagreed. When O'Neill said Burke was not given the information because he was not a signatory on the account, and did not have access to any documents on the account (despite being, as Ahern had said, a trustee of the building trust), Ahern did not give clear answers.

When O'Neill and Judge Mahon put it to Ahern that most of what he had been asked in the tribunal's letter of 30 November was within his knowledge, and that the bulk of its queries could have been answered by him immediately, Ahern appeared to become annoyed. The request made in the letter constituted a 'gigantic undertaking', he said. Making it clear that he had 'total confidence' in Judge Mahon, he continued:

> No matter what you say to the counsel for the tribunal they come back with twenty more questions. I started off being asked about my own accounts and my own personal accounts and then my daughters' and then Celia Larkin's accounts, and then we get into my mother's accounts and father's accounts, and maybe my grandmother's accounts—she died about one hundred years ago. Where does it stop, chairman? I mean, this is Fianna Fáil Government central, and I don't control the BT account. I am not the BT account. I didn't take out any money. I didn't put [property developer] Owen O'Callaghan's money into it or anybody else's money into it. I don't know what the relevance is.

Ahern accepted that he could have answered some of the questions in the letter immediately. O'Neill asked if Ahern appreciated that asking the tribunal to go to the constituency organisation to get information that was in Ahern's knowledge, and that he hadn't disclosed when asked, would delay its inquiries into the B/T account. Ahern said he didn't accept what O'Neill had said. O'Neill said there had been 'extensive correspondence' between the tribunal and Ahern on the matter, but the chairperson asked him to move on, and the correspondence was not read out. O'Neill then turned to the issue of the loan that the previous day Ahern had said had been made to a member of the staff.

'Who was the member of staff referred to?'

'Celia Larkin,' Ahern replied.

This was a huge development in the political controversy concerning Ahern. According to his own evidence, political donations given to him had in turn been given to his girlfriend to help her buy a house. In the middle of the property boom, and in the wake of all that had been learnt about Charles Haughey and Ray Burke, it was an enormous blow to Ahern's reputation and a severe weakening of his hold on the position of Taoiseach.

As soon as Ahern revealed that the 'staff member' who received the loan was Larkin, Hugh Millar, the solicitor who had dropped a letter into the tribunal earlier that morning, rose and interrupted. He had been there the previous day but had not said anything. He said he was there to represent Larkin and a surviving occupant of the property that Larkin had bought with the help of the £30,000 from the b/t account. His clients objected to what he said was an intrusion into their personal affairs and a matter that was not covered by the tribunal's terms of reference. The chairperson didn't agree with this point, saying the tribunal's interest was in establishing the beneficial ownership of the b/t account. Millar also said the matter should be dealt with by way of private inquiry before it became the focus of public hearings; and he said the letter he had delivered that morning, which contained his clients' outline of the circumstances behind the purchase of the house, should be read into the record if the matter was to be dealt with in public hearings. In the course of his submissions he said he had first been contacted by his clients on the afternoon of 19 February, three days earlier.

O'Neill did not want the letter read out before he had completed his examination of Ahern, but the chairperson decided that it should be read into the record. The letter said the price of the house was £40,100, with the cost above £30,000 coming from its elderly tenants. It included the statement that Ahern had no involvement in agreeing the loan to Larkin.

When questioning resumed, Ahern acknowledged that Larkin was his partner but said the relationship had nothing to do with the transaction.

Celia Larkin was head of our constituency office. She was the senior person in our constituency office and had been for many years. She was known to all of the officers, and known to all of the house committee; had been a senior officer in a neighbouring constituency in previous times. She was a person who ran for Fianna Fáil in local elections. She was a person who served on the National Youth Committee of Fianna Fáil. She was a person of good standing in Fianna Fáil. And her family had a difficulty.

It was on that basis that the money was given, he said.

Ahern said that, to the best of his recollection, he first learnt of the matter after Larkin had completed the purchase of the house. He was unsure whether Brennan, Ahern's friend and solicitor, had acted for Larkin in the purchase. (Documents in the Registry of Deeds showed that he had.) There was no charge on the house deeds registering the loan, but Ahern said he imagined that if Brennan had been involved there would be a document somewhere recording the loan. No such document was ever produced. Asked when the loan had been repaid, Ahern said, 'I asked one of the officers yesterday, and they said in the period since Christmas.'

Under questioning from O'Neill, Ahern agreed that Larkin had not worked in St Luke's since 1987: since that date she had been working in his offices in Leinster House and Government Buildings. According to Ahern, 'she did all the work on the annual fund-raising dinner. So she worked with the House Committee. She did all of the organisation of the annual dinner. So she worked with that committee.'

O'Neill proceeded to ask Ahern about other withdrawals from the B/T account. Some, Ahern said, were for annual functions held in St Luke's, including functions held for the persons who contributed the money to buy it.

> In the early years they had a dinner with the trustees who were the 25 people or so that formed the trust to purchase St Luke's in the first place. And some of the people that were involved in the construction of St Luke's. They had an annual dinner for the first three or four years . . . The dinner for the trustees ceased somewhere along the way. They didn't continue that.

He agreed that there were common rules that applied to each Comhairle Dáil Ceantair and that these rules included the stipulation that there must be two treasurers overseeing each constituency's financial affairs. He also agreed that the B/T account was not a Comhairle Dáil Ceantair account and was therefore not under the control of the Dublin Central treasurers. The account was under the control of the cumann, he said, 'but the treasurers would have been aware of that.' No document to support this statement was ever produced. The account, in fact, was not under the control of any cumann. The O'Donovan Rossa Cumann had about twenty to twenty-five members, Ahern agreed, and neither Tim Collins nor any of the other 'trustees' were members.

Ahern was asked about his conversation with Collins before he gave evidence. O'Neill asked if Collins had told him that he had other accounts in the Irish Permanent, Drumcondra, and Ahern said he had. He said he hadn't asked Collins if he had any joint accounts in the branch. He gave a similar reply when asked if Des Richardson had any accounts in the Irish Permanent in Drumcondra.

Ahern's evidence was that he was busy trying to balance his obligations to the tribunal with his busy schedule as Taoiseach and that his constituency organisers and the surviving trustees of St Luke's had independently decided that they would deal directly with the tribunal rather than doing so through him. Furthermore, his evidence was to the effect that this stance was adopted against his wishes.

Evidence heard later by the tribunal strongly questioned this claim and showed that this whole apparent development was something that Ahern controlled at all times. It seemed that he was using tricks he had learnt over the course of his political career. These manoeuvres bought him time, but in the end they were no match for the tribunal's powers of discovery and its right to call witnesses. This no doubt contributed to the frustration and anger that was at times evident during the closing period of his tenure. He was Taoiseach, but that fact couldn't save him.

Chapter 5 ∽

| THE BOOKKEEPER'S BOOKS

In the spring of 2001 Ronan Murphy, a senior partner with the accountancy firm Price Waterhouse Coopers, met the trustees of Fianna Fáil in relation to the annual audit of its accounts. Murphy's firm had audited the head office and party leader's accounts for many years. Among those present at the meeting was Bertie Ahern, the Minister for Finance and a party trustee and treasurer. A few weeks after the meeting Murphy was contacted by Fianna Fáil head office and told to expect a call from Ahern. In the event he was called by Sandra Cullagh from St Luke's, and when he went to see her she told him that Ahern wanted an account of the Dublin Central constituency brought up to date.

Murphy and some colleagues proceeded to conduct an exercise with one of the constituency accounts, the constituency No. 1 account. It wasn't an audit but an income and expenditure statement. This meant that, working on whatever documentary evidence or oral explanations were available, the accountants drafted a document showing, and giving explanations for, the flow of money into and out of the account. The explanations for the sources of the income, and the reasons for the expenditures, were accepted at face value and were not independently verified by the accountants.

The account had been opened in 1983, and the accountants were asked to do the accounts preparation work for each year since. Murphy saw where Ahern himself had started to do some of the work before engaging PWC. The accountants were given a suitcase full of documents linked to the account. However, although they were told that all lodgements to the account arose from political fund-raising, there was no documentary evidence to support this statement or which identified particular donors.

The bill for bringing the account up to date (that is, to 2001) was £2,950, and the PWC invoice, at Ahern's suggestion, was sent to Fianna Fáil head office for payment. The exercise was repeated each year thereafter, up to 2005.

The account that Murphy did the work on was in the names of Joe Burke and Bertie Ahern, but all the information he received came from Ahern directly, or from him through Cullagh. Ahern gave Murphy no explanation for wanting the work carried out or of what the account was for.

Murphy was not told about other bank accounts that would later come to the attention of the tribunal. He was not told about the B/T account, the account called the CODR account or the account into which money arising from the sale of the Amiens Street building had been lodged. Nor was Murphy told about a deposit account and a current account maintained by the Comhairle Dáil Ceantair.

When he later gave evidence to the tribunal, Murphy accepted that the exercise he and his colleagues had conducted could not be considered a picture of the income and expenditure of the Ahern constituency operation, because PWC had not been told about the other accounts. It was a picture of income and expenditure through one particular account. In so far as it might be presented as a picture of the income and expenditure of the constituency, it had no value. Des O'Neill, counsel for the tribunal, said it had been told that there were another seven accounts that held funds relevant to the constituency operation, and he put it to Murphy that, on that basis, the exercise conducted by him and his colleagues 'seems pointless'. Murphy said that they did what they were asked to do and that no reason for the work had been given.

O'Neill selected the year 1992 and illustrated how the accountants had been told that the £34,835 lodged to the constituency No. 1 account had arisen from political fund-raising. However, during the same year, according to what the tribunal had been told, £19,000, which had been lodged to the B/T account, arose from political fund-raising and more particularly from the holding of a golf classic. Murphy agreed that, on the basis of what he was being told, the B/T account would have to be taken into consideration if a general picture for fund-raising for 1992 was to be constructed. He did not disagree when O'Neill said the document produced by PWC was 'meaningless from the point of view of analysing the affairs of the constituency.'

Ahern's evidence about the B/T account was given on 21 and 22 February 2008, and, as we have seen, it was given before the related documents had been handed over to the tribunal either by him or by his constituency organisation.

Deirdre McGrath, a senior manager with PWC, had been working on the audit of the accounts of Fianna Fáil head office and of the party leader since 2006. On 7 January 2008 she got a call from Cullagh in St Luke's, who said Ahern wanted McGrath to update the income and expenditure statements on the No. 1 account for the years 2005 to date. McGrath agreed to go to St Luke's at 9:30 on the following Monday morning, 14 January.

On the day McGrath got the call from Cullagh, Ahern's solicitor, Liam Guidera, wrote to the tribunal on Ahern's behalf describing the circumstances in which the Davy political donation of £5,000 had ended up in the B/T account, but he said the issue was more correctly a matter for the constituency organisation.

The day McGrath arrived at St Luke's to begin her work on updating the No. 1 account was the day the tribunal sent a lengthy letter to Guidera seeking answers from Ahern about the B/T account, the house committee and a range of matters relating to Ahern's Drumcondra operation. It also notified Ahern that the tribunal was considering making orders of discovery in relation to these matters. When McGrath got to St Luke's she and her colleague, Brian O'Gorman, were given cheque stubs and bank statements so that they could begin work on updating the No. 1 account.

On Monday 21 January 2008 Denis O'Connor, a senior partner with PWC, received a phone call from Seán Dorgan, the general secretary of Fianna Fáil. O'Connor was told the Taoiseach's office would be contacting him regarding work Ahern wanted done on some accounts. Later in the week O'Connor got a call from Cullagh in St Luke's, and it was arranged that O'Connor would meet Ahern there on Friday 25 January at 1 p.m.

Ahern told O'Connor that he wanted an income and expenditure statement, but not an audit, prepared on another constituency account. The account was the B/T account in the Irish Permanent in Drumcondra, though Ahern at all times referred to it as the 'building trust' account. The period to be covered was from the opening of the account in 1989 to date, though there had been no lodgements or withdrawals since 1996 other than the addition of interest. Ahern told O'Connor that the account was used primarily for the upkeep of St Luke's and that the trustees on the account were Burke, Collins, Reilly, Brennan and Keane. Only the first two named were still alive.

Ahern gave O'Connor the bank statements on the account and said that he would be talking to people over the weekend and that he would see what information concerning the account he could get. It was agreed that they would meet again the following week, that O'Connor would bring McGrath with him and that she would also work on the account.

O'Connor was not told that the tribunal had contacted Ahern a month earlier asking him to answer certain questions and to produce documents concerning transactions on the account 'as a matter of urgency'. The following week O'Connor was contacted by the Taoiseach's office and asked to attend at St Luke's at 3:30 on Thursday afternoon, New Year's Eve. McGrath accompanied him. Ahern was there and had with him a notebook, in the middle pages of which he had some handwritten notes, which the accountants presumed concerned information he had gathered in the period since he had met O'Connor. Ahern had little with him by way of third-party documentary evidence, though he did point out that there was a copy of a cheque for £30,000 made out to a solicitor, Patrick O'Sullivan. Notes taken by O'Connor recorded Ahern saying that O'Sullivan acted for 'the family of a staff member, Celia Larkin, whose three aunts were about to be moved out of their house. He was told the money was a loan and would be repaid with interest on the sale of the house after the death of the last occupants.'

The copy of the O'Sullivan cheque was the only third-party documentary evidence available concerning the account. Ahern said two lodgements, in 1992 (£19,000) and 1995 (£10,000), related to golf classics. A withdrawal of £20,000 on 26 August 1994 was cash to pay for work that was to be carried out on St Luke's but which in the event was not carried out. A lodgement of the same amount on 26 October 1994 was the relodgement of the August withdrawal, the accountants were told.

The accountants went away and got to work. On 5 February 2008 Ahern called O'Connor and said three withdrawals, in 1989, 1990 and 1992, related to summer functions held for members of staff and constituents in St Luke's. He said a number of lodgements of £5,000 were political donations from donors whose names he could not remember. Ahern said a sum of £2,285.71— which, along with a cheque for £5,000, formed the initial lodgement to the account—may have come from an Irish company called Walls. He then said it might have come from Michael Wall (the Manchester man who had entered into an arrangement with Ahern in 1994 concerning his home in Beresford Avenue). He then changed his mind again and said it was Michael Wall's. Ahern at this time was imparting information to the accountants that the tribunal had for some time been seeking from him as a matter of urgency and that he was later to tell the tribunal—by way of his solicitors—was a matter that should be taken up with the constituency officers. Ahern never told the accountants that the work they were doing was being done in connection with his appearances before the tribunal, though they assumed this to be the case.

In a letter to the tribunal on 5 February 2008 Ahern, through his solicitor, argued that the questions and the intended orders of discovery described in the letter of 14 January were more properly matters for the Dublin Central Comhairle Dáil Ceantair. This was the same day he was in contact with O'Connor giving him information about the lodgements and withdrawals on the B/T account.

On Monday 11 February, Cullagh phoned McGrath and said there were some additional accounts that Ahern wanted work done on, and, as a result, McGrath attended at St Luke's on the Wednesday. She was given documents relating to accounts associated with the 1989 and 1992 elections, including bank statements, lists of donations, compliments slips from donors and a small number of purchase invoices. Cullagh asked that the work be done on site. McGrath understood that the work had to do with Ahern's dealings with the tribunal.

The following day McGrath was asked if she could meet Ahern on Friday 15 February, and she did so at two in the afternoon in St Luke's. Ahern said he was still looking for information on four lodgements of £5,000 to the B/T account, but he thought some of them might be from the same source. During the meeting, McGrath later told the tribunal, they were interrupted by Cullagh, who said Tim Collins had been on the phone regarding information he was searching for in connection with the accounts being prepared. Ahern asked Cullagh to ask Collins to keep looking.

Ahern asked McGrath to print out the work she had done on updating the No. 1 account and also to begin work, on site, on another account, the CODR account. He called it the Cumann O'Donovan Rossa account, although it was later to emerge at the tribunal that the account had no link whatsoever with the cumann. Ahern asked her to cover the period 1988–2004 but later amended this instruction and asked her to work up to 1995 only. Ahern assisted her and provided her with bank statements and a bank deposit book. He told her that one withdrawal of £30,000 from the account was for Walsh Maguire Engineers and was a payment on account for work on the renovation of St Luke's.

On 18 February, McGrath handed over bound draft reports on the B/T, CODR and No. 1 accounts, as well as the 1989 and 1992 election accounts. The books were collected by arrangement from the PWC offices by a driver from St Luke's two days before Ahern appeared at the tribunal and said he had 'exhorted' the constituency officers to co-operate with its urgent request for information. McGrath later told the tribunal that the vast bulk of the information in her final work on the accounts was contained in the draft accounts delivered on 18 February. She also said she had encountered no difficulties arising from constituency officers saying she could not be given information before it was cleared with the constituency's solicitors. All the information, of course, had come to her through Ahern.

McGrath also said she had not known that the 1992 'Fianna Fáil election account' referred to in her draft report was, in the bank documents, called the 'Tim Collins Fianna Fáil election account' or that the reference to Collins had been 'redacted or obliterated' from the documents given to her. Nor did she know that the address had also been altered. It had read 'Tim Collins, St Luke's,' on the bank documents but simply 'St Luke's' on the documents shown to her. Furthermore, she did not know that in 1992 a separate election account had been opened under the auspices of the Comhairle Dáil Ceantair officers.

McGrath told O'Neill that Ahern had told her the initials on the CODR account stood for Cumann O'Donovan Rossa. The address for the deposit account was the Secretary, CODR, 146 Lower Drumcondra Road. O'Neill said the secretary of the cumann had told the tribunal that the account had nothing whatsoever to do with the cumann. McGrath said she hadn't known this.

In time it became clear that Ahern had, under oath in the witness box, misled the tribunal about his knowledge concerning Celia Larkin's 'repayment' of the money that had been given to her from the B/T account. He had told Judge Mahon that the money had been repaid in the period 'since Christmas' and that his knowledge came from constituency officers. In fact, as Larkin revealed in her evidence, she had dealt directly with Ahern in relation to the matter. The money had been repaid with interest, and Ahern had supplied Larkin with the figure that constituted the original amount plus the interest that would have been received had the money remained on deposit in the Irish Permanent. Not only that: Larkin had borrowed the money from Ahern before writing her cheque to the constituency.

Ahern was asked about this in June, when he was back giving evidence again. O'Neill read into the record his evidence from 21 February and explained that, on that day, the tribunal had not known that the payment to the solicitor, O'Sullivan, had to do with a loan to a member of staff at St Luke's, or that that person was Larkin. Ahern, when asked about the matter, had given a clear impression that his knowledge that the money had been repaid 'recently' had come to him from the trustees. Yet Larkin's evidence made it clear that she had dealt directly with Ahern and had left a signed blank cheque into St Luke's. This was filled in later by Cullagh when Larkin supplied her with the figure, which in turn Ahern had supplied to Larkin. Celia Larkin also said that Ahern had loaned her the money so that she could make the payment. Larkin's evidence on the matter was read out by O'Neill, with Ahern in the witness box.

> You were the person, not the trustees, who had all of the dealings with Ms Larkin. You calculated the interest that was due and to a particular date. Your secretary completed the cheque supposedly on the 4th of February of this year.

Given all this, how could Ahern, when asked by the chairperson when the money had been paid back, have replied, 'I asked one of the officers yesterday, and they said in the period since Christmas'?

Ahern said Larkin had paid the money back to the treasurers, leaving the cheque in St Luke's. 'I wasn't sitting around St Luke's watching what day anyone would come in. I wasn't there at all. I was in Government Buildings.'

On 20 May 2008 the tribunal heard from a number of witnesses who had worked in the Irish Permanent, Drumcondra, during the 1990s. First up was Lisa Jordan, a senior administrator in the bank's head office, who had worked in Drumcondra since June 1991. She said she had been aware of the b/t account and of the fact that it was Collins who operated it. She said the passbook on the account was kept in the branch, and when Collins came in to do a transaction the book would be fetched from safe keeping.

> I would remember Mr Collins coming into the branch. He would have been a chatty customer . . . I recollect an occasion prior to . . . 1993 that Mr Collins, in a jocular manner, when asking for the passbook on the b/t account, referred to it . . . as the Bertie Ahern/Tim Collins account. I am certain that this was said in a jocular manner.

Asked about her recollection, she said someone had gone to retrieve the passbook,

> and they were a bit confused as to where it was, and he said, 'Oh, it's the Bertie/Tim account', and they were like, 'What's it under?' you know? So I would have said, 'It's just the b/t.' And that's it.

Jordan said she did not recall dealing with anyone other than Collins in relation to the account. She had never heard the account being referred to as the building trust account, nor was she ever aware of the account having any connection with Fianna Fáil.

While Jordan's evidence dealt almost exclusively with the B/T account, it was mentioned that her statement also included the following:

> I was aware that Mr Collins operated an account number 50165547 in the name of himself and Desmond Richardson. In 1992 I dealt with transactions on this account on the following dates.

The reading into the record stopped there, though a tribunal barrister Henry Murphy said Jordan had gone on to set out 'twenty transactions between the 3rd of January and the 5th of October 1992.'

When the matter was raised briefly in evidence Jordan said the Collins and Richardson account was referred to in the branch as the 'D/T' account (indicating Des and Tim). A transaction dated January 1992, which bank documents showed she was involved with, contained a reference to the account in initials: D/T. The transaction involved a cheque that was being made payable to a third party, and Collins's signature appeared on the bank record.

The next witness was Elizabeth Smyth. Jordan believed that Smyth had heard Collins's remark in the early 1990s concerning the 'Bertie and Tim' account. Smyth had worked in the Drumcondra branch from 1991 to 1996. 'I remember Tim Collins well,' she said.

> I would describe Mr Collins as gregarious, with a word for anybody. I would have seen him not only in the branch but around Drumcondra and in Kennedy's public house, where he would often be on a Friday evening with Mr Ahern and other friends of Mr Ahern.
>
> It was my understanding from conversations in the branch, including some with Mr Collins, that the B/T account was an account operated by Mr Collins and that the B/T stood for Bertie and Tim. I recollect Mr Collins would ask for the passbook for the account, which was kept for safe keeping in the branch. I do not recollect any reference to the B/T account as being a building trust account. I believed the only connection of the B/T account to Fianna Fáil was that Mr Ahern was a minister and a Fianna Fáil TD.

Smyth said that, in the branch,

> it was known that the account belonged to Mr Collins and that
> Bertie Ahern was also on the account but that Mr Collins did all the work
> on it. He was the one that came into the branch, he would be the one to
> ask for the book and so on . . . In the branch it was common knowledge
> that [B/T stood for] Bertie and Tim . . . The reason why I remembered it
> in the sense as much as I can was that it was Bertie Ahern who was a
> minister at the time. So I was quite young at the time, so it was impressive
> to be working on a minister's account . . . I think it was spoken about at
> the branch as to who or what B/T stood for and what it was about,
> because you couldn't just keep doing withdrawals or lodgements to an
> account and not know who or what the set-up of the account was. So I
> have a vague recollection that it was discussed in the branch, and my
> impression of what I can remember was that it belonged to Bertie and
> Tim and that's what the B/T stood for.

Blair Hughes, the manager of the Irish Permanent, Drumcondra, from 1993
to 1996, also gave evidence about the B/T account. He said he used to sit at a
desk on the ground floor of the open-plan area of the branch office. 'If I was
in the branch and saw Mr Collins I would approach him and have a chat. I
would on occasion complete a withdrawal or lodgement docket for Mr Collins
while talking to him and hand it to the teller to complete the transaction.'

Hughes said he knew that Collins operated an account in the branch under
the initials B/T. 'I had no reason to believe that this account was operated for
or on behalf of the Fianna Fáil party, the local cumann, or that it related to a
building trust.' He said he assumed it was Collins's account. 'I just made an
assumption that B and T stood for Bertie and Tim. I had no other evidence
to say it was anyone else's account.' He said he knew of the association between
Ahern and Collins—knew them to be close friends rather than political
associates. 'I may have been advised by people in the branch when I arrived
that had experience with it [the account], I don't know. But I cannot
remember actually discussing it with anybody. It was just an assumption on
my part, whether that be right or wrong.'

Tim Collins gave evidence on 13 March 2008. Collins had a relatively small
business at about the time he opened the B/T account, but he prospered during
the years of the economic boom and the associated property bubble. He
eventually became a successful property scout and property investor, among
other things, and was a witness before the planning tribunal on matters other

than those concerning Ahern. Since he had not been named as a contributor to any of the Ahern dig-outs, he had not been called during the earlier hearings, concerned with Ahern's finances.

Collins told the tribunal that the B/T account was set up as a contingency fund—a 'sinking fund' that would be there in case money was ever needed for St Luke's. He agreed that funds used for St Luke's had come from other accounts when there had been money available in the B/T account and also that, although there had been significant withdrawals from the B/T account over the years, there were never any withdrawals for the purpose of maintaining or renovating St Luke's.

A number of facts appeared to be at odds with Collins's description of what the B/T account was for and of how the Davy Stockbrokers cheque came to be lodged to it. Firstly, there was the question of why the cheque wasn't lodged to any account until two-and-a-half months after it was issued. It was issued on 11 November 1992 and lodged on 31 January 1993. At the time it was received, the fund-raisers could not have known that they were going to receive funds in excess of what could be required for the campaign. Collins said he had no recollection of discussing the Davy cheque with Ahern or of how it came to be decided that it would be lodged to the B/T account. According to Collins:

> The B/T account, and I will say this until the day I die, is a sinking fund in the event of anything ever happening to Mr Ahern, that the trustees that would be left alive wouldn't have to pick up any tab on the house, any debt that would be left on it. And that was my view at the time and [also the view of] another person on the committee.

O'Neill pointed out that the bound PWC report on the B/T account, which had been given to the tribunal by solicitors acting for the Comhairle Dáil Ceantair and the trustees, had described the purpose of the account as administering funds 'for the maintenance and upkeep of the property known as St Luke's.' When Collins was asked if he had given a description of what the account was for to the accountants from PWC he said he hadn't spoken to anyone from PWC. He also said he hadn't seen the documents prepared by PWC before they were given to the tribunal.

Asked about the building trust, Collins said the trustees were the same as the St Luke's trustees, save that Brennan was a trustee (of the B/T account) and Richardson wasn't. 'Richardson wasn't on the house committee,' Collins said by way of explanation for Richardson not being on the building trust.

'Did you intend opening an account for the building trustees?' O'Neill asked.

'No. It was for the house committee.'

'I see. Is there any reason why you didn't have H/C then, perhaps, as the name of the account, because it's not an account of the building trustees?'

'I have no . . . There is no reason why it's not H/C, it's just that I put B/T for building trust.'

Collins said he had no reason for not giving St Luke's as the address on the account, nor had he any reason for electing to have the statements on the account kept in the branch. The account was opened nineteen years before Collins appeared to give evidence, and the address on the account from 1995 had been of Collins's home. He had not mentioned the account in a sworn affidavit of discovery that he had made to the tribunal in 2006. The discovery order included an obligation on him to reveal all accounts into which he had lodged funds. This meant that both Collins and Ahern had left the B/T account out of the list of accounts they had declared to the tribunal after having been served with orders of discovery. Collins said he hadn't forgotten about the B/T account, which was still in existence with funds on deposit in it, at the time of his sworn affidavit in 2006; but he accepted that the wording of the order of discovery encompassed the B/T account.

Asked when he had last discussed the account with any of the people he said were trustees of the account, Collins replied, 'Oh, it's many years ago. I'd say I've been out of circulation around there now for about thirteen years.' The sole surviving member of the house committee from the mid-1990s was Joe Burke. 'I haven't spoken to Joe Burke in a long while,' Collins said.

A mortgage of £75,000 on St Luke's was taken out in 2000, at a time when there was £47,000 in the B/T account and, according to the evidence given to the tribunal, a loan of £30,000 plus interest out to Larkin. The mortgage was used for substantial work on St Luke's. Collins's reply seemed to be that it was decided that constituency workers should be let raise funds to repay the mortgage. He said to O'Neill:

I understand what you're saying . . . that we should have paid it off with the money that was there; but we always wanted to have a sinking fund there, and that's why we kept it there. When the work had to be done, let the people go out and fund-raise to pay for that.

Collins was asked about the cash withdrawal of £20,000 the tribunal had been told was made to pay people who were going to carry out work on

St Luke's but which had been returned some months later after it was decided not to go ahead with it.

> I took the money out, and Joe Burke, being a builder, I left the money for Joe to see could he have it sorted out. And he got professional advice on it over the period of time to say that the job was too great and too big, that that wouldn't be able to sort it out . . . He wanted cash to be able to pay people if he wanted to get a job done in a hurry.

Collins said he left the cash for Burke in an envelope in St Luke's.

> My recollection is that I brought it to St Luke's and left it in the office. And whoever was there, I can't recall who was there, [I] said, 'There, make sure Joe Burke gets that.'

He said he had no recollection of relodging the money.

Collins was asked about the joint account he had in the Irish Permanent in Drumcondra with Des Richardson. This account had also been left out of the sworn affidavit of discovery that he had made in 2006. He accepted that he should have told the tribunal about the account. 'I had completely forgotten about that,' he said. The names on the account, opened in July 1991, were Des Richardson and Tim Collins. At the time the two men were involved in what Collins said was a small architectural practice called Pilgrim Associates. The account was operated until 1993. Of the 151 withdrawal slips the tribunal retrieved from the bank's archives, the name of the account was described as D/T on 46 of them, O'Neill said. The initials stood for Des and Tim, Collins agreed, but he said it was not the case that B/T stood for Bertie and Tim.

When Liam Cooper, a party activist, gave evidence, he told the tribunal something of the history of the O'Donovan Rossa Cumann. He had been active in Fianna Fáil politics in Dublin Central since the early 1980s and was a member of the cumann. It was one of the oldest in Fianna Fáil and could trace its ancestry to Fenian times. It was originally a Fenian cell, he claimed, named after Jeremiah O'Donovan Rossa, who, he pointed out, was buried in Glasnevin Cemetery. The cell subsequently became a Sinn Féin cumann in the early twentieth century. Following the foundation of Fianna Fáil in 1926 the Sinn Féin O'Donovan Rossa Cumann transferred *en masse* to Fianna Fáil. 'It has been the focal point for Fianna Fáil activity in the Drumcondra area since the 1920s.'

Cooper was a long-time secretary of the cumann and had served at officer level in the Comhairle Dáil Ceantair, including as treasurer. At the time he gave evidence he was chairperson of the cumann. He said he had never been a member of the trust that was involved with St Luke's.

> Nor have I ever been involved in fund-raising for this trust. I am aware, as is every other Fianna Fáil member in the constituency, that the trustees ran regular fund-raisers to provide for the expenditure of running the office in St Luke's and the upkeep of the house.

He explained that what he called the 'house committee' was involved in raising funds for St Luke's and that the committee was independent of the Comhairle Dáil Ceantair structure. He was asked what knowledge he would have had in the period 1994–2001, when he was a treasurer of the Comhairle Dáil Ceantair, of the various accounts that were operated by the house committee. 'I actually anticipated that you would ask me that,' he said. 'So, with your permission, I have a note here for myself so that I can be deadly accurate.' He was asked not to refer to the note and to tell the tribunal from memory what accounts he knew the committee to be operating. He named the building trust account, the CODR account and the long-term deposit account with the ACC Bank in Westmoreland Street that held proceeds from the sale of the party premises in Amiens Street.

Although he was aware of the existence of the B/T account, he said he wasn't aware of the balance in it, or even of the fact that the balance was in thousands rather than hundreds of pounds, which was the norm for most of the accounts with which he was involved. He said he might on occasion briefly mention the B/T account to members of the committee, and might inform constituency AGMs that there had been no movement on the account. It was put to him that there was nothing in the records of the Comhairle Dáil Ceantair that had been shown to the tribunal that recorded the B/T account being mentioned in any capacity. Cooper did not dispute the assertion. 'I can't explain that,' he said.

Joe Burke returned to the witness box on 14 May 2008, the same day that Cooper gave his evidence and the day after Collins's appearance. Burke had been written to on 8 April and asked for a narrative statement on matters relating to the B/T account, but he hadn't supplied it by the time he was called to give evidence. An overweight man who looked both boyish and unhealthy, Burke tended to play with his gold watch while giving his testimony, opening and closing the clasp of the watchstrap. On New Year's Day 2008 Burke had been rushed to hospital after he was found slumped over the wheel of his Mercedes in Ringsend, having taken an overdose. He had been on a drinking spree the previous day, and events at his home that night had led to the gardaí being called by a young woman he had met in a nightclub. Bertie Ahern had appointed Burke's partner, Maria Corrigan, to the Senate in 2007. Burke had asked Ahern to make the appointment.

Burke told the tribunal that he had not had any dealings with PWC, nor had he looked at the documents they had produced before he entered the witness box. As a trustee of St Luke's and a member of the house committee, Burke had been served with an order of discovery, which included any documents recording the source of lodgements made to the B/T account. The constituency treasurer, Dominic Dillane, had appeared at the tribunal the day before Burke and given evidence in relation to the affidavit of discovery he had sworn and that arose from that order. Dillane had been acting as representative for the Comhairle Dáil Ceantair and the trustees, but Burke confirmed that he had not discussed the matter of the B/T account with Dillane. 'I haven't. That would be correct, yes,' he said.

The PWC report on the B/T account identified various sources for lodgements, but, other than two substantial lodgements it said had resulted from golf classics in 1992 and 1995, Burke said he had no knowledge of them. He said he would have had knowledge of them at the time. 'My memory doesn't serve me well today,' he said. He said he had discussed the account with Ahern after Ahern had received a letter from the tribunal on 30 November 2007 asking about the account.

Burke had no specific recall of any of the withdrawals from the B/T account other than the payment made in relation to Celia Larkin's purchase of a house and the cash withdrawal of £20,000 and subsequent relodgement of an identical amount. In relation to the payment associated with Larkin he said that the fact of the transaction was not discussed with anyone in Fianna Fáil other than his fellow-members of the house committee.

If the account-holders had the option of expending the money as they saw fit, he said, 'why would I have to go to anybody in Fianna Fáil to tell them what I'm doing?'

'Because,' said O'Neill, 'apparently this was a trust for the benefit ultimately of Fianna Fáil.'

'At the end of the day, if Mr Ahern leaves politics, yes, that's correct,' Burke replied. 'And since he hasn't left politics and we weren't about to hand over to Fianna Fáil, there was no reason to go to anybody to explain what we were doing.'

In relation to the cash withdrawal of £20,000 and later cash lodgement, Burke said he had collected the cash from St Luke's and put it in a safe in his house so that it would be available if needed for the work on St Luke's. However, it transpired that it was a larger job than was originally envisaged. 'The money was handed back.'

O'Neill asked why the money was withdrawn in cash. 'The old saying is very simple: It's always nice to see the colour of your money. It was as simple as that.' Burke said the money was left back to St Luke's, where he had originally collected it, although he might have used some of the original cash in another transaction.

During Collins's evidence it was disclosed that there had been another development in the inquiries, again arising as a result of documents retrieved from banking archives. The documents showed that the cash lodgement of £20,000 to the b/t account in October 1994 had been immediately preceded by an unusually large amount of sterling being exchanged in the branch. The British and Irish pounds were at par. Someone had brought £20,000 cash in sterling into the branch, changed it for Irish currency and lodged the cash to the b/t account.

When the new evidence was raised with Burke he said:

At the time, in 1994/1995, I was doing a huge amount of pub refurbishing in Ireland. I remember at one particular time we had about eight or ten pubs. We would have been buying a lot of memorabilia and salvage and that in England. Since I didn't have any bank account in England, I would have been using sterling. And when the question came to me, Did I give it back in sterling, I was kind of stumbled as to say I did or I didn't. But it's possible that I did.

He said he would have put the cash in an envelope and given it in St Luke's to whomever was there so that Collins could collect it. He would not have told the person he gave it to that it contained a large amount of cash, Burke said.

I've always the policy that if you tell someone that it's cash in an envelope, it will cause them to fret and worry. If you don't tell them anything, they'll just think it's documents. It's the policy I have until today, by the way ... I just left the envelope and possibly used the words 'That's to be collected by Tim Collins.'

Asked by Judge Mahon why he would have used sterling he had purchased for use in England to repay a debt in Drumcondra, Burke said:

> I'll tell you very simply, chairman. The Christmas season was coming up and all our works were finishing. Our pubs would have been finishing. It would probably have been a conscious decision for me to get rid of whatever surplus cash that was there that wasn't required for the rest of the year. As simple as that, chairman. Very simple.

Burke said the withdrawal and subsequent lodgement had occurred without the generation of any documents to record the transactions. Likewise, he did not have any documents in relation to the golf classics that he said occurred in 1992 and 1995 and resulted in, respectively, the lodgement of £19,000 and £10,000 to the B/T account. Bank records showed that the £19,000 lodged in 1992 arose after a cheque for £20,000 was brought into the bank, the lodgement made and £1,000 taken away in cash. There were no associated documents. 'But are you asking me, "Did it happen?" Yes, it happened.'

O'Neill pointed out that in June 2006 Ahern had informed the tribunal that certain large lodgements to the constituency No. 1 account were the proceeds of golf classics and annual fund-raising dinners. The No. 1 account, the tribunal was told, was funded solely by these events. Burke could not explain why the proceeds from the golf classics in 1992 and 1995 had gone into the B/T account in those years, rather than into the No. 1 account, or how such round-figure amounts could emerge as the profits from the holding of golf classics. He said he presumed that the lodgements occurred because the account needed the money at the time, but O'Neill said the balances did not show this. While the B/T account had funds in it, the No. 1 account ended up in the red at the end of each year, he said.

O'Neill put up a note on the overhead projector showing the manuscript minutes of a house committee meeting of 22 February 2008. The note said that the committee in the period 1986–96 did not formally exist and that Burke ran the annual golf classic. 'From 1997 to now, house committee has been officer board with Joe Burke.' Burke didn't dispute the accuracy of the note. 'Without a formal house committee. Yes. Yes. Without a formal. Yes. The word being formal,' he said.

In March 2008 Ahern travelled as Taoiseach to the United States, where he attended a St Patrick's Day function in the White House and presented the President, George W. Bush, with a crystal bowl of shamrock. On 19 March, while Ahern was still abroad, Blair Hughes, the former manager of the

Drumcondra branch of the Irish Permanent, gave evidence to the tribunal. One of the lodgements Hughes was asked about was the £20,000 sterling lodged to the b/t account on 24 October 1994, the month before Albert Reynolds's resignation as Taoiseach and his replacement by Ahern.

The documents linked to the lodgement were put on the overhead screen, and Hughes described how they recorded £20,000 being lodged in cash, the code for the teller who processed it (c87), where it occurred and the transaction number assigned to it (transaction 54).

The tribunal then displayed another document, which Hughes explained was a foreign currency purchase form that had been used to buy £20,000 sterling from a customer. The customer, Hughes explained, was given £20,000 in Irish pounds in return. The code for the teller who processed the transaction was the same (c87), and the transaction number was 55. The person who carried out both transactions had signed his name to both documents, and Hughes said the signature was that of an employee, Michael Murnane.

Hughes was asked if the documents showed that someone had come into the bank and lodged £20,000 sterling to the b/t account. 'Correct,' he answered.

But there was more. Other documents on the screen showed £6,000 sterling being brought into the branch on 9 March 1994. The lodgement was divided between Ahern's personal account (£4,000) and the accounts of his two daughters (£1,000 each). The documents also showed that on 9 May 1994 a sum of £5,450 sterling was brought in and divided between Ahern's and his daughters' accounts. The next day £50 sterling was lodged to Ahern's account. On 28 October 1994, two days after the £20,000 b/t lodgement, £4,000 sterling was lodged to Ahern's account.

In total, then, £35,500 sterling in cash was lodged to the Ahern and b/t accounts in the Irish Permanent in Drumcondra over a period of eight months in 1994, the year immediately following Ahern's finalisation of his separation agreement with his wife and his re-engagement with the Irish banking system. These lodgements were on top of the sterling cash that had been indisputably lodged to his account with the AIB in O'Connell Street, which Ahern said he had been given in Manchester.

After Hughes's evidence, which was based on documents that had been supplied to Ahern on 5 March, Ahern's counsel, Colm Ó hOisín, did not opt to ask any questions. He said his client wanted to reserve his position and was still considering documents he had been receiving as recently as five days earlier.

Ahern had provided no explanation up to the subsequent sitting of the Dáil in April 2008, when he was due to be questioned by the opposition about how sterling had turned up in his Irish Permanent account. Instead of going into the chamber and answering questions he announced his decision to retire as Taoiseach in May, which would provide him with the time to make an arranged address to the joint houses in Washington and to finish off with a meeting with the Rev. Ian Paisley at the site of the Battle of the Boyne. Ahern didn't answer the question about the sterling until he was back in the tribunal witness box in June, by which time he was no longer Taoiseach and it was already becoming clear that the economic boom had been badly mismanaged. When he arrived at Dublin Castle he made less effort than hitherto to be pleasant with the photographers gathered to snap him going in. He gave sworn testimony that some of the sterling in his building society account had been won on the horses. As soon as he mentioned horses there was loud and derisive laughter from the crowded public gallery. It was a moment of public humiliation. Having experienced years of adulation and praise, Bertie Ahern was on his way to becoming a target for anger and revilement.

PART THREE

Power

Chapter 6 ᗍ

| DEPUTY

When All Hallows Missionary College was founded in 1842, with the intention of providing a pathway for pious and talented young Irishmen who wanted to propagate the faith abroad, Drumcondra was a rural landscape with few inhabitants and little by way of claims to fame. *The Missionary College of All Hallows* by Kevin Condon, published by the college in 1986, contains a map of the area from the 1840s showing the bridge across the River Tolka and a small gathering of houses on the south bank. Over the bridge and north up the slope of Santry Road is a building on a turn into a narrow road that curves as it makes its way towards Goosegreen Lane, part of which is now known as Grace Park Road. The building on the corner is the Cat and Cage pub. The narrow road winding up towards Goosegreen Lane is now called Church Avenue and is best known for the fact that Bertie Ahern grew up there.

The avenue gets its name from the Church of St John the Baptist, a modest Church of Ireland building with a small surrounding graveyard whose granite headstones, for the most part, lean like the Tower of Pisa. Beyond the church the road follows a solid stone wall that is part of the southern perimeter of the All Hallows grounds, a wall that once marked the perimeter of the lands of a reasonably grand residence called Drumcondra House, which dates from the 1720s.

All Hallows was founded because of the determination of a priest called John Hand. Condon relates that Hand was from Oldcastle, Co. Meath, the son of a poor farmer who, as Hand progressed through his ecclesiastic career, appears to have been evicted from his lands and to have fallen on hard times, ending up working as a herdsman. Hand attended a seminary outside Navan and, later, St Patrick's College, Maynooth. On his ordination he worked with a school in Usher's Island, on the banks of the Liffey, before being assigned in 1838 to the parish of Phibsborough. The church, St Peter's, was a modest one, and Phibsborough was a village on the fringe of the city. Migrants came in from the countryside to settle there, and it was a place of great poverty.

Hand was impressed by the work of the French Association for the Propagation of the Faith, which visited Ireland about that time, and he began to lobby his archbishop and the hierarchy about his idea for the establishment of a missionary college. A proposal submitted to a bishops' assembly in Dublin in 1841 was rejected, but Hand persisted and, in time, was sent to the Continent to study how the missionary colleges there were run. Within a year he returned with a rescript, or written papal decision, giving him the authority to open a missionary house in Dublin.

Drumcondra House had been built by Sir Marmaduke Coghill, a member of the Irish Parliament before the Act of Union in 1800. Its later owners included John Claudius Beresford, who was known as a fearsome hunter and torturer of rebels during and after the 1798 Rising. Hand negotiated a lease on the house and its twenty-four acres with Dublin City Council. The Lord Mayor of Dublin, Daniel O'Connell, was a supporter of, and contributor to, the project.

The finance for the operation of the college came from subscriptions raised from the faithful. Hand died after a wet and cold fund-raising tour of Co. Meath in 1846. He was buried in the grounds of the institution he founded.

On the day I visited the college a man pointed out that the grounds are on a hill and that you can look from the doors of what once was Drumcondra House towards the city and the Dublin Mountains beyond. He said the church authorities liked to have their institutions on hills, to serve as a reminder to the faithful below. He listed a stream of institutions on higher ground in cities around Continental Europe, saying that, before the creation of organised police forces, fear of God was a particularly important factor in social control.

Within fifty years of its foundation All Hallows had produced more than a thousand missionaries. They went to Britain, North and South America, the West Indies, Australia, New Zealand, India, South Africa, Mauritius and elsewhere, with many of the graduates becoming bishops in their adopted dioceses. Half the permanent Catholic missionaries in Australia in the second half of the nineteenth century came from All Hallows, according to Condon. It was a major instrument in Irish institutional Catholic power.

Bertie Ahern's father, Con, was born in 1904 and came from Ballyfeard, near Kinsale, Co. Cork. He ran messages for the Irish Volunteers during the War of Independence, and when, in 1922, de Valera and his associates rejected the Treaty agreed with the British by Michael Collins and his fellow-plenipotentiaries in London, plunging Ireland into civil war, Ahern sided with the anti-Treaty forces and joined the IRA. The Civil War in Cork was a noticeably bloody affair. According to Bertie Ahern, his father was interned in the Curragh camp, twice went on hunger strike and remained a hard-line republican into the 1930s. Up to the 1970s the Gardaí still considered Ahern to have republican sympathies. According to Bertie Ahern's friend and long-time supporter Paddy Duffy, 'the father had been a member of the old IRA. There was a Southern, rebel Cork atmosphere in the Aherns, certainly about the father.' Bertie Ahern told RTE radio in 2004 that his father was a tough man, who, if someone got on his nerves, would 'clock them as quick as he'd look at them.'

Con Ahern came to Dublin in the 1930s and studied for the religious life for a brief time with the Vincentians, the administrators of All Hallows since 1891. He was assigned to work for a year on the college farm, where his skills from his younger days in Ballyfeard were noted, and in time he left behind his idea of the priesthood and began to work full-time on the farm, eventually becoming farm manager. It was a very large operation, and his responsibilities included the college lands and other lands further north in Co. Dublin. A rift within his family appears to have occurred at this time, with Con Ahern growing resentful that his younger brother David had got possession of the family farm while he had been attending the seminary.

In Bertie Ahern's memoirs he describes childhood days working and playing on the All Hallows lands, climbing trees, herding cattle and talking to the seminarians, who came from around Ireland and abroad. He describes it as the best playground a boy could ask for. The affection appears genuine.

In 1937 Con Ahern married Julia Hourihane, a young children's nurse born in 1911 into a struggling rural family from Castledonovan, Co. Cork. The couple had five children: Maurice, Kathleen, Noel, Eileen and Bertie, who was born in September 1951. The farm manager's job with the college brought with it tenancy of the house in Church Avenue, which the family later purchased. Back when John Hand had bought Drumcondra House there were three large houses in the area: Drumcondra House, Drumcondra Castle and Belvedere House. All became significant Catholic institutions. The castle is now St Joseph's Centre for the Visually Impaired, and Belvedere is the central residence of St Patrick's teacher training college. All Hallows was, and is, only one of a range of significant Catholic institutions in the Drumcondra area. From Church Avenue you can look south across the Tolka Valley and see the huge Clonliffe College and the rooftop of the Archbishop's Palace poking up through the surrounding trees. To the immediate north of All Hallows, up Grace Park Road, is the Hampton Carmelite convent. In his memoirs Bertie Ahern said his favourite day in the liturgical calendar as a boy was Holy Thursday, when the family followed the tradition of visiting seven churches. It was easy to do so in the Drumcondra area.

It is perhaps interesting to note that Ahern's background involves strong links with republicanism and the Catholic Church, two institutions that predate the state and that are notable for their views on the limited extent of its authority.

The houses in Church Avenue and other surrounding streets are residential islands in a sea of Catholic institutions. Many of them are built on what were church lands, and most of the streets are named after bishops and archbishops of the city, a practice that had ended by the time Ahern's house in the Beresford estate was being built. Ahern's modest detached house can be seen clearly from the grounds of All Hallows, and it is built on what were once college grounds worked on by his father. You can even see the rooftop of the conservatory Celia Larkin had built onto the back of the house, using funds the Mahon Tribunal was told had been handed over in cash, in a briefcase, during a meeting in St Luke's on a weekend in December 1994 when Ahern had been sure he was about to become Taoiseach.

Ahern attended St Patrick's National School, in the teacher training college complex directly across Drumcondra Road from Church Avenue, and St Aidan's Christian Brothers' School in Whitehall, a fifteen-minute walk up Drumcondra Avenue, away from the city. In his memoirs Ahern spends little time on his schooldays, saying simply that he had first hated the school, which was rough, but later came to like it and worked hard. Academically he was an average student. He was interested in sport, history and politics—subjects that featured strongly in the home. His sister Eileen, who spoke in the documentary 'Bertie' by Mint Productions, broadcast on RTE television in 2008, said that his favourite book was James O'Donnell's *How Ireland is Governed*, published by the Institute of Public Administration.

During Ahern's teenage years a neighbour, Noel Booth, who was the chairperson of the local O'Donovan Rossa Cumann of Fianna Fáil, drew him into providing a helping hand during the 1965 general election campaign. He helped put posters up on lampposts, and on polling day shook hands for the first time with Charles Haughey in a Drumcondra polling booth. By the time of the 1969 general election, when he again helped out with the canvass, Ahern was a member of the party and the cumann.

After his Leaving Certificate, and with the help of his sister Eileen, Ahern got a summer job with the Dublin District Milk Board. When an opening came up for an accounts clerk he secured the position and soon afterwards joined the Federated Workers' Union of Ireland. He studied accountancy at night in Rathmines College, though his memoirs are not clear on whether or not he finished the course. (Later, when he was Taoiseach, he would state on his cv that he was an 'accountant' and that he had also studied at the London School of Economics. When the *Sunday Tribune* looked into the matter it could find no evidence that he had attended the LSE. The short controversy ended without Ahern being able to show that the doubts raised by the paper were unfounded, and the claim that he had studied at the LSE was quietly dropped from his cv. The matter is not mentioned in Ahern's memoirs.)

In April 1974, before he had finished his studies in Rathmines, Ahern got a job as an accounts clerk in the Mater Hospital, a twenty-minute walk from his Drumcondra home. There he met Tony Kett, who was to be a lifelong friend and supporter and whom Ahern later appointed to the Seanad. Kett, Ahern and others set up their own soccer club, the All Hamptons, which became the focus of a sporting and social group that often met for drinks in the Cat and Cage and other local pubs after games on a pitch in the All Hallows grounds. As noted by his friends and himself in the 'Bertie' documentary, Ahern was interested in both Gaelic games and soccer and was involved with his friends in the running of the All Hallows club. 'We had hot showers when a lot of League of Ireland teams didn't,' he told the documentary-maker, Steve Carson. About his footballing style he said, 'We were physical guys. We could handle ourselves . . . I didn't like guys getting past me, so I suppose I got a reputation, but I was never sent off, never got a red card.' His friends said Ahern had a talent for organisation and wanted to be captain of whatever team he was on. Organisational ability, toughness and determination were to be hallmarks of Ahern and the team of supporters who travelled with him through his political career.

One of those he met through the football club and the social scene that grew around it was Miriam Kelly, a bank clerk who lived with her family in Clonliffe Road. They began to date, became engaged and were married in St Columba's Church in September 1975, on Ahern's twenty-fourth birthday. The service was conducted by Father Martin O'Connor, who was known to them through football and the All Hallows grounds. Miriam was twenty-one. In his memoirs Ahern says they went to Malta on their honeymoon and were back just in time for that year's all-Ireland final. They moved into their new home at 133 Pinebrook Road, Artane, where one of their neighbours was Joe Burke.

Another person who came to know Ahern at about this time was Paddy Duffy. A teacher in the De La Salle primary school in Finglas (which the present writer attended in the 1960s and early 70s), he became involved with the local Erin's Isle GAA club and, through the club, came into contact with the local Fianna Fáil organisation. Duffy is a very well-educated man, notably so for a member of Ahern's inner circle of supporters. He joined the Christian Brothers as a trainee at the age of twelve and studied in Bray and in Marino teacher training college. On graduation he taught for a while at O'Connell's CBS on the North Circular Road before being sent to Rome to study philosophy and theology in Italian and French. This was 1967–70, a period when, according to Duffy,

> Rome was in a ferment. It was the time of the whole renewal of the church begun by Pope John XXIII; it was all about bringing the congregations up to date and renewing the faith . . . just after the Second Vatican Congress.

Duffy lived in the Christian Brothers' monastery in Rome, 'where they taught the elite', as the church was going into a period of upheaval that, in the Western world at least, would be marked by a collapse in vocations.

> It was wonderful. I had a wonderful time with the brothers . . . There were thirty-two of us in the group, all highly energised in terms of vocation. Twenty-eight of the thirty-two left at that time—it was the beginning of the collapse. The door was open. Over five or six years thousands left—it all happened very quickly.

As a result of his work with Erin's Isle, Duffy got to know the Fianna Fáil TD in Finglas, Jim Tunney, as well as many of the members of the local party organisation.

> The apparatchiks ran the local organisation at the time like Opus Dei; that's how perfect it was at the time. You didn't sneeze but the organisation knew. At the very first meeting I attended I met Bertie Ahern.

Although he was slightly older than the others, Duffy grew friendly with a group of men in their twenties who were active with the local party machine.

We were all working, which was something in those days. He [Ahern] was working in the Milk Board, later the Mater. He and his mates were mad on soccer, All Hamptons was their club, whereas I was more Gaelic-aligned. There was no social segregation. Things are much more so now. The talk was politics or football, hardly any talk about work, whereas now people are almost immediately into what they are doing in their work situation.

The attitude was there were these very great oak trees of politicians in the political landscape and we were very much the young lads. We thought we knew everything. We talked and we consumed politics . . . The organisation was very old, like a family, well knitted, people had been around for years. Everyone had been vetted, I don't mean in a communist way, but almost. You held the true faith of Fianna Fáil, or you didn't. Disloyalty to the party would never be tolerated.

In the 1970s Ahern's O'Donovan Rossa Cumann was in the Dublin Finglas constituency. When Duffy first met Ahern, the future Taoiseach was a youth delegate for his cumann who attended the monthly meetings of the Comhairle Dáil Ceantair. The latter body selects the constituency's delegates to the party's annual ard-fheis and also its candidates in local and general elections. The Dublin Finglas Comhairle Dáil Ceantair meetings were attended by between 100 and 150 people. Duffy says he grew to notice some valuable traits in Ahern.

From the early stages it was clear to me and the other younger lads that Bertie knew and understood the mechanics of the organisation. One of the early signs was that at different comhairle meetings people would be selected to go here and there and everywhere, even as delegates to the ard-fheis, and almost imperceptibly we came to realise that Bertie was very good at working out if something would pass—that he had this innate capacity to understand people and the way they would vote. This is something that I never really got to the bottom of myself. It is a very rare combination of psychological insight and numerical dexterity or adaptability.

Such positions as officer for the comhairle would be fought over ferociously, according to Duffy, because the honour was so great. Over the years he and others noted Ahern's ability to predict who would get elected. Ahern would learn, sometimes by heart, the rules of the party and the local organisations, and he used this in conjunction with his flair for assessing people.

We all came to understand that Bertie was able to smell the wind . . .
Bertie would be able to say what he thought about every one of a hundred
delegates, within one or two, which is a very, very special gift, because
how you really see into somebody's soul—I don't mean in a Freudian
way—but how you really know how people are going to blow is very
difficult, and a great gift to have.

Duffy's view is that Ahern was exceptional in his family in some ways. For a
start, no-one else spoke with the Dublin accent Ahern had. In addition,
Ahern had a pronounced capacity for figures, statistics and rules and for the
study of systems and structures as they were applied to human organisation
and endeavour. The ability to retain detail, however, was something he
shared with his father, who was noticeably good at learning and retaining
racing form, the progeny of horses and the records of trainers and jockeys.
Ahern was not as interested in horses as he was in football, Duffy says. 'Even
up to today if you asked him who won the all-Ireland cup in 1934 he would
be able to tell you. And probably the score. He was very interested in learning
all that.'

The multi-seat proportional representation system creates great rivalry
not only between candidates from different parties but also—and sometimes
even more so—between candidates belonging to the same party. Within
constituencies there is a natural desire for the sitting deputy to want to
maintain his or her position both within the constituency organisation and
in the public eye. The favour or control of a sufficient number of cumainn
gives support to the politician at the comhairle level and ensures selection
for future elections. Up-and-coming members with ambition and ability are
at one and the same time positive portents for the future of the constituency
organisation and a potential threat to the position of those at its apex. Such
tensions exist in all parties but tend to be particularly acute in Fianna Fáil,
because of its passion for winning and holding power and its extraordinary
record in doing so.

One of the decisions around which these tensions become focused is the
choosing by the constituency of the number of candidates to be put forward
at election time. Sometimes the sitting TDs will insist that no other candidate
be put forward. At other times they and the constituency organisation
might believe that it is in their interest to run a new candidate to sweep up
votes in particular parts of the constituency where the sitting TDs are weak,
so that those votes could be transferred when the new candidate was
eliminated from the count, or to fend off the threat of a candidate from a

rival party. Sometimes head office has a different view from that held by the constituency organisation. The debates over such matters can be heated and prolonged.

As the 1977 general election approached there was just such a debate within Fianna Fáil in Dublin Finglas. (The constituency had just been created and would be abolished before the next general election.) The sitting Fianna Fáil TD for Finglas was Jim Tunney. Danny Bell, a local councillor since 1974, was the second party candidate in the constituency. The National Executive decided that a third candidate should be added to the ticket to soak up votes in the Drumcondra area, and Ahern was chosen. At the time, as Paddy Duffy pointed out, no-one knew that the Fianna Fáil election manifesto, including as it did an over-generous series of pledges designed by the Trinity College economist Martin O'Donoghue, was going to lead to a landslide for the party.

> Bertie really got on the ticket as the sweeper, as a young lad who definitely had no chance whatever, because he was so far away from these people [Tunney and Bell]. He got on the ticket and that was that. And what nobody realised was that Bertie had talents that even he didn't realise he had. That's one of the great things in life, that if you get the opportunity you can show your paces, but very often you don't get the opportunity— you never get the chance . . . I and the others were very happy that this young turk had been selected. We thought it was hilarious in some ways. Bertie set about getting a couple of his friends [involved], basically friends who worked with him or who were in All Hamptons, or friends of the family. I might have written some of the literature—the brochures and that sort of thing.

Joe Tierney, a Cabra activist with Fianna Fáil whose first involvement with politics was in support of Vivion de Valera in a 1945 by-election, when Tierney was eight, said Tunney was paranoid about Bell making inroads into his support in Finglas. 'Ahern was only brought in because his name began with an A, and he would be over Danny Bell on the ballot paper,' he said. A one-time member of the National Executive who was to have a stormy relationship with Ahern, Tierney said he took against Ahern from the start. 'Because I saw him operating in Finglas in 1977. He would go into a neighbourhood as soon as it was canvassed by Fianna Fáil, and turned it around so it was just for him. He was never a party man.'

Ahern set up an operations base in the front room of his parents' two-up, two-down home. According to Duffy he and his team of supporters devised a system for getting elected: canvass, canvass, canvass. They made the occasional foray into Finglas, which Tunney and his camp did not appreciate. On the morning of the poll Ahern and his supporters took the unusual step of conducting a leaflet drop in the hours before breakfast—something that was to become a feature of Ahern's campaigns. In those days canvassing on polling day at the polling stations was still allowed, and Ahern's supporters continued to work up to the time the polls closed. The next day the count took place in Bolton Street Technical College. At 8:30 p.m. the returning officer announced that Ahern had reached the quota and had taken the second seat, which Bell might have been expecting. According to Duffy,

> it came as a great delight to us, of course, and as a great shock to everybody, that this tousle-haired young man was elected that nobody had ever heard of. That was the beginning, if you like, of the official road.

In his memoirs Ahern said he made his way back up to Church Avenue for a hug from his mother and a firm handshake from his father. Then it was down to the Cat and Cage, which was packed with cheering supporters, and later on to Santry Stadium, where more well-wishers were gathered. It was the early hours of the morning before he got back to his Artane home.

According to Duffy, within months of the election he and others met in the Ahern household to discuss with the new TD what he would try to achieve with the power he now held. As he tells it, there was no particular political philosophy, set of policies or national objectives that galvanised the group. Rather, the focus was on career advancement, with the question of policies being placed in that context. Those at the meeting included Kett, Burke, Chris Wall (active in the Clonliffe Harriers, based in Santry Stadium, where Ahern's brother Maurice was a leading light) and Paul Kiely (who worked in the Mater Hospital).

> It was totally new to us. None of us had been this close to a TD, and the question was what to do with this new-found position, which opened up endless possibilities, none of which we could ascertain. We felt there was great potential in it, but we actually didn't know what that potential was. It was an opportunity to do something, but what we didn't know at that stage. As a result of that particular meeting, I remember typing up a four or five-page document called 'How to become Taoiseach in Twenty Years', and what we had in that document was the result of our discussion—how we thought that Bertie could be promoted to become junior minister,

senior minister and then Taoiseach. I have searched high and low, and I can't find it. I definitely had it until I moved house eight or nine years ago. It was a simple document, but it indicated that from that early time he and those of us around him saw the possibility of Bertie becoming Taoiseach.

To the best of my memory, it really was a programme to become involved in key issues and to bring the best people possible around him to work with him on the key issues, and by doing that to gain his name and acclaim, and then, with the happy bounce of the ball—because we all realised that politics is a very uncertain sport—that he would get promotion and he would make it. One of the early ones that we mentioned, which was very clear to us, was industrial relations. Which was an absolute disaster at that stage, with millions of work days being lost every single year.

Ahern was a member of the Federated Workers' Union of Ireland and found the workings of trade unions and industrial relations generally of interest. 'Bertie said from early on that he was interested in that,' said Duffy. He said he could recall discussing trade union matters with Ahern in the very earliest period of his political career, 'scoping out' the whole movement and identifying who the main players were. 'Bertie deliberately got to know and befriend, and understand, most of the trade union leaders. That was a very deliberate policy.'

Ahern was to play a role in the rationalisation of the trade union movement, while the creation of social partnership would be a core element of his political achievements; but Duffy said this wasn't planned. What was discussed at the early stage was more 'inchoate', he said. 'The germ of the idea, the necessity of going towards those sort of objectives, was there and was spoken about.'

In his memoirs Ahern wrote that there was no truth in the story that within weeks of his being elected a twenty-year plan was drawn up that envisaged his becoming Taoiseach.

There is a curious sense of resentment that emerges at times from Ahern's memoirs. He wrote of going to Leinster House for the first time and having to find for himself what desk he could use, of not being congratulated by anyone or 'even' having his photograph taken. In the period 1977–9 the Taoiseach, Jack Lynch, never said one word to him, Ahern wrote. Kind words were said by the Labour Party's Brendan Corish and Fine Gael's Liam Cosgrave, and this was, he wrote, his induction into the 'oldest rule' in politics:

politicians in other parties are the opposition, but your real enemies are in your own party.

When Lynch appointed Tunney a junior minister in his Government, Tunney had to give up his seat on the Dublin City Council, but he was unhappy at the prospect of Ahern, who had done so surprisingly well in the general election, replacing him. Tunney tried unsuccessfully to block him. Ahern took particular pleasure in topping the poll in the 1979 local elections. By then the popularity that had brought Fianna Fáil such a landslide victory in 1977 had evaporated. The oil crisis had thrown the economies of the Western world into shock and the Irish economy into a tailspin. The national finances quickly deteriorated, and there was an outbreak of bitter industrial strife. Party backbenchers grew uneasy, with mutterings about Lynch and his leadership. Lynch had been a compromise candidate for the party leadership at the time of the resignation of Seán Lemass, and his elevation parked for a time the contest between Haughey and George Colley. Ahern in his memoirs wrote that, at an event in November 1979, Colley came over to him and said hello, the first time he had done so since Ahern's election as a TD two-and-a-half years earlier. Colley was in the neighbouring constituency of Dublin North-Central but had 'not once' spoken to him until then, Ahern wrote. He decided that Colley's motive was that he wanted to curry favour in the coming leadership battle.

Ahern saw much in Colley's background that he admired: he was old Fianna Fáil, his father having been involved in the Easter Rising and the IRA. He had attended 'Joey's' school, run by the Christian Brothers in Fairview, not far from Drumcondra. Yet he always felt, he wrote, that, when he was speaking to him, Colley was 'looking down' on him. Ahern did not perceive any such sense of superiority emanating from Haughey, who had grown up in a modest home in the north Dublin suburb of Donnycarney. Indeed, they may well have shared a sense of resentment towards those they considered to have been born into greater privilege. Haughey's father had been a member of the old IRA, had joined the army but then had been invalided out. Haughey's very successful ministerial career had suffered a severe setback as a result of the Arms Crisis in 1970, which centred on the importing of guns for the Provisional IRA. Ahern said he supported Haughey over Colley because of the superiority of the former's ministerial record, though it is likely that the matter was more complex. Paddy Duffy emphasised the 'republican' issue.

It was quite clear that our preferred side of that equation was Haughey. None of this was worked out: it was just the way things were. From early on, Chris Wall and Bertie in particular would always have mentioned Haughey as being the most republican of the two. It was unspoken in many ways, but there was never any question of our giving our loyalty to Colley over Haughey. It was always Haughey.

Ahern's ability to 'smell the wind' may also have been a factor. The 1977 general election was a landslide for Fianna Fáil, giving it a comfortable absolute majority in the Dáil—the last it would see in the period of Ahern's political career. Geraldine Kennedy was at the count centre in the RDS in Dublin and came upon a happy-looking Haughey. She asked him why he looked so pleased, given the huge number of deputies who had just been elected under Lynch's leadership. 'But they're all my people,' replied a smiling Haughey. Kennedy quickly secured a commitment from him that if he became leader he would grant her his first interview as Taoiseach.

According to Duffy, when he and Ahern were considering any matter they would keep in mind three aspects: the national agenda, the party agenda and the local agenda. It was critical for the progress of Ahern's career, Duffy said, that each of these was taken into account when deciding on Ahern's moves as his career unfolded. 'You had to keep position on all those to keep your momentum moving and to try and move up the ladder.' There was a very strong focus on getting things done.

> Like everything else in Ireland, perhaps, we spent not enough time thinking about what we should be doing: we spent a huge amount of time trying to do it. Because everything takes so much time. Getting political preferment, in particular, is a big job.

Ahern's election had been a surprise in 1977. He kept his head down in the Dáil and negotiated the rise of Haughey and Haughey's eclipse of Colley without creating enemies. (In his memoirs he said that he acted much as he had done when he had entered the tough environs of St Aidan's as one of its youngest pupils: he kept his head down and observed.) His primary concern was to solidify his support in his constituency, recognising that all political careers are founded on an ability to get elected. He established a well-run 'ward-boss' system, a network whereby each road or district in his constituency had someone who operated as the eyes and ears of the organisation and as a conduit for communications with Ahern and his closest associates. All the real or perceived needs or concerns of constituents were given attention, and in return Ahern hoped for electoral support.

Changes to constituency boundaries in 1980 saw Ahern end up in Dublin Central, one of the poorest, if not the poorest, constituency in the country. He was no longer in a contest with Tunney but was up against Haughey's leadership rival, George Colley. According to the former political editor of the *Irish Times*, Denis Coughlan, Haughey put Ahern into Dublin Central so he could 'shaft' Colley and thereby damage his prospects in the party leadership stakes.

Gerald Kenny was a member of the Thomas Davis Cumann at about this time. Centred in the Berkeley Road and Phibsborough area, it was the strongest and largest cumann in the constituency, according to Kenny. An employee of a security firm, who later set up his own business, Kenny joined Fianna Fáil in 1972, having been involved in providing security to the 1971 ardfheis, where tensions were high as a result of the Arms Crisis. His parents had been in the party. He said he liked, and likes, Ahern but was a supporter of Colley. He agrees with Coughlan's view on what Haughey wanted Ahern to achieve in the constituency.

> Bertie put Colley in second place in the first election. Then opposed the nomination of his widow, Mary Colley. Bertie would try not to let it be seen that he was trying to shaft someone. But Haughey wanted any of the Colleys out of it.

Ahern and his supporters knew that Colley was a formidable opponent. According to Duffy, as the 1981 election approached, the 'Ahern army' was approximately 100-strong. The election would see 'the survival of the fittest.' The 'army' was almost professional in its drive, he said, and was determined that every door in the constituency would be knocked on three times during the campaign. The plan was to canvass the whole constituency, even though this broke the rules governing how it was to be divided up with Colley.

The intensive canvassing and the work since 1977 paid off. Ahern topped the poll, winning almost 19 per cent of the first-preference votes. By comparison, Colley garnered only 6.8 per cent. Nationally, Fianna Fáil failed to get enough deputies returned to remain in Government. The national focus was understandably on the outcome of the election and the formation of a new Government, but there was still time for the media, and those in politics, to register Colley's humiliation at being elected after his young constituency colleague. Duffy said he had mixed feelings about this.

We were really surprised. We were a bit shocked that we did so well and that poor old George Colley had been defeated. It was sort of a bitter taste, in a way. We recognised he was a good man, and it was shocking, and you could only imagine being on the far side . . . but I think everyone in the country knew then that this guy, Bertie Ahern, had something special. So I think that really brought Bertie to national political prominence for the first time.

The early 1980s was a period of great political turmoil. The oil crisis had combined with Fianna Fáil's 1977 budget strategy to create a noxious economic mix. The public finances and the economy became the core of political debate. There was a whiff of sulphur about Haughey, who many distrusted because of his unexplained wealth, the Arms Trial and what Garret FitzGerald of Fine Gael called, with an unfortunate choice of words, his 'flawed pedigree'. Haughey would be a divisive figure in the party, and in society generally, during his entire period as party leader, but Ahern managed to position himself solidly in the Haughey camp without creating any animosity in the anti-Haughey wing of the party, or indeed more generally. This achievement can be attributed to his affability, to his apparent modesty and to the care he took to avoid confrontation. His focus was on getting on, and during his first period in the Dáil he made some progress in that regard.

About a week after Haughey's elevation to the position of Taoiseach in December 1979, Ahern was appointed as his party's deputy chief whip. Soon afterwards the chief whip, Seán Moore, fell ill, so Ahern became the *de facto* chief whip. The post involves ensuring that party members are present for votes in the Dáil—a considerably more difficult job in the era before mobile phones. Ahern also had to compile regular reports for the parliamentary party, have frequent contacts with Government ministers and talk regularly to Haughey. The latter began to refer to Ahern as 'the kid'.

Haughey called an election for June 1981, and it turned out to be the first of three general elections within eighteen months. Ahern and his supporters fought all three, and his vote-winning record was further enhanced with each poll.

It was about this time that Ahern and his supporters launched a programme they later referred to as 'Operation Dublin'. According to Royston Brady, a former Ahern ward boss and one-time European Parliament candidate for Dublin, the exercise involved seizing control of some cumainn that were not particularly active and the closing down of cumainn that were particularly inactive. The exercise in Dublin Central resulted in a situation where the bulk of the party organisation came under Ahern's control. 'If you weren't willing to play ball, you were gotten rid of, whether you were staunch Fianna Fáil or whether you weren't,' Brady said. 'That didn't come into it.' Ahern disputes this analysis in his memoirs, though a similar picture was described by some of Ahern's inner circle in the 'Bertie' televsision documentary.

Gerald Kenny's recollection is that Ahern organised the cumainn so that they favoured his position.

> We were joined with O'Donovan Rossa, and the MacEntee-Cusack Cumann based around the markets and formerly in the control of Tom Leonard TD. Leonard had been gifted the seat at a convention, instead of Mary Colley. The three cumainn were to come together. I got [the] position of chairman. The secretary and the chairman essentially run a cumann. Tony Kett got secretary. That meant there was no position for MacEntee-Cusack, and they walked out *en masse.*

Joe Tierney said that, while the reorganisation was presented as a citywide exercise, the focus was in fact on Dublin Central, where he and others had resisted the efforts of Haughey and Ahern to impose John Stafford as an election candidate in the 1983 by-election caused by Colley's death. Haughey, he said, turned into a 'raging lunatic' when the local organisation thwarted his efforts, which were supported by Ahern. Then, in the 1985 local elections, the organisation put in a Moore Street trader called Ernie Beggs rather than Ahern, who had to be added to the ticket by the National Executive. At the end of Operation Dublin 'they had wiped out 16 cumainn and taken control away from me. By me I mean the organisation. He [Ahern] didn't reorganise anything. He just wiped them out.'

Kenny said he thought he might be able to rectify matters afterwards with disaffected party members, but it didn't turn out to be the case.

> So they effectively locked out a bunch of ardent and absolute Fianna Fáil loyalists, and it was just 'Who cares?' These were genuine, authentic people—people who were in the party because they thought the party was good for the country. And they were even insulted. Battle stories were told about how cutely it was done. It was totally ruthless and was geared towards garnering power as quickly as possible. There was to be no opposition.

The February 1982 election, which saw Fianna Fáil under Charles Haughey return to power, led to Ahern being appointed Government chief whip. For the first time he was on the inside track in Leinster House. His memoirs make it clear how much he enjoyed knowing more than his colleagues in the party about what was going on. He had to work with his own party, with the Workers' Party, which was supporting the Government, and with the independents, who included a constituency rival, Tony Gregory.

Ahern was highly suited to the position of chief whip, according to the former Labour Party leader Pat Rabbitte.

> He was ideal. He had all the skills that were needed for that position. He was diplomatic, reticent, he was underspoken, he would keep the lads in line without being dictatorial or lacking understanding of their problems. He was a very emollient face for the media during a turbulent time in the party's history. I can't envisage anyone else going out to the media and being asked how many voted against Haughey [at a parliamentary party vote on his leadership] and saying, 'I don't know, I had my head down taking the minutes.' I mean, no-one else could get away with that kind of thing. He would phone Seán Barrett as the Fine Gael chief whip and they'd meet over two pints of Bass, and they'd fix the business for the next week in the bar, and Bertie would be manoeuvring and so on. Very often I found in my dealings with him that I came out second best, and I would only find out afterwards. You never quite knew what he was looking for when he asked to see you, but you'd find out four weeks later.

The Haughey Government soon fell, and in November 1982 there was another general election. Ahern won twice as many first preferences as Colley, who was elected after the distribution of Ahern's surplus. Garret FitzGerald formed a coalition with the Labour Party, and Fianna Fáil found itself in opposition. Ahern, by now acknowledged as a close associate of Haughey's, was appointed party chief whip and spokesperson on labour affairs, a position that saw him 'marking' Ruairí Quinn. Ahern was a TD and Dublin City councillor, a senior figure within the party organisation and a poll-topping politician with a constituency machine to rival the best in the land. He was probably the first Irish politician to make canvassing a permanent activity, not just something that occurred when an election was called. This was to mark the entirety of his political career, firstly at the constituency level but subsequently on a national basis.

As well as being involved in the 1981 and 1982 general elections, Ahern was also involved in a by-election in 1983, though not as a candidate. George Colley died of a heart attack in September 1983, so a by-election had to be held in Dublin Central. A number of deputies died at about this time, including Brian Cowen's father, Ber Cowen, and Ahern later said this was probably to some extent attributable to the stress created by all the political upheavals. There was great tension in the party, with passionate disagreements between those who supported Haughey and those who felt that he was unfit for office. Those who opposed Haughey wanted the candidate in the by-election to be Colley's widow, Mary Colley, while Haughey wanted the candidate to be a local businessman, John Stafford. Neither one was eventually selected, with Ahern arguing that putting either candidate forward would simply focus the poll on the divisions that existed within the party. He was in favour of another candidate, Tom Leonard, whom, he argued, the party could unite behind.

Paddy Duffy has a different take on the matter. He said that he, Joe Burke and Chris Wall, having been tutored well by Ahern, met Haughey to discuss the matter, but the reasons put forward to Haughey were not the real ones motivating Ahern and his supporters.

We persuaded him that Tom Leonard was the man, because we wanted a weaker candidate, one we could control, and very reluctantly Haughey agreed, and we went down to Kennedy's [pub in Drumcondra] afterwards, and we were all standing round. Tony Kett was there as well, and Haughey said, 'Give the lads a drink,' and we all had a pint; and then afterwards, because Haughey would only have one drink, Haughey said, 'I don't appear to have any money. Here, Bertie, look after that.'

It was after this failure to have his will imposed on the constituency organisation that Haughey began to refer to Ahern and his supporters as the Drumcondra Mafia.

The Clontarf Fine Gael TD Richard Bruton was working for his party's candidate, Mary Banotti, during the by-election. He said Leonard was 'a decent skin' but was never a serious contender for a successful political career. Ahern never liked competitors close to him in his constituency, Bruton believes. 'He followed the old adage that the greatest threat to a sheep was the sheep grazing beside him. He never had any competitive sheep in the same pasture as him!'

Leonard polled very well and won the seat. However, he was never a threat to Ahern's dominance of the constituency and did not contest the 1987 general election, in which Dr Dermot Fitzpatrick was elected as the second Fianna Fáil TD in the constituency.

As part of his consolidation of his political position, Ahern during these years also established a fund-raising network. The unprecedented series of general elections put a severe strain on the finances of all politicians and political parties. According to Duffy, it was in the early 1980s that people like Des Richardson and Tim Collins, figures who became important money-men in the Ahern organisation, appeared on the scene, though he said he is not clear on the details. Celia Larkin, a full-time civil servant, also got involved. More ambitious fund-raising activities got under way, and a full-time constituency office for Ahern was opened over Fagan's pub, close to Drumcondra Bridge on the Tolka.

Strangely, there were two parallel financial structures in the constituency: one involved the local elected officers of the party, who came through, and belonged to, the Dublin Central cumann and comhairle structure; the other involved Collins and Richardson, and much larger sums of money. Not only were Richardson and Collins not elected officers of the constituency, accountable to the constituency organisation, they were not even members of the party. They nevertheless became involved in the running of the finances of Ahern's Dublin Central organisation, which soon became the best-funded constituency organisation in the country. Duffy says:

> In some ways in Bertie's life there were slightly different circles. The people I have mentioned were there from the beginning. Our remit was to always talk politics. Later on there was another, connected circle, in a different context, and that would include Des, Tim Collins; Joe Burke would probably have been in that as well—a business or sort of financial side. But the two of those [circles] never met. There was no connection between the two of them.

Some members of the various factions in Ahern's set-up were also involved in his social life, which mainly centred on pubs in Drumcondra and Beaumont. Ward bosses, such as the two Paddy Reillys, and key supporters, such as Kitt, Burke and, later, Dermot Carew, would meet Ahern socially in these pubs. Richardson rarely joined them, according to Duffy, who himself had a young family and other interests and also rarely went to the pub with Ahern.

The Labour Party deputy Joan Burton, whose Dublin West constituency adjoins Ahern's, believes that Ahern was good at asking for money. At the time, political fund-raising was almost entirely unregulated, and Ahern would have been keenly aware of the importance of a war chest in the battle for electoral success. According to Royston Brady, each ward boss was in charge of raising funds from potential targets in their own area, but a percentage would have to be forwarded to Ahern's constituency operation.

Burton emphasised another aspect of political fund-raising: the effect it has on a politician's self-esteem.

It is a huge boost to any politician when a range of people come forward and give money. In a way it doesn't matter if it's ten euro or ten thousand, but obviously if it is ten thousand . . . There is no politician on earth who is not flattered by people coming forward and saying I would like to support you.

You have this intense sense, in Fianna Fáil, that 'We are the business, we are doing the business,' and I think he [Ahern] was very good at that. I think he learned that at the hands of Haughey, and I think he was ruthless about doing it—letting people know that money was expected. I would say he made it very clear that he expected [people] to contribute handsomely.

The decision to open the office above Fagan's was taken despite the fact that the party had a building in Amiens Street which was available to Ahern and other party figures from his and nearby constituencies. It had been in the party's ownership for decades. Royston Brady's father, Ray, a taxi-driver who also played music in pubs, got to know Ahern in the early 1980s and became one of his key supporters. On Saturday mornings Ray Brady would usher in the waiting constituents to see Ahern in an office in the Amiens Street building, and it was at the end of one such morning that Royston Brady, then in his early teens, was first introduced to Ahern. A number of members of the Brady family became Ahern supporters. Royston's brother Cyprian ran Ahern's constituency office for twenty years, was appointed to the Seanad by Ahern in 2002 and was elected a TD in Ahern's constituency in 2007. He was elected on Ahern's transfers. A sister also worked in St Luke's.

Brady said from early on he noted that Ahern was very 'eccentric' about money, and mean. He said that, during one election in the 1980s, when he was still a teenager, he and a friend, Andrew Farrell, spent polling day handing out Ahern leaflets. They had been promised food, but it failed to materialise, and in the afternoon, when they were famished, his friend confronted Ahern near the Gardiner Street polling station and asked for money. Ahern gave them a fiver, and they went and bought some chips and Cokes in nearby Dorset Street. They had some change and were thinking of using it to buy cigarettes, but when they came round the corner they were confronted by Ahern looking for his change.

Farrell now lives in Arizona, but he confirmed the story when we spoke by phone. He said that he and Royston and Royston's brothers used to hand out leaflets for Ahern at election time but also between elections,

> to let people know that Bertie was still around, still looking out for them. I did it to help Royston out and his dad. And we were thinking also that Bertie might get us in somewhere—get us fixed up with a job—though with me personally that never worked out. I moved away. I think the main reason we were doing it was a good job at the end of it, you know. I think that's why a lot of people do it. I'd say the majority of people hope to get something out of it.

He said the only thing he ever got from Ahern was a FÁS job painting the railings around the Stardust Memorial in Coolock.

Farrell confirmed the story about the chips. He said he and the others would begin as early as five in the morning on polling days. They used to call themselves the BBC: Bertie's Breakfast Crew. In his memory it was not until later in the day, maybe back in St Luke's, that Ahern asked them for the change. He said his picture was taken that day and ended up in a book called *Dubliners*, written by Colm Tóibín and with photographs by Tony O'Shea. (Tony has kindly agreed to his photograph of Farrell being reproduced in this book.)

As has already been noted, the Fianna Fáil premises in Amiens Street were sold in 1989 in circumstances that remain unclear. Joe Tierney, a former elected officer of the Comhairle Dáil Ceantair in Dublin Central who remains active in the constituency, said the sale of Amiens Street occurred without the membership being consulted and without the treasurer knowing what happened to the money that was paid.

> It should have been put to the floor for a vote. That's how it should have been done. And the constituency treasurer should have known what happened to the money. But that never happened.

———

A sense of Ahern's ambition and drive, as well as of his take on the nature of a political career, was placed on the record in November 1984 when the front-bench spokesperson on labour attended a party conference in the Gresham Hotel organised for female would-be local election candidates. Haughey also attended, but it was the address from Ahern that was given prominence in Denis Coughlan's report for the *Irish Times*. 'Bertie tells FF women: sell your soul', read the headline. His view was fairly grim.

> Keep your balance. Keep well in with everybody. Say hello to your local TDs and councillors even if you hate them, and you might get nominated at your local convention. You have to walk the line, take the middle ground. You may hate your TDs but you must do what is required. We all have to swallow humble pie, and I have been doing it for years, but if you keep at it you can break through and get selected to the convention.
>
> If you do it the other way, you haven't a chance. And if getting there means selling your soul a little bit, there isn't a profession in the world where you don't have to change your principles. If you play it right and keep your balance, you can get to the convention.

Ahern told the women there was a built-in antipathy towards women in Fianna Fáil and expressed the view that the National Executive could do more to ensure that good candidates were selected at local conventions. Once through the convention, all candidates, be they men or women, 'have to take all the nonsense, the hard talk, the face-to-face and door-to-door criticism, while taking your own stand on particular issues.' The last point was an alternative take on his frequently expressed view that what he loved most was going out and meeting the people in his constituency, though, in fairness, it may well be that the delivery made the address amusing. Ahern has a great gift for humour.

The Gresham meeting was in preparation for the 1985 local election. Ahern's breakthrough into national prominence came from his position as a councillor rather than that of a deputy. He first got a seat on Dublin City Council when he replaced Jim Tunney in 1977. He contested and won the 1979 local election and topped the poll. In the 1985 local election the party's National Executive added him to the ticket after Stafford and others joined forces locally and outvoted Ahern's selection for the north inner-city ward. Ahern fought a hard battle against Tony Gregory in the campaign and took great pleasure in coming out on top. Fianna Fáil generally did well, with Ahern's brother Noel being among the new councillors elected. Ahern became the party leader in the council chamber and in 1987 was appointed Lord Mayor of Dublin, succeeding Tunney.

He threw himself into the role and seemed to accept just about every local and national invitation that came into his office. (He had no interest in any foreign engagements that arose, and his Artane neighbour Joe Burke, who had also been elected a councillor and was Ahern's Deputy Lord Mayor, usually travelled for him.) Ahern began to apply to the citywide, and indeed national, stage the insight and practice he had developed locally. His work rate was phenomenal and was part and parcel of an attitude whereby everything was a form of canvassing. The public took to the image of the somewhat tousle-haired 'true Dub' devoted to politics and public life, and from this period on Ahern lived his life in the full glare of the media. He became a public figure, even a political celebrity, with the media focused to an unusual extent on his appearance and character rather than on the substance of his work.

It was during this period, when he was living in the Mansion House, that Miriam Lord of the *Irish Times* began to write about him regularly.

He was so welcoming, so nice, but he was always a bit of a mess, always real dishevelled. Senan Maloney wrote a great piece at the time in the *Herald*. He was leaving a gig in the Mansion House, and he looked in the back of the Lord Mayor's car and it was filthy with crisp packets and old papers and so on, and he wrote a piece, the headline was 'Poor Old Dirty Bertie'.

As already noted, at about this time Celia Larkin became more involved in the administration of the Ahern machine. What began as a close role as a supporter changed during the period 1982–7 into an intimate relationship, and by the time Ahern moved into the Mansion House his marriage was coming to an end. Ahern's drive and focus was such that he had developed a life-style for himself in which everything else took a back seat to his political ambition. In his memoirs he wrote that he was torn between continuing his career in politics and accepting an opportunity he said he had to become chief executive of the Mater Private Hospital, while continuing to do freelance tax consultancy work. He saw the choice as one between politics and money. With hindsight, he wrote, it was in fact a choice between politics and family.

Chapter 7 ∾

| MINISTER

Bertie Ahern met Ruairí Quinn in the members' bar in Leinster House on a night soon after the 1987 general election that brought Haughey and Fianna Fáil back into power. Quinn, who, like Ahern, had been first elected to the Dáil in 1977, was considered by many to be closer to Ahern than most opposition politicians, and indeed closer than most deputies from Ahern's own party. When Quinn was Minister for Labour during the 1982–7 Government, Ahern had marked him as Fianna Fáil spokesperson on labour. When Ahern was appointed opposition spokesperson Quinn sent him a copy of the briefing document he had been given when he was appointed minister. He felt Ahern had a right to it. The two men worked well together, and in his memoirs Ahern is generous in his praise of Quinn and in the regard he has for him.

According to Quinn, in 1987 they discussed Ahern's position. Ahern told him that Haughey was thinking of appointing him Minister for Health. 'I said, "Are you out of your mind? Look at what has to be done. You've shadowed labour, you know the territory."' Not long afterwards Ahern was appointed Minister for Labour. It was an appointment that greatly suited him and that placed him at the heart of the establishment of the social partnership process—a development recognised by many as a key contributor to the subsequent Irish boom.

After Ahern's appointment, he and Quinn met at the Coq Hardi restaurant in Ballsbridge, a favourite of Haughey's in those years, to discuss Ahern's takeover at the department. Ahern asked if there were any projects in the department that Quinn wanted finished, and Quinn briefed him on the work he had been doing. According to Quinn, Ahern ran with the policies and plans that Quinn had already put in place and initiated very little himself by way of legislative change.

Quinn said in all his dealings with Ahern he found him to be very matter of fact, with 'no sides'.

> I never got any sense from him that he had any great political ideas or any projects he wanted to do. To this day I don't know what he stands for. I haven't the slightest idea. He basically seems to me to be the ultimate chameleon.

Because of sharp cutbacks in Government spending overseen by the Minister for Finance, Ray MacSharry, there was a period of intense industrial unrest. Ahern maintained a high profile within Leinster House and outside it as he became associated with the settling of a series of important disputes. Some of his core skills were particularly useful in this regard: his toughness, his ability to make people feel he was sympathetic to them, his capacity for absorbing detail, his concealment of any view or position he himself might have on matters, his patience and his capacity for work. The unions saw him as someone they could do business with.

Ahern developed a reputation as a successful mediator and as someone with a record of successful interventions in seemingly intractable industrial disputes, often carried out in the early hours of the morning. In his memoirs, writing about Northern Ireland, Ahern made the point that participants always prefer agreements if they are arrived at in the hours after midnight. He also took a swipe at employers, who, he said, tended to cave in the minute industrial action was taken and immediately want the Government to settle the dispute.

Pat Rabbitte, a trade union official before he became a full-time politician, believes that the image Ahern created during this period—a friend of the trade unions and a skilled mediator—was just another example of the serial misrepresentation that marked his political career.

> He made so much of his trade union contacts which were largely non-existent. He used to put it about that he was a shop steward for the Workers' Union of Ireland, prominent in its machinery, a trade unionist first. There was no basis for that. In reality, if he ever held a union card it was only briefly and it was only to have the card. He had a minimal role

as an activist, but he used that to develop a very good relationship with the trade unions, especially during the Haughey years. They were the years of the anorak and the long hair. He developed a relationship with, for example, Billy Attley [former SIPTU general secretary]. He was never quite so close to the Transport Union, as it was at the time. There were a number of celebrated industrial disputes down those years. People like Des Geraghty will tell you. Take the engineers or the electricians: Bertie always had someone inside who would keep him in touch with how things were going, and he would arrive just as the breakthrough was happening, and he would be there to take the kudos after the all-night session. He had an uncanny knack for that.

Gradually it added a great lustre to his personality as a conciliator. And there is no doubt that it is one of the strongest aspects of his personality, his conciliatory demeanour and his capacity to talk people into agreement. People liked him—people like him—even though they never got close to him.

No doubt about it, if you believe there ought to be a Minister for Labour, Bertie was ideally suited to it. He managed to convey that he was the unions' man, while the employers knew that he was really their man. And that's a rare achievement. Bertie always had contacts with prominent people in the business community and he used those links very adroitly. He was always well informed.

There is no doubt that Ahern brought the employers and the unions together to a degree that was unprecedented. It was not something that happened by accident; rather it was a policy adopted by Fianna Fáil while it was in opposition. The genesis for the idea came from the labour movement.

In 1986 Ahern and Haughey had visited the leadership of the Irish Congress of Trade Unions in their offices in Raglan Road, Ballsbridge, to discuss a plan being developed by Congress. It wanted to redress the chronic unemployment situation and suggested an arrangement with the Government and the employers whereby the unions would provide industrial peace and moderate wage demands in return for an easing of the tax burden on employees and Government policies aimed at job creation. Ironically, the trade union movement was not getting on well with the FitzGerald Government, even though the coalition included the Labour Party. Fine Gael has never been seen as sympathetic to the movement, while the Labour Party, despite receiving financial support from it, has often felt that it is not the trades unions' favourite party.

In government, Ahern took the Congress plan and ran with it. His involvement with the partnership process, and his dealings with the unions and the employers, was one of the great springboards of his political career.

Duffy described the partnership model as 'a sound Christian democratic basis for life and for living in a nation.' He said a book could be written that would deal solely with the amount of personal input Ahern had in bringing the trade union movement into the role of being an equal partner in the economic management of the country and with 'how that consensus transformed the country for fifteen, seventeen, eighteen years.'

According to Duffy, the use of patronage played a role in Ahern's long-term dealings with the trade union movement and in his rationalisation of a movement that had a lot of small, long-established unions.

Ahern facilitated patronage in the sense that they were all brought into the new system. Many of the trade unions were given money to rationalise. They were looked after in terms of being on all the boards of every institution that was ever created, so that the whole model of patronage was created where the representatives of the workers were now actually sitting on all these boards. They were brought right into the parlour and the office. It was no longer a case of agitating from outside the door and on the street. By the time he was finished they were all part of the new system. That took an unbelievable amount of work over twenty years to accomplish. It took unbelievable powers of persuasion, to persuade people to merge—to give up status. And moving on from there, to bring in the employers. He did the same work again with all the employers. He got to know all the main employers and, of course, from a very early stage he took a huge personal interest in the labour-relations machinery. He relished the detail of how that worked and became a personal friend of all the people who were selected and promoted to do those jobs.

Another development Quinn noted during Ahern's reign with the Department of Labour was the move by the state training agency for the tourism industry, CERT, from its head office in Clonskeagh to new offices in Amiens Street, in Ahern's constituency. Two architectural firms worked on the new head office: Arthur Gibney and Partners and Pilgrim and Associates. Tim Collins and Des Richardson were both involved with Pilgrim, which has featured in the proceedings of the Mahon Tribunal. To explain about Pilgrim, it is necessary to temporarily abandon the narrative of Ahern's political career.

Pilgrim was set up by Collins and the architect Tim Rowe in the late 1980s. They met when working on a hospital. Collins's speciality was laying floors, but his function in the new business was finding clients for what was to be a small architectural practice. Richardson became a director of the company but was not so involved in its day-to-day business. Richardson told the tribunal that his main function was providing workers when they were needed, through his employment firm, Workforce.

Collins and Richardson, according to the latter, had met doing political fund-raising and became associates and friends. Richardson, a tall, strong-looking man who often wore pin-striped suits, gave the impression in the Mahon Tribunal witness box of being tough and clear-minded. Collins was a quieter man, less willing to engage. At the time of his appearances as part of the tribunal investigating Ahern's finances, Collins was unwell and submitted doctors' certificates as part of his dealings with it.

Collins became a director of Workforce, and, as we have seen, he and Richardson were both trustees of St Luke's and directors of Pilgrim. Collins gave evidence to the tribunal about matters other than Ahern's money. He was called as a witness to modules in which the tribunal investigated testimony from Frank Dunlop that he had given bribes to Dublin councillors in the hope of getting land that belonged to clients of Pilgrim rezoned. Collins at all times denied that he had any knowledge of such payments.

One module involved lands at Cloghran, in north Co. Dublin, bought for approximately £180,000 in 1989 by a consortium of three men, including John Butler, who Collins said was a long-standing friend. Butler was associated with a scaffolding company called Scafform, which did work for the Fianna Fáil ard-fheis and also provided services to Joe Burke's pub-renovation business. In 1989 Collins was involved in Butler's sale to Richardson of 50 City Quay in Dublin. Butler regularly attended Ahern's annual fund-raising dinners, held in the Royal Hospital, Kilmainham, during this period. Up to 350 people would attend the dinners, which are usually considered to have been Richardson's brainchild. The men who were the trustees of St Luke's, as well as the solicitor Gerry Brennan, were the main organisers. Ahern's partner, Celia Larkin, may also have had a role, Richardson told the tribunal. According to Dunlop's evidence to the tribunal, some of the clients he brought to the Ahern dinners were people on whose behalf he was making corrupt payments to Dublin councillors. The clients told the tribunal they had not known he was making the payments.

Pilgrim started to work for Butler and his associates in relation to the Cloghran lands. Collins said Butler and his partners ran a restaurant called the Courtyard in Donnybrook, Dublin.

Well, you see, how it came about was they wanted to replicate the Courtyard on the north side of Dublin, and that was how I earned my living, driving around looking for properties, trying to match them up, and I found a site and I thought it would be suitable and I brought it to them.

Collins said he just cold-called on the owners of the land.

I don't know. I just drove in off the back; it was at the back of the Coachman's Inn. I drove in one day, and this man, I asked him would he think of selling.

Collins's hope was that he would at one stage be rewarded by Butler and his partners.

I would hope to get a finder's fee at some stage . . . Nothing written down. I trusted the people I was dealing with.

Pilgrim worked on a plan to have a hotel built on the lands, though no plan appears to have been submitted to Dublin County Council. In 1992 Collins was instrumental in introducing Butler to Frank Dunlop. He said that it was generally accepted that Dunlop knew the councillors and was good at public relations and that he had introduced other landowners and developers to Dunlop. When it was put to him at the tribunal that he had told Dunlop that he knew that councillors would have to be paid, he said, 'That's a lie.' In the end the lands were sold in 1996 for approximately £1.6 million. This was a sixfold increase in value.

Collins gave evidence to a number of tribunal modules that looked into parcels of land owned by different parties who in turn became clients of Pilgrim and whom Collins introduced to Dunlop. In all cases Dunlop said he had made corrupt payments, but Collins, Rowe and their clients denied that they knew this was happening. Collins also told the tribunal that in or around 1994 he and Rowe moved to Project Management, a large architectural firm run by Ambrose Kelly, where Collins again practised as a land agent and a purveyor of clients while Rowe worked as an architect. Kelly gave evidence to the tribunal, in particular about his dealings with Liam Lawlor, the Fianna Fáil TD who was the focus of extensive corruption inquiries by the tribunal. In his evidence Dunlop said he had made corrupt payments to Lawlor in relation to the securing of council support for a development at Quarryvale, near Lucan, Co. Dublin, now Liffey Valley Shopping Centre.

Richardson told the tribunal that he came to know Dunlop in or around 1993, when Ahern asked him to work full-time on raising money for Fianna Fáil. At the time Ahern was Minister for Finance, party treasurer and chairperson of the Fianna Fáil finance committee. The position he created for Richardson was a new one. The party owed £3½ million. Richardson said his original intention had been to restructure the party's fund-raising operation at home and abroad and return to his own work after about two years.

The party had its own structures based at its head office in Upper Mount Street, with a finance officer and audited accounts, but Richardson operated outside this framework. He set up office in the Berkeley Court Hotel in Ballsbridge and ran his own operation, informing head office of his progress and handing over the money raised. It is not a parallel operation in the sense of the one Ahern had developed within Dublin Central, though it has echoes of it. Richardson was involved in both.

An example of what he did was given during the tribunal's hearings when evidence was heard about a dinner in a house in Cork in March 1993. Approximately twenty businesspeople attended, ten of whom apparently made cash or cheque payments on the night, leaving the money in envelopes on a hall or dining-room table. Among those in attendance was the Cork property developer Owen O'Callaghan, who had a role in drafting the invitation list. Dunlop was acting for O'Callaghan at the time in relation to the Quarryvale project. He said O'Callaghan did not know about the corrupt payments he was making, and O'Callaghan denied any knowledge of them.

Dunlop met Richardson before the dinner to help him draft a few words on Fianna Fáil's financial needs and its future aspirations. On the day after the dinner, Richardson made two lodgements of £25,000. He could not recall later why he had lodged it in two instalments.

When Ahern became party leader in December 1994 he asked Richardson to stay as the party's fund-raiser until the following election. Richardson was extremely successful in getting people to hand over money. He cleared the party's debts and so contributed in no small way to Ahern's political success. He remained the party's key figure in raising funds from supporters up to 1999.

Richardson told the tribunal that, soon after his appointment as a fund-raiser, Dunlop offered to help him if he required it in any way. He said Dunlop, who had served as Government press officer during Haughey's time in power, subsequently helped him with the drafting of letters looking for support and had also helped with the writing of speeches. The two men ended up going into the lobbying and public relations business together.

One of the difficulties with the evidence Richardson gave in relation to the various companies he worked with was that he was negligent in making filings to the Companies Registration Office. In February 1992 a company called Willdover was incorporated, with a registered address at 50 City Quay. It was owned by Richardson, but he never filed the documents to show that he was a shareholder and director. 'The intention was there but it never happened.' He invoiced Fianna Fáil for his work for the party using Willdover, he said. The pattern appears to have been an invoice for £5,000 each month, though Richardson said the amount would include recompense for money he had spent on party matters.

Richardson was also involved with a company called Berraway, which was incorporated in April 1992. Again, he did not register his position as a director or shareholder of the company. Initially it was involved in property development, with a Co. Meath man, Éamonn Duignan, as one of the three partners, Dunlop being the other. A banking document displayed at the tribunal showed the three men signing it as directors of Berraway in September 1993, though Richardson said he was never a registered director. In or around June 1994 Berraway began renting office space from Dunlop, at 25 Upper Mount Street, the building used by Dunlop for his firm Frank Dunlop and Associates. Dunlop's firm was a very lucrative business that had a lot of *bona fide* blue-chip clients who used Dunlop as a political lobbyist, but it also involved Dunlop running a substantial sideline as the organiser of political corruption in the Dublin planning process. He later pleaded guilty to corruption and was sentenced to two years in prison, with six months suspended. Dunlop also provided continuing advice and services to Fianna Fáil, including operating as director of elections.

Soon after Berraway moved to Dunlop's building, Richardson, Dunlop and Duignan began using a partnership structure for their property development ventures, and Berraway came under Richardson's sole control. He opened an account in the company's name with the Montrose branch of the Bank of Ireland in Donnybrook. Then, about the time when Ahern became party leader, Richardson began using Berraway to invoice Fianna Fáil. According to his evidence, he also began invoicing the party a flat fee of £5,000 per month, with expenses incurred during his work being dealt with separately.

In 1997, the year Ahern became Taoiseach for the first time, Richardson and Dunlop went into business together. According to Richardson, Dunlop suggested that they sign a one-year contract that would involve Richardson using the contacts he had made to find clients for Dunlop's PR business. Richardson invoiced Dunlop for his contributions, using Berraway, even though Dunlop was a registered shareholder in Berraway. Richardson told the tribunal that he did not know how Dunlop ever became registered as a shareholder. During 1998 Richardson and Dunlop were meeting each other almost weekly, the tribunal was told. By this stage the tribunal was established, but, as Dunlop later told it, he was sceptical of its ability to expose corruption.

Berraway was dissolved in 1999, about the time Dunlop first disclosed to the Flood Tribunal (as it was then called) that he had been involved in a series of corrupt payments to councillors on behalf of a range of clients over an extended period. Naturally, his lobbying business collapsed. According to a report in the *Sunday Business Post* in 2000 by its former editor Tim Harding, more than €1 million passed through the Berraway account between 1996 and 2000. The funds appear to have arisen from payments from clients rather than from profits arising from any business ventures.

In December 2007, when Ahern was still Taoiseach and the tribunal was conducting public hearings into his finances, I wrote an article in the *Irish Times* about this web of relationships involving Dunlop, Richardson, Ahern and Collins. I was prompted to do so because Dunlop had mentioned in evidence how he had had regular contact with Ahern during Ahern's time as a minister and Taoiseach. He would call Ahern, and Ahern would call him. Dunlop would introduce clients to Ahern and discuss with him matters of concern to Dunlop's clients. 'Bertie would go out of his way on some occasions to facilitate any requests I made of him,' Dunlop said.

I wrote about these links because of what Dunlop had disclosed about his long-time engagement in corruption, because of his business dealings with Richardson and because of the roles played by Richardson and Collins in the money side of Ahern's political career and the whole unhappy question of legitimate political fund-raising. The morning the piece appeared, Dunlop came up to me at the press table before the start of that day's evidence and mentioned the article. He seemed annoyed. 'So it's not okay to have friends now, is it not?' he said, or words to that effect. I said Ahern must have been very surprised when he found out what Dunlop had been up to over all those years. That seemed to deflate any annoyance Dunlop was feeling. He laughed and walked to the witness box. When he got there he paused, looked back at me, smiled, and then entered the box to give his morning's evidence.

_____

By the time Ahern had become minister, Gerald Kenny was running a small and not particularly successful security firm while also being an active member of Fianna Fáil in Ahern's constituency. A year or so after Ahern had first been elected as a deputy, Kenny had met Ahern at Ahern's request in a pub near the Botanic Gardens. Ahern, he said, talked to him about his business, which was not doing as well as Kenny pretended it was.

> As far as I was concerned, Ahern was Haughey. I was of a different persuasion [a Colley supporter], but Ahern is a very easy guy to get on with. We met in the Tolka House. I didn't really have a clue what he was talking about. He was telling me that what he was earning between the Dáil and the Mater Hospital wasn't really enough to pay his bills, his mortgage, the expenses of the constituency, and so on. But actually he was asking if I was interested in his being a consultant, a business consultant, to my company, and I was saying, 'What would I need a consultant for? I have a mickey-mouse business.'

Nothing came of the suggestion. However, after Ahern was appointed Minister for Labour, Kenny's business was again raised. According to Kenny, Ahern told him there were a lot of security contracts available in agencies that reported to his department.

> He rang me and we met. I can't remember where, it could have been the Tolka again. Later on I know I met him in the Department of Labour in Mespil Road. We were on our own. He started going on about this, that and the other, and I remember him saying very strongly that if there is something going a Fianna Fáil man should get it. He proceeded to tell me that there were going to be security contracts available in FÁS, and he wanted to know if I would be interested. He said, 'You'll get the money, and I'll get the jobs.' In other words, whoever he sent to me would get the job. Electorally it made sense. Then he said, 'What you need to do now is meet Paddy Duffy, and he will arrange how things will work out.' Paddy is probably the shrewdest of them all. We didn't know each other at this stage, but I got to know him later.

Kenny said he later met Duffy in the Skylon Hotel in Drumcondra. He was in the habit of giving the party about two hundred pounds a year, channelling it through his cumann so that it would get the benefit. His view was that if you were going to get involved in a political party you should be willing to contribute money to it. When he met Duffy he was expecting to be asked for an increased donation. Duffy discussed Ahern's constituency operation with Kenny and outlined to him how difficult it was to fund it and how much money it cost. By the end of the conversation it was agreed that Kenny would give two thousand pounds a year. It was about twice the amount he had been expecting. He said he paid the money by taking out ten seats at a hundred pounds each at the annual Kilmainham dinner and giving the other thousand to one of Ahern's close associates. He could not remember who but he thought it might have been Joe Burke.

Duffy, when asked about this meeting, said that he could not remember it and that it appeared unlikely. He said he had nothing to do with the Kilmainham dinners or the financing of the St Luke's operation. His role was with policy and strategy matters associated with Ahern's career. The people who were involved in running the financial side of Ahern's operation had been clearly demarcated in the tribunal hearings, he said. 'The structure was that the people who organised that whole area were clearly known, and nobody outside of that group had any hand, act or part in any of that.'

In relation to the FÁS issue Duffy said that there was very high unemployment at the time and that many people in Fianna Fáil and the other parties were asked for help. Ahern tried to help anyone who approached him in that regard. 'Bertie would be well known for having worked hard, maybe harder than others, at trying to get people jobs, particularly at the lower level. Certainly I would have met a lot of those during my time—ushers and doormen, that sort of role—and they were very grateful.'

Kenny said his company, County Security Ltd, got a contract for supplying security to the FÁS offices in D'Olier House, D'Olier Street, opposite the former offices of the *Irish Times*. (D'Olier House is rented to the state by an Irish company that is in turn owned by a Cayman Islands trust set up by the property developer John Byrne, who was a long-time friend of Haughey's. The trust was set up by Haughey's bagman, Des Traynor, architect of the infamous Ansbacher deposits in the Cayman Islands.)

According to Kenny, D'Olier House 'possibly needed a doorman for the door and a good alarm system, but we started off with two men during the night and two during the day . . . And it was a small place. It was farcical.' One of those he employed at Ahern's request was Ray Brady, father of Royston and Cyprian. Royston Brady, when asked about it, confirmed that his father, who had previously worked as a taxi-driver, was employed providing security at the D'Olier Street offices in the 1980s before getting a job in Dublin Castle.

Kenny, who said he last met the Brady children when they were young teenagers, described Ray Brady as a gentleman.

> He was extremely honest, a religious man. He said one strange thing one night when we were discussing his salary. Ray was working for me in FÁS in D'Olier Street at the time. Every so often there would be a blow-up about wages. Ray was giving out about Bertie. Obviously Bertie had promised him something else, because, really, security jobs weren't that good, though it was a job. Ray said, 'You know, Gerry, how much I love that man, but he is the meanest man in Ireland.'

By this time Kenny had become interested in psychology and was studying in Trinity College, Dublin. He was not paying as much attention as he should have been to his business, and County Security Ltd got into financial trouble. He reduced his payment to Ahern's constituency operation to one thousand pounds. Then he decided the company would have to fold. When he told Ahern, he said, a number of people became involved in managing the situation.

> I think it was a bit alarming for him because he had a number of people working for him through me, and he arranged basically how the company would be liquidated. He sent me to a guy over on Percy Place, then to a second guy. I had a one-to-one meeting with a man where we discussed whether we could keep the business going or shunt it to someone. A meeting was arranged in an impressive office in Merrion Square, a recruitment agency, I think. There were about four people there. Des Richardson officiated.

During Ahern's time as Minister for Labour his image was that of the scruffy, workaholic politician no-one could dislike. Miriam Lord recalls going for Christmas drinks to the Department of Labour with a colleague from the *Irish Independent*, where she then worked. They talked to Ahern.

> He was standing with his back to the wall and drinking a beer. My colleague was an experienced journalist who knew him over the years and, as she was speaking to him, she was brushing dandruff and lint off his jacket, like a mother would do with a child. And then she straightened his tie, ever so slightly, and he continued to speak, like a little boy. If she had taken out a handkerchief and spat on it, and rubbed it on his face, I

wouldn't have been surprised. It was only afterwards that she realised what she had been doing, and she was embarrassed and she said, 'I've just been rubbing the shoulders of the Minister for Labour.' And then she thought: 'Ah why wouldn't I? It's Bertie. Somebody has to look after him.' People just felt very at ease with him.

In May 1989 Haughey, who had been running a minority Government with the support of independents, decided to call a general election. The election featured regularly in the Mahon Tribunal and the Moriarty Tribunal (inquiring into payments to Michael Lowry and Charles Haughey) during the 1990s because of the large amount of money given to Fianna Fáil politicians in the course of the campaign. Some of this ended up in personal bank accounts. One of Fianna Fáil's fund-raisers, Paul Kavanagh, gave evidence to the Moriarty Tribunal that some who gave money to Haughey were indifferent as to whether he put it in his own pocket or gave it to the party.

The 1989 general election saw Ahern poll the second-highest number of first-preference votes in the country, coming in far ahead of his fellow-candidates in the constituency, Dr Dermot Fitzpatrick and John Stafford. The electorate rejected Haughey's gamble for an absolute majority, and he managed to get back into power only by doing a deal with the PDs. Ahern and Albert Reynolds negotiated the deal on behalf of Fianna Fáil. When Haughey announced his new Government, Ahern was still Minister for Labour.

In 1991, when tensions were particularly high between the coalition partners because of suspicions about Haughey, Ahern and Reynolds successfully conducted a review of the Programme for Government with their coalition partners. Shortly afterwards Ahern was in a room in Government Buildings, briefing the journalists Sam Smyth, Stephen Collins and Gerald Barry, when Haughey poked his head round the door. He pointed a finger at Ahern. 'He's the man,' he said. 'He's the best, the most skilful, the most devious, the most cunning of them all.' The comment was duly recorded and has dogged Ahern ever since, though perhaps it did him as much good as it did harm.

As was the case throughout Haughey's time as leader, there were tensions within Fianna Fáil. Reynolds and a group that became known as the country-and-western set were intent on ousting Haughey. A motion of no confidence was put down for a parliamentary party meeting. It was defeated, and afterwards Haughey sacked Reynolds. Ahern replaced Reynolds in the Department of Finance and so became the second most powerful figure in the Government and a contender for the future leadership of the party.

However, when Haughey resigned a year later, Ahern opted not to fight Reynolds for the leadership. Reynolds became Taoiseach and jettisoned a huge proportion of the Cabinet. Ahern was one of the few left standing.

During Ahern's time as Minister for Finance he had to deal with a very serious crisis involving Ireland and the European Union's plan for a single currency. International speculation forced sterling out of the Exchange Rate Mechanism and caused a collapse in the value of the currency—a huge blow to the Irish economy, which depended so heavily on exports to Britain. Ahern came under enormous pressure to devalue the Irish currency within the ERM. Speculators bet huge amounts against the Irish currency. As well as working with a number of senior civil servants, Ahern worked at this time with Padraic O'Connor, the NCB executive who would later become embroiled in one of the dig-out scenarios presented to the Mahon Tribunal to explain lodgements to Ahern's bank accounts. The currency crisis straddled the collapse of the Reynolds coalition with the PDs, a general election and the negotiation of a new coalition arrangement, this time with the Labour Party. Ahern held out against the currency speculators for a period, stating that Ireland would not devalue and was determined to remain within the ERM. In the end, in January 1993, he announced a 10 per cent devaluation, and the crisis came to an end. Ahern received wide praise for his handling of the issue, and though the devaluation cost the state money it immediately led to a fall in interest rates and gave the economy a competitive boost that had important long-term consequences.

One of the more notable and controversial initiatives of Ahern's career during this period was the introduction of a tax amnesty in the early months of the Fianna Fáil-Labour coalition. The measure allowed people with tax debts to settle their liability by paying 15 per cent of the amount owed, and it also provided for elaborate measures to ensure the right to secrecy of those who availed of the amnesty. The legislation creating the amnesty made it a criminal offence for anyone to avail of the deal without declaring all their liabilities; but, as it later transpired, the secrecy measures made it all but impossible for an offence to be proved.

Ruairí Quinn's explanation of how the amnesty got through a Government that included the Labour Party is surprising. 'Bertie wasn't going to allow it to happen, and then he just announced it at the cabinet.' This is similar to the account given by the Labour Party adviser Fergus Finlay in his book *Snakes and Ladders* (1999). He wrote that the party had been given the impression that, although Reynolds wanted the amnesty, Ahern wasn't going to go along with it and had assured the Labour Party that it would not go ahead. Then, when the matter came up at a Government meeting, Ahern presented the amnesty proposal, and it went through without debate. Greg Sparks, a principal with the accountancy and financial consultancy firm FGS, acted as an adviser to Dick Spring during that Government. He recalled getting a phone call from Ahern at about 1 a.m. on the Tuesday morning the meeting was to be held. Ahern was seeking to ascertain the Labour Party stance on the proposed amnesty, which, of course, was being kept secret. At the time the Labour Party had a system whereby measures due to come up at Government meetings would be considered beforehand by the party advisers and programme managers and then discussed with the Labour Party ministers before the meeting. Sparks recalled one minister, Mervyn Taylor, banging the table and saying 'over my dead body' in relation to the amnesty proposal.

> Then off they went into the cabinet meeting and there was total surprise when they came out four or five hours later and it had been passed. Now, there is cabinet confidentiality, but, from what I can make out, Albert was the main advocate for it. Bertie didn't want it, and we didn't want it. Dick was waiting for Bertie to object to it, and Bertie was waiting for Dick to object to it, and neither of them objected to it, and, because of that, it went to the cabinet and it was passed. I have to say it seems very, very strange, but that is the way it was explained to me.

Sparks thinks that, perhaps because it was early in the lifetime of the Government, neither Ahern nor Spring wanted to expend political capital going up against Reynolds, and so each held back. He does not believe that Ahern was in fact in favour of the measure, while presenting himself to the Labour Party as being against it. 'I have no doubt but that Bertie was against it. No doubt at all.'

Pat Rabbitte, who was then a member of Democratic Left (the breakaway group from the Workers' Party) and on the opposition benches, is not so sure. He believes that Ahern had no principled objection to the measure.

> If Bertie had meant anything of what he pretended about his empathy with the trade union movement he could not have promoted the tax amnesty . . . Ruairí Quinn has gone on the record to say that Bertie gave them to understand that he would stop it. Then it was suddenly proposed at the cabinet and it was through. I don't understand that.

The Labour Party successively opposed changes to the capital acquisitions tax regime that their coalition partners wanted to introduce. It was while reading through Government papers one weekend that Sparks noted a short passage regarding the tax, which applies to gifts above a certain value. The proposal was that the tax would be capped, that is, that there would be a threshold above which increases in the value of the asset or money received would not increase the associated tax bill. Sparks and Fergus Finlay flew down to Co. Kerry and had a meeting with Spring in a hotel in Tralee to discuss the matter. Ahern, who was in the area, turned up, and he and Spring went to a hotel room to talk. The measure was dropped, and the media never got to hear what had happened.

Another issue that arose when Ahern was Minister for Finance involved planning and tax concessions. In an effort to stimulate building in blighted urban areas there was a scheme whereby identified urban areas could be 'designated' so that developments in those locations could benefit from tax concessions.

The department responsible for overseeing the scheme was the Department of the Environment, where Michael Smith was minister and Emmet Stagg of the Labour Party was minister of state. Ahern, as Minister for Finance, had an ancillary role. Neither Smith nor Stagg would speak to the present writer about an episode in which plans associated with prospective designations were moved from the Department of the Environment to the Department of Finance. The Mahon Tribunal conducted private, confidential inquiries into the matter as part of its intended module on allegations relating to the tax designation scheme. Evidence was never heard in public because of a ruling of the Supreme Court. Although evidence on the matter will not now be heard, Stagg, who gave a statement to the tribunal, would neither talk about the matter nor explain why he didn't want to. 'I just don't,' he said.

According to one of Stagg's party colleagues, his statement to the tribunal was that 'the maps had gone up to the Department of Finance; the maps showing the areas that were going to possibly be included, key insider information. These had disappeared.' The issue for the tribunal was whether confidential information might have been made available to persons who should not have had access to it.

When Stagg discovered that the files had been moved from the department, he contacted Smith, who in turn had to take steps to have the documents returned to his department, which they were. Another source, who does not want to be identified, has also confirmed that the tribunal inquired into this matter in private.

The reason public hearings into the tax designation allegations were never heard is worth noting, since it is not the only private inquiry concerning Ahern that did not go ahead. In 2004 the tribunal, responding to the concerns of the Oireachtas about the growing scale of its costs, drafted a list of matters that could be the focus of future public inquiries. No new items were to be added to the list. This became known as the J2 list.

The tribunal drafted a list of items it *might* hold public inquiries into in the future rather than a list of items it *would* hold public inquiries into. Later, in a case taken by the Fitzwilton Group, which was seeking to prevent the tribunal conducting public inquiries into a payment to Ray Burke, the Supreme Court ruled that, because the tribunal had drafted a list of items it might, rather than would, inquire into, it was now barred from conducting public inquiries into the items on the list or into any new allegation.

The J2 list was never published, but in July 2007 Ahern's senior counsel, Conor Maguire, in the course of making an argument that the tribunal should not be holding public inquiries into Ahern's finances, mentioned it. An edited version of it had been supplied to Ahern by the tribunal, and it included items that it felt might be relevant to him. The first of these was the most strange.

The tribunal, Maguire said, had listed a possible public inquiry into the affairs of fourteen people, including Ahern, and 'all matters involving separately or together, directly or indirectly' these fourteen people and 'persons, companies, trusts or entities controlled or operating for any of their benefits, individually or otherwise.' The names of the other thirteen people were not disclosed, and Ahern would not comment on it at the time.

The other allegations Maguire mentioned related to tax designation and 'Green Property Group/rezoning or tax designation'. Maguire's submission was unsuccessful. The public inquiry into Ahern's finances was a subset of the tribunal's inquiry into Quarryvale, which had begun before the instruction from the Oireachtas that the tribunal draft a list of allegations it would be inquiring into in the future.

———

The Reynolds Government eventually fell apart because of the bad relationship between Reynolds and Spring. The final break was a complicated scenario involving the extradition of a paedophile priest, Brendan Smith, the appointment of the Attorney-General, Harry Whelehan SC, to the High Court, and concerns over the reasons for the extradition of Smith to Northern Ireland encountering a months-long delay, despite a series of warrants being submitted to the Attorney-General's office.

The tensions within the coalition and within Leinster House reached hysterical proportions, with rumours flying and with a growing conviction that the Government was about to fall. At one point Pat Rabbitte referred in the Dáil to a new revelation that would 'rock the foundations of the state.' This never emerged, but the coalition Government did sunder. Reynolds resigned as Taoiseach and party leader, saying he did not want to do anything that might destabilise the fledgling Northern Ireland peace process. Ahern replaced him as party leader. Máire Geoghegan-Quinn had thrown her hat in the ring in an attempt to win the leadership but withdrew before a vote, and Ahern was appointed unopposed.

The Dáil was not dissolved. Reynolds remained as acting Taoiseach as Ahern worked to see if he could negotiate a new coalition with Spring. Matters progressed to the extent that a draft list of ministers in the new Government was agreed between them. According to Sparks, Spring and Ahern got on well, and a Labour Party-Fianna Fáil coalition with Ahern as Taoiseach might have worked well. Ahern, in his memoirs, wrote that he was very angry that the Reynolds Government had been allowed to collapse in the way it did, because of the amount of good work he believed the Government was achieving. Going on his subsequent attitude to presiding over a coalition Government, it is fair to presume that, if a Government had been formed, Ahern would have used his considerable political skills to maintain good relations with the Labour Party.

Sparks said he had a very good experience working with Ahern and with Ahern's adviser, Gerry Hickey. Ahern, as Minister for Finance, had agreed to the establishment of a tax strategy group, which came up with policies based on a more long-term view of taxation policy. The work of this group also, for the first time, involved the Revenue Commissioners being consulted on changes to the tax code. Sparks felt that Ahern had taken a political risk in supporting Labour Party policy on a residential property tax. 'That blew up in his face. There was fierce opposition.' However, he said it showed that Ahern was ready to take political risks for policies he believed in.

Sparks felt Ahern was determined to work with the Labour Party and was essentially sympathetic to many of his coalition partners' ambitions. From his dealings with Ahern, Sparks felt that he did not have strong political convictions and that this made him receptive to the arguments of others.

Fianna Fáil is not a policy-driven party. Bertie was more the type of person who is open to views being given to him and being selective as to whether they were runners or not. I think it is his strength and ended up becoming his weakness.

It was while Ahern was negotiating a new coalition deal and his first Government with Spring that he was involved in his dealings with Michael Wall concerning the house in Beresford Avenue. It appears that, having become party leader unexpectedly early, Ahern was bounced into dealing with his unresolved living arrangements. The need to have a home became an immediate political imperative.

The Mahon Tribunal was later told that the house was selected by Michael Wall and Celia Larkin. Michael Wall, a squat, bearded Irish emigrant with a successful coach business in Manchester, said that he selected the house because it was near the airport and he was considering setting up a new business in Dublin. The solicitor who acted in the purchase of the house was Ahern's solicitor, Gerry Brennan, and later Brennan drafted a will for Michael Wall that would have left the house to Ahern. (If Ahern predeceased Michael Wall, it would be left to Ahern's daughters.) It was for this and other reasons that the tribunal investigated whether or not Michael Wall was in fact acting as a nominee for Ahern when the house was purchased in Michael Wall's name.

Michael Wall travelled from Manchester to Dublin two-and-a-half weeks after Ahern became leader of Fianna Fáil, carrying a briefcase filled with cash, which, he told the tribunal, he had taken from his office safe. He said he did not know exactly how much was in it but that it was approximately £30,000 sterling, though it might have included some Irish currency. He said he went to the Ashling Hotel near Heuston Station, checked in, took some cash from the briefcase, put it in his hotel wardrobe and went off to the Royal Hospital nearby for the annual fund-raising dinner for Ahern. The dinner was usually attended by more than three hundred people, and there must have been a particularly excited atmosphere on that night, as everyone expected that Ahern would be anointed Taoiseach the following Tuesday.

On Saturday afternoon Michael Wall went up to St Luke's, where he and Ahern adjourned to Ahern's office. Michael Wall said he put the briefcase on the office table and told Ahern it was for the renovation of the house in Beresford Avenue. None of those who gave evidence on the matter expressed the view that there was anything bizarre or troubling about a prospective Taoiseach being given a briefcase full of cash in this way. The tribunal was told that Larkin came in bearing tea. There were bundles of cash on the table, and Ahern was going back and forth with handfuls of it, bringing it to a safe in a back room. Again there was no mention at the tribunal of Larkin expressing shock or concern at what she saw. Ahern said he put the money into his safe without counting it or discussing with Michael Wall how much was there. Given that everyone believed that Ahern was on the cusp of becoming Taoiseach, this has to count as the most bizarre testimony given to any of the tribunals.

Ahern had to catch an early flight to Brussels on the Monday morning to attend a meeting of European finance ministers. He told the tribunal that he left the briefcase in his office in St Luke's for Larkin so that she could bring it and its contents to the O'Connell Street branch of the AIB. She told the tribunal that she lodged the money without looking inside the briefcase or counting it. By this version of events, no-one knew how much was in it when it was handed to the branch official for lodgement.

On the Sunday of that weekend Geraldine Kennedy, the political correspondent of the *Irish Times*, was at home preparing lunch for some friends when she had a conversation on the phone with the paper's editor, Conor Brady. They discussed the Brendan Smith extradition controversy, and Brady expressed the view that there was still some digging to be done in relation to the story. Kennedy abandoned her lunch plans and began making calls. By that evening she had gathered the material for what became the next morning's front-page lead. Ahern read the story while on his way to Dublin Airport. When he rang Dublin upon his arrival in Brussels he was told that the story had taken off and that there was a renewed sense of crisis in the corridors of Leinster House.

Kennedy's story described a new and different sequence of events concerning the matters that had led to Reynolds having to resign and that created serious concerns within the Labour Party as to whether or not it could trust Fianna Fáil. To reassure the Labour Party, Ahern needed to get a copy of a report concerning the crisis written by the new Attorney-General, Eoghan Fitzsimons, so he could give it to Spring. But Reynolds was still Taoiseach, and Fitzsimons felt that he needed the approval of the Taoiseach before he could hand it over. Reynolds was in Budapest. According to Sparks, Reynolds refused to take the calls he was getting from Ahern. 'It was very interesting. Back and forth. Back and forth.'

A different version of this story appears in *One Spin on the Merry-Go-Round* (1995), Seán Duignan's account, based on his diary, of his time as Reynolds's press officer. He recounted that Fitzsimons's report was at first faxed to the wrong hotel in Budapest. It arrived too late for Reynolds to see it and have it sent to Ahern before Reynolds addressed a session of the Commission on Security and Cooperation in Europe. After his speech, according to Duignan, Reynolds went through the Fitzsimons report line by line before finally sending it on to Ahern. The report confirmed the new sequence of events reported by Geraldine Kennedy (though Duignan said the information in Kennedy's report would already have been known to the Labour Party).

Even when he got back to Dublin and to Government Buildings, Ahern wasn't able to satisfactorily settle the dispute with Spring. He met his party ministers and discussed the crisis but could not find a way to stop matters unravelling. After midnight he left Government Buildings and made his way back to St Luke's. At 2 a.m. the phone rang. It was Spring. The conversation was short and to the point: the Labour Party was pulling out of the coalition.

The Reynolds Government fell, and Ahern's efforts to form a new arrangement with the Labour Party also fell, because of the controversy concerning the extradition of Brendan Smith and the appointment of Harry Whelehan to the High Court. There is no suggestion at all that anyone in Fianna Fáil was trying to shield Smith. The affair had to do with trust rather than any definite event or policy difference; yet it was a watershed in recent Irish history. In his memoirs Ahern said he was sorry that the relationship with the Labour Party soured, since there had been the possibility of a realignment in Irish politics. Sparks thinks the Labour Party and Fianna Fáil could have got on very well. 'I do think if Dick and Bertie had been able to come to an agreement, the way politics would have developed over the next fifteen years would have been totally different.'

Ahern came within a hair's breadth of forming his first Government as Taoiseach with the Labour Party as his coalition partner. Because that didn't happen, and because the Labour Party ended up going into coalition with Fine Gael and Democratic Left, Ahern tilted to the other side of the political spectrum and teamed up with Mary Harney and the PDs. This had enormous and arguably decisive implications for the political management of the Irish boom.

Chapter 8 ∽

| TAOISEACH, 1997–2002

On 26 June 1997 Bertie Ahern stood to address the chamber after the members of the 28th Dáil had elected him Taoiseach. At forty-five he was the youngest politician ever to be elected to the position. In the gallery were his two daughters, his mother, other family members and his long-time supporters. 'I assure the wider public that I have an honour which has been bestowed on only a handful of people,' Ahern said.

> It carries responsibility and is a job at which a person must work extremely hard. I like working hard, but this job is harder than any other, and I look forward to it. Having spent twenty years here, and having had an interest in politics since a very young age, it is hard to put into words the honour of this position. The only way I can repay it is to work every hour of every day to show I merit it. I will do that on behalf of my party, the Dáil and the people of the country.

The other party leaders, as is customary, wished Ahern well, as they did the members of the Dáil who were going to form Ahern's first Government: Charlie McCreevy (Finance), Mary Harney (Tánaiste and Minister for Enterprise, Trade and Employment), Dermot Ahern (Social, Community and Family Affairs), David Andrews (Defence), Noel Dempsey (Environment and Local Government), Micheál Martin (Education), Ray Burke (Foreign Affairs), Joe Walsh (Agriculture and Food), Síle de Valera

(Arts, Heritage, Gaeltacht and the Islands), John O'Donoghue (Justice, Equality and Law Reform), Jim McDaid (Tourism, Sport and Recreation), Brian Cowen (Health and Children), Mary O'Rourke (Public Enterprise) and Michael Woods (Marine and Natural Resources).

The Attorney-General was David Byrne SC, the barrister who some weeks earlier had helped Ahern with the document concerning the ownership of St Luke's. Byrne's appointment occurred despite efforts by Harney to have Michael McDowell, who had lost his seat in Dublin South-East by a small number of votes, appointed to the position.

Ahern's first Government was an effective one, according to Micheál Martin. Ahern would

> have a lot of work done before cabinet, in terms of bilaterals with ministers, and between ministers and the Minister for Finance, and himself, before cabinet, and that was effective. The first Government was a particularly successful Government. I think it did a lot of good work. I think it had a lot of energy, and Ahern was on top of most issues.

Fianna Fáil's performance in the election was in fact the second-worst in its history. (The worst was in 1992, under Reynolds.) The share of the national votes in 1997 was 39.33 per cent, compared with 39.11 per cent in 1992. Ahern's popularity rating before the election was only slightly ahead of those of John Bruton and Dick Spring. Harney was the most popular political leader going into the election but had a disastrous campaign. Fianna Fáil's improved vote management meant that it gained more seats than it did votes. It entered the 28th Dáil with an extra 9 seats, or 77 in all (83 was needed for a bare majority). The PDs won only 4, compared with the 10 with which they had entered the campaign. Fine Gael did well, winning an extra 7 seats, but the bottom fell out of the Labour Party's support: it lost 16 seats and entered the Dáil with only 17 TDs. Fianna Fáil could have negotiated a stable coalition with the Labour Party, but Ahern chose instead to create a coalition Government with the PDs that was dependent on the support of independents. According to the political journalist Pat Leahy, many senior figures in the party still felt very sore about how they had been treated by the Labour Party in 1994.

Ahern had thrown himself into the job of leader of the opposition with his trademark capacity for long hours and herculean effort. He managed to mend much of the damage caused by the internal party rifts that had persisted through the Haughey years and the damage to morale that had come with the unexpected loss of power in 1994. But in relation to parliamentary performance and the holding of the Government to account he was not perceived as being particularly successful. He also struggled with his media image. Power automatically brings media focus, but as leader of the opposition a politician has to win positive coverage by sharp criticism and by the creation of the impression that they would make a better Taoiseach.

It was Pat Rabbitte's view in the mid-1990s that Ahern did not have what was required to be a party leader. He held this view despite having a high regard for Ahern's ability and having been a spokesperson on labour and finance, respectively, when Ahern had been Minister for Labour and Minister for Finance. 'I had a lot of regard for his capacity, for his diligence in terms of doing his homework. He had an extraordinarily single-minded, purposeful approach to politics.' Nevertheless, the notion of Ahern being Taoiseach was regarded in the Dáil as 'somewhat risible', according to Rabbitte.

This was in part because of the image Ahern had created over the previous twenty years. The image of the plain man, with the ordinary tastes, the 'Howa yez, lads?' ordinary Dub. The friend of the trade unions, the bedraggled appearance, the long hair. He just didn't look leader material. It is an awful job anyway, but he was poor. He was no match intellectually for John Bruton. Not that Bertie wasn't a very bright man, a very intelligent man: he was. But in terms of parliamentary wingcraft, allied to some intellectual substance about convictions in politics, he wasn't a match for Bruton.

For Rabbitte, it was only when being in office brought the lustre of Taoiseach to his persona that Ahern became a credible leader.

The hair was cut, a personal make-up artist was maintained, the presentation was practised, and he became a different man entirely to when he was leader of the opposition during the rainbow Government.

Ahern's preparations for the 1997 general election included efforts to distance himself from the low standards of the Haughey era, which were then being pried into by the McCracken (Dunne's Payments) Tribunal. He told the delegates to the April 1997 ard-fheis that there would be

no place in our party today for that kind of past behaviour, no matter how eminent the person involved or the extent of their services to the country ... Even if in the particular instance there were no favours sought or given we could not condone the practice of senior politicians seeking or receiving from a single donor large sums of money or services in kind.

No-one who betrayed the public trust was welcome in the party. 'I say this with every fibre of my being.'

The way Ahern set out to change his image impressed Joan Burton.

I take my hat off to him. He improved his speech. That showed a massive amount of dedication. And he was lucky with having Celia Larkin. I have no doubt that she did his makeover. That was tremendously important.

Ahern.went from being a rough-looking, not well-dressed politician to being a contender for the title of best-dressed Taoiseach. Burton said, 'I think people like that. I think people like people in high public office dressing appropriately for the job.'

According to Richard Bruton, it is important not to attach too much significance to what Ahern did before achieving power. He recalled a black poster in the 1997 campaign that had Ahern staring out of the gloom. After the campaign it was praised for being a masterful image, but if Fianna Fáil had not managed to get back into Government people would have been criticising the poster. 'Nothing succeeds like success.'

Within months of Ahern coming to power he found himself forced to establish two tribunals of inquiry: one (Moriarty) to look into payments to Michael Lowry and Charles Haughey; the other (Flood, later Mahon) to look into corruption in the planning process in Dublin. Meanwhile, news stories about payments to Ray Burke put Ahern under increasing pressure and raised questions about his decision to appoint him a minister in the first place. Ahern was later forced to ask the Flood Tribunal to investigate Burke's finances. A furious Burke resigned not only from the Government but from the Dáil. The media and the opposition watched to see if Burke's rage would lead to any scandals about Ahern coming to public attention.

For Rabbitte, Ahern's establishment of the Moriarty and Flood Tribunals meant that he was a member of the Government while inquiries were under way that might discover some of the skeletons in his own cupboard.

Very, very few politicians in Leinster House would have been able to carry around in their stomach what Bertie Ahern carried around during his period as leader. He knew these things, we didn't know them, and he was always alert to [the danger]. That's why Ray Burke resigned. Bertie had promised Ray Burke that there would be no tribunal, no matter what happened; and then events, dear boy, happened, and he conceded a tribunal and Burke went mad and resigned on the spot from the House as well as the Government. Burke had a few real set-tos with Bertie, because they knew a lot about each other, and Bertie harboured these things and performed swimmingly as Taoiseach. Very few members of Dáil Éireann would have been able to do that [knowing that Burke was out there] and knowing himself about some of his own dealings, and so on. It was for that reason that he sometimes became tight-lipped and wary, in that fashion, because he was trying to figure out [what to say or do].

With regard to the country's economic management, Ahern's biggest decision in 1997—perhaps in his whole political career—was the appointment of Charlie McCreevy as Minister for Finance. There was a political logic to the move, in that McCreevy was close to the PDs, with whom Ahern was going into coalition, both personally and in terms of political philosophy. Moreover, Ahern appears to have come to the conclusion that the country was in the mood for centre-right politics. McCreevy was an idiosyncratic individual with strong libertarian views and, amazingly, had almost free rein for the implementation of fiscal policy. According to Pat Leahy's book *Showtime: The Inside Story of Fianna Fáil in Power* (2009), which is based on extensive interviews with members of that Government and its senior advisers, Ahern was just about consulted by his Minister for Finance, while the rest of the Government was ignored. Ahern was not given to strong views on policies anyway, and the tax-cutting measures that McCreevy implemented over the following period went down well with the public and created unprecedented popularity ratings for Ahern. The boom that was taking off as Ahern came to power continued and gathered pace through his first Government. He marshalled his considerable political skills towards being given the credit, creating the impression that it was he and his Government that had brought about the transformation of Ireland.

The taxation and spending policies McCreevy implemented were the defining elements of the first Ahern Government. Ruairí Quinn, who handed over the reins in Finance to McCreevy, had very negative views on the appropriateness of his successor's policies and believed that McCreevy paid little heed to Ahern's views on the matter. For Quinn, Ahern was 'intellectually intimidated' by McCreevy. Ahern was over-impressed by the fact that McCreevy had attended Gormanston College, a fee-paying boarding school, had gone to university (he was in the same class as Joan Burton) and was 'a bright qualified accountant'. Ahern had gone to his local school and then went straight into the work-place after his Leaving Certificate. For Quinn, Ahern's falsification of his CV, to say he had studied at the LSE, was evidence of 'a big inferiority complex' and was in sharp contrast with the attitude of Ray MacSharry, who gave the impression that he was proud of what he had achieved, given that he had finished his formal education when he left secondary school.

McCreevy was a 'very maverick sort of character', Quinn said. He did what he wanted and at times didn't even inform Ahern about what he was planning. And Ahern didn't feel strong enough to challenge him.

> McCreevy was a Eurosceptic. He didn't want Ireland to go into the currency union, but it was party policy and he had to go along with it. The holy grail of the single currency for me was that you get into a low-interest, low-inflation, stable currency that didn't devalue and fluctuate. So money had to earn its keep. It was no longer profitable to put money on deposit at 10 per cent. So there was enough money coming into the economy. The banks were lending as they hadn't done before. Interest rates dropped even before we joined. McCreevy just ignored all that, as did Bertie.

For Quinn, the tax changes McCreevy introduced, and especially those introduced in his first budget, unbalanced this situation. An 'avalanche' of money began to flow into an economy that was already creating a thousand new jobs with every week that passed.

When Quinn's view of the freedom with which McCreevy operated was put to Micheál Martin, he didn't necessarily disagree. He said a Minister for Finance has to be allowed act without interference from his Taoiseach. He cited as an example his experience during the second Ahern Government, when he was Minister for Health and McCreevy was presiding over a post-election tightening of public expenditure. According to Martin, Ahern, who always maintained his interest in the Mater Hospital and would regularly meet consultants and others to discuss how it was faring, was concerned about how the health cutbacks in 2003 were affecting the hospital.

> We lost three hundred beds in the Mater and places in Dublin. Bertie was very upset. He'd say to me, 'Have you gone to Charlie?' I'd say, 'I have, but there's no give.' And he would say, 'Ah, Jesus!' And I'd say, 'You're the

leader. He's the Minister for Finance.' He would have wanted me to win against Charlie.

However, Ahern would not go directly to McCreevy and instruct him to change a particular decision or policy. He never 'undermined' McCreevy in that way, Martin said. 'The conventional wisdom is that you never undermine your Minister for Finance, because that is the end of the minister in terms of credibility.' Martin was sure that Ahern would have organised endless official representations to McCreevy, but he's equally certain that he never made a direct approach.

For Greg Sparks, Martin's analysis of the relationship between a Taoiseach and the Minister for Finance was too simple. 'In the final analysis, the Minister for Finance is there on the Taoiseach's permission.' Sparks's experience was that alliances were formed in the Government in relation to particular issues; how these played out influenced what a Minister for Finance would or could do in relation to the Government's work. 'You could play other ministers against finance. You got everyone else on side before going to finance. You played one off against the other.'

For Sparks, McCreevy's independence in the Government *vis-à-vis* Ahern and his Fianna Fáil colleagues arose from McCreevy having political views that were more suited to membership of the PDs than of Fianna Fáil. McCreevy was a long-time friend and admirer of Harney's, and at the time of the formation of the PDs he surprised observers by not leaving to join the new party.

Joan Burton, who studied commerce in UCD with McCreevy, said he is 'very right wing and abhors the state. He wants to minimise the involvement of the state.' This was a sentiment shared by the PDs. For Sparks, the relationship between Harney and McCreevy, with McDowell later as Attorney-General, created a circle around Ahern that isolated him as Taoiseach and affected his ability, and that of his Government colleagues, to control the Minister for Finance. 'That was a very powerful axis for the Taoiseach's office. The dynamic there was far too powerful. The Taoiseach was captured.' The fact that McCreevy felt an affinity for the politics of the PDs, and was particularly friendly with Harney, also affected his loyalty to his party leader. 'If loyalty is with the leader of another party, that exposes the Taoiseach, because it makes the finance minister that bit more impregnable.'

For Sparks, it was because Ahern lacked strong political convictions that he was particularly susceptible to the arguments of McCreevy, Harney and McDowell. 'I would think Charlie McCreevy had a far greater influence over him as Minister for Finance than he should have had.' It is an observation supported by Pat Leahy. McCreevy and Harney essentially controlled the Government's economic policy, according to Leahy. They found Ahern easy to get around, and McCreevy could persist with his radical views on taxation as long as he kept Ahern happy with increases in social welfare. Besides, their concern that the Government might not last meant that they front-loaded their most radical reforms. This view is also supported by the television documentary 'The PDs: From Boom to Bust', in which the journalist Sam Smyth interviewed leading PD members, McCreevy and others. In it, however, Ahern rejects the suggestion that McCreevy introduced policies without adequately consulting him.

McCreevy's first budget was presented in early December 1997. There were increases in the old-age pension, in child benefit and in other social welfare payments, though the increases in unemployment benefits were modest. It was the tax cuts that made the headlines. The higher and standard rates of income tax were each cut by 2 per cent, to 24 per cent and 46 per cent, while income tax allowances were also increased. There was a surprising cut in the rate of capital gains tax. The reduction from 40 to 20 per cent meant, for instance, that someone who bought land and then sold it on at a profit would now be able to keep 80 per cent of the profit made. The decision was McCreevy's and caused consternation at senior levels within the department. It was the first of such major decisions that would be taken over the course of McCreevy's tenure in the department. McCreevy did little or no consulting with his Government colleagues before the budget announcement. He did keep Ahern and Harney briefed, with Ahern standing up to McCreevy and insisting that the social welfare increases that were to be announced had to be greater than McCreevy wanted them to be. McCreevy acquiesced.

Ahern's political judgement proved to be on form, as the social welfare increases served to dampen the message carried by the tax reforms. This was so, even though the tax-cutting measures cost the exchequer £500 million, while the social welfare increases cost only £100 million. The opposition criticised the tax measures, claiming that they would disproportionately benefit the better off. Quinn said the budget combined 'economic madness' with 'political selfishness'. Ahern said it was equitable and a 'budget for everyone'. The highest absolute gains will always be to the better paid, he said. This was a presumably deliberate confusion of what was at issue.

John Bruton, in a speech delivered the day after the budget, made a series of prescient observations. The budget involved larger changes in income tax and PRSI than budgets introduced by the rainbow Government, yet it would see lower-paid workers gain less, he said. Workers on the average industrial wage would gain less than they did from the budget of the previous year that Bruton's Government had introduced. Those on higher incomes would benefit significantly more than those on low and middle incomes. Bruton said that, in fairness to the Government, this was what had been promised in the election campaign, but he then asked why any government would set out to do something that was manifestly unfair. Before answering his own question, he said everyone agreed that all parties, including those in government, had a sense of social concern.

> The reason is that this budget was not driven by a desire to achieve social justice but by the needs of marketing. It is easier to market the concept of a reduction in tax rates because little has to be explained. Two pence in the pound speaks for itself. On the other hand, it requires an effort to explain that an increase in personal allowances and a widening of the tax band benefits those on lower incomes more than a reduction in the top rate . . . It was a form of intellectual and political laziness on the part of the government, a willingness to pursue the easy marketing approach of concentrating on tax rates rather than the more difficult, in marketing terms, but much fairer, in political terms, approach of increasing tax-free allowances and widening tax bands.

The policy being pursued was not consistent with the proclaimed values of Fianna Fáil, Bruton said. He added that it was the vision of trade union leaders such as Peter Cassells, who had argued for wage restraint during the 1980s, that had played the key role in the creation of the boom. But social partnership

> will be put under strain in the next two years. One of the things that will put it under strain will be increased house prices. That inflation in house prices is being contributed to by the tax policy of the government, which puts so much emphasis on reductions in income tax for those on higher incomes who are the people bidding up the price of houses.

Social partnership and the idea of wage restraint would come under great pressure, Bruton said, as people who were getting married found that they could not afford to buy a house on the wages they were earning.

According to Bruton, the Taoiseach and his party did not have to choose a policy that benefited the rich but they did so to guarantee the support of the PDs. They got into government on the strength of that, and they delivered on it, but it was wrong and a political mistake. It was also an economic mistake, Bruton said.

Quinn told the Dáil that he was one of the few deputies who had sat through George Colley's budget speech in 1978. 'As has often been remarked since, that was a great party, and we spent about fifteen years paying for it.' He said it was extraordinary that McCreevy and Harney, who had spent most of their political lives denouncing the profligate nature of the 1977 manifesto, were now back in the Dáil repeating that 'economic madness'.

> The circumstances today are uncannily similar to those in 1977. This year, as in 1977, a good and prudent Government handed over office with an economy in excellent shape and starting to boom—in the recent case the boom is well under way. Instead of nurturing the economy, the Lynch Government felt impelled to deliver on its extraordinary promises, and the rest is history. Within a short time the economy overheated and crashed viciously, with the weak, the poor and the most vulnerable bearing the burden of recovery. The 1998 budget threatens to repeat that serious tragedy.

Quinn said the effect of the budget was to completely change direction. The Government had inherited a budget surplus, a robust economy and a partnership agreement that envisaged how the fruits of the boom would be distributed in society in the years to 2000. The effect of the budget was to change matters so that the more you earned the more you got.

In particular, Quinn criticised the decision to reduce the capital gains tax rate by half, to 20 per cent. 'So much for the work ethic . . . The budget sends out a message that people should switch from work and enterprise, for which they will pay 46 per cent at the margin, to trading and dealing in property, for which they will pay a mere 20 per cent in tax and no PRSI or levies.' The measure would reorient the country in the direction of 'traders and hucksters instead of promoting wealth, enterprise and employment.' The new rate 'sends a signal to investors to intensify the purchase of property where the greatest gain can be maximised. This will cause further asset fluctuation and drive out the ordinary house-buyers,' Quinn said. 'It is scandalous, stupid, brazen and unnecessary.'

Quinn also raised the fact that the state was embarking on 'the important but hazardous entry into economic and monetary union.' He argued that the Government needed to generate large surpluses, since it was going through the high period of the economic cycle, but was instead introducing tax measures that disproportionately favoured the better off. 'It is the poor and the weak who will have to pay when the party comes to an end.' The country, he said, had to have a debate about the discipline needed to accommodate being in Economic and Monetary Union so that the citizenry could understand what was required. (Later analysis of what went wrong during the boom years would identify this as a critical, if not *the* critical, challenge the Ahern Governments had faced.)

For Quinn, the budget indicated a decision not to use the positive economic circumstances the Government found itself operating in to seriously redress inequity and social exclusion. 'I am deeply, passionately angry,' he said.

Ahern saw matters differently. 'This is probably the most remarkable budget of modern times.' It was 'historic for many reasons,' he said. The 'amount we have been able to do' was a reflection of the economic growth of the past ten years. The broad budget balance meant that the state would not be borrowing to add to the national debt. 'I did not think I would ever see that.' The Government, he said, had delivered on its social partnership commitments by agreeing by the second year what was to be given over three years, and it had fulfilled its promise to the electorate by announcing one-third of the tax reliefs promised over five years.

The budget gave a huge boost to the economy and to the growing feeling among the work force that the era when the Irish could be depicted by the international media as the 'poorest of the rich' was now firmly in the past. The widespread feelings of optimism were added to by the renewed good relations between the Irish government and the republican movement, boosting hopes of an eventual solution to the North's problems.

During its early period, the Government, and Fianna Fáil in particular, was buffeted by a series of scandals involving the Haughey legacy, Ray Burke, planning corruption and other matters. But as the economy continued to improve it was difficult for the opposition to make inroads into the Government's ratings. Ahern and his party were also buoyed up by the election near the end of 1997 of its presidential candidate, Mary McAleese. In the wake of the poor performance of the Labour Party's candidate, Adi Roche, Dick Spring resigned as party leader. Quinn took over the role and by the end of the year had negotiated the merger of his party with Proinsias de Rossa's Democratic Left.

When Pádraig Flynn had to resign from the European Commission because of inquiries by the planning tribunal into a payment made to him,

Bertie Ahern after he was first elected to the Dáil in 1977. (© *RTÉ Stills Library*)

Bertie Ahern and Charles Haughey in All Hallows College after the funeral mass for Con Ahern, December 1980. (*Courtesy of Frank Millar, Irish Times*)

FIANNA FÁIL CANDIDATES
DUBLIN CENTRAL

AHERN
BERTIE
(T.D. T.C. ALD.)
CHIEF WHIP MINISTER OF STATE
DEPT. OF AN TAOISEACH & DEFENCE

COLLEY
GEORGE

(T.D.)

LEONARD
TOM

(T.C.)

Leaflet from November 1982. George Colley died months later, and Tom Leonard won the seat in the resulting by-election. (*Leaflet supplied by Alan Kinsella*)

On the way into Leinster House, January 1983.
(*Courtesy of Peter Thursfield, Irish Times*)

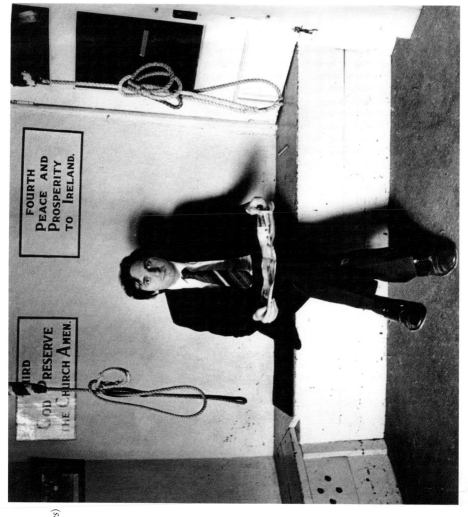

St George's Church,
Temple Street, Dublin,
July 1983. (*Courtesy of
Tom Lawlor, Irish Times*)

Ahern takes over as Lord Mayor of Dublin from Jim Tunney, July 1986. (*Courtesy of the Irish Times*)

Andrew Farrell near Gardiner Street polling booth, June 1989. (*Courtesy of Tony O'Shea*)

Ahern leads Fianna Fáil talks with the Labour Party after the November 1992 general election. Ruairí Quinn is facing Ahern. (*Courtesy of Frank Millar, Irish Times*)

Ahern with Joe Burke on the morning of budget day, January 1994. (*Courtesy of Matt Kavanagh, Irish Times*)

Ahern entering Government Buildings in June 1994, only hours after being told by Dick Spring that he was pulling out of the proposed coalition. (© PA *Archive/Press Association Images*)

Ahern invites the media in to photograph him with his mother, Julia, then eighty-six, during the June 1997 general election campaign.
(© *PA Archive/Press Association Images*)

Ahern and Celia Larkin at the Dublin count, June 1997. His running-mate, Marian McGennis, is on his right. (© *PA Archive/Press Association Images*)

Ahern leaving the Dublin count after the June 1997 general election. (© PA *Archive/ Press Association Images*)

Ray Burke (Minister for Foreign Affairs), Bertie Ahern and Tony Blair at the door of 10 Downing Street, London, July 1997. (© PA *Archive/Press Association Images*)

Ahern enters the Fianna Fáil ard-fheis, November 1998. (*Courtesy of Frank Millar, Irish Times*)

Charlie McCreevy, Mary Harney and Bertie Ahern in February 2000 at a meeting of the social partners to conclude the Programme for Prosperity and Fairness. (*Courtesy of David Sleator, Irish Times*)

Ahern after giving evidence to the Moriarty Tribunal, June 2000. (*Courtesy of Frank Millar, Irish Times*)

Ahern and Charlie McCreevy during the 2002 general election. (*Courtesy of Matt Kavanagh, Irish Times*)

Ahern's daughter Georgina, Royston Brady, Bertie Ahern and Joe Burke at the launch of a new ferry in Dublin Port, August 2003. (*Courtesy of Cyril Byrne, Irish Times*)

Ahern at the Galway
Races, August 2006.
(© *Matt Browne/Sportsfile*)

Paddy Duffy, whose association with Ahern goes back to the mid-1970s, photographed in 2005. (*Courtesy of Matt Kavanagh, Irish Times*)

Tim Collins, with Dominic Dillane behind him, Dublin Castle. (*Courtesy of David Sleator, Irish Times*)

David McKenna and Des Richardson in Washington for Ahern's address to the US Congress, April 2008. (*Courtesy of David Sleator, Irish Times*)

The Rev. Ian Paisley and Bertie Ahern greet each other at the site of the Battle of the Boyne, May 2007. (*Courtesy of David Sleator, Irish Times*)

Bertie with Noel Ahern, Cyprian Brady and Maurice Ahern in St Luke's, Drumcondra, in December 2010 on the night he announced that he would not be standing for election. (*Courtesy of Dara Mac Dónaill, Irish Times*)

he was replaced by David Byrne. Ahern then invited Michael McDowell, who had just finished chairing a report for the Government on new structures for financial regulation, to take on the position of Attorney-General. McDowell went to Government Buildings to meet Ahern and emerged to tell reporters that he had accepted the position. He had not yet rejoined the PDs, but he was inching back towards a political career. His move into the centre of power no doubt added to the influence of the political outlook of the PDs on the Ahern Government.

The appointment meant that McDowell, who had a deep interest in Irish history and politics, was centre stage for some truly historic developments. The efforts of the Irish and British Governments to bring about a resolution of the conflict in the North had deep roots. From the point of view of nationalism, the process began with contacts between John Hume of the SDLP and Gerry Adams of Sinn Féin in the mid-to-late 1980s. The two sides became involved in a debate over the future direction of nationalist effort, and papers swapped between them featured heavily in Sinn Féin publications and internal party debate. What Adams had in mind when he entered the talks cannot be known, but it is certainly the case that much of Hume's criticism of republicanism became internalised within the Provisional movement. By the late 1980s discreet contacts with the Irish Government had opened, and when Reynolds became Taoiseach he took the process and ran with it. He had an excellent relationship with the British Prime Minister, John Major, and won the trust of the republicans. Reynolds, a wealthy businessman with a penchant for risk-taking, threw everything into winning the prize of peace.

The engagement with the republicans was a fraught one for a democratic Government, as the Provisionals continued to run an illegal and murderous militia. Ahern's extraordinary ability to project feelings of sympathy and understanding stood him in good stead, as did his legendary patience. As Ruairí Quinn noted, 'he has this skill to be able to spend so much time on people and to accommodate them and to take so much boredom. I mean, God knows, to have spent so much time listening to Gerry Adams for all those years.'

Ahern's interest in, and feeling for, republicanism helped him get on with the Provisionals, and no doubt his father's history and political outlook played a role in this. In his memoirs Ahern said he had gone to the British embassy on the night it was burned down after the Bloody Sunday killings in Derry in January 1972. He said some of his friends had joined the IRA after the killings, and he obviously intended to give the impression that he sympathised with their decision.

When Ahern became Taoiseach he immediately immersed himself in the effort to conclude a deal in Northern Ireland. He had met the British Prime Minister, Tony Blair, during the former's period as leader of the opposition, and they had hit it off. Rabbitte noted the close relationship that developed between Ahern and Blair.

> It was extraordinary that he met a similar character in Blair. Blair was the quintessential Englishman, albeit born in Scotland. He too was an exhibitionist, a performer above all else. An exceptional performer. But as Robin Cook [former British Cabinet member] said to me—we had breakfast here [in the Dáil] one morning after he spoke to our [Labour Party] conference—and I asked him, 'What is Blair like?' and he said, 'Well, the first thing you have to recall is, he is not one of us.' Meaning he was not a Labour politician, in the sense that Robin Cook or Gordon Brown or Michael Foot, or so on was. He was a tremendous public performer, and he had this smiling affability, and he and Bertie took to each other as soul brothers.

In the first weekend of April 1998 Ahern returned from an Asia-Europe summit in England, raced to a constituency Mass in Cabra and went on to bed. The next morning he went to St Luke's and from there to Government Buildings for a meeting with a delegation from the SDLP. It was while there that he got a call to say that his mother, Julia, had suffered a heart attack and had been rushed to the Mater. He spent time at her bedside before she died on the Monday morning without having regained consciousness.

Julia Ahern was buried in the republican plot in Glasnevin Cemetery, beside her husband, Con. The graveside service was nearing its end when Ahern had to leave to travel to Belfast to attend the talks in Hillsborough Castle. When he arrived the waiting journalists put down their microphones and cameras and expressed their sympathies. The atmosphere inside the building was intense, with side meetings going on here, there and everywhere and with the participants including some of the most unsavoury people on the island. At one point, according to Ahern, he was in a room with some loyalists and republicans when one of the former turned to him and said they had worked out that he was the only person in the room who hadn't killed anyone.

Agreement was eventually reached on Friday 10 April. It was Good Friday, and the news was greeted with elation throughout Ireland and was reported around the globe. Ahern signed 'the Belfast Agreement signed on Good

Friday' wearing a black tie. On his way back in from Dublin Airport his car drove past Church Avenue just as it had a week earlier when his mother had still been alive. He subsequently appeared on 'The Late Late Show', where he spoke about the difficult negotiations leading up to the agreement and of his having to persist with the effort in the midst of grieving for his mother.

His ratings in an opinion poll in the *Irish Times* later that month were the highest he was ever to achieve and the highest achieved by any Taoiseach in recent times. The survey found that he had a satisfaction rating of 84 per cent. This was well ahead of the best scores ever recorded for Haughey (67 per cent), FitzGerald (63 per cent) and Reynolds (63 per cent). Fine Gael and Labour Party supporters were more behind Ahern than the population as a whole had ever been behind those former Taoisigh. Three-quarters of the respondents from both parties said they were satisfied with Ahern's performance. The historic breakthrough in the North was the main factor behind this unprecedented level of support, coupled as it was with—as Ahern was to put it in a later context—the fact that the Irish boom was 'getting boomier'.

According to Joan Burton, Ahern's success in the North added to his power.

He gained, understandably and deservedly, massive international respect and massive national respect out of the whole Good Friday thing. He had, then, vastly enhanced powers. As he was held in enormous respect, he could do more. It added a vast new dimension to his power. Once he had done that, then he was dealing on an equal basis with Blair and with Bill Clinton, and that added hugely to his aura. I don't know if that emboldened him then to move further away from the public interest and feel much more powerful in responding to vested interests. I suspect it did.

Rabbitte believed that people such as the Northern loyalists must have been very impressed by Ahern's informality and apparent willingness to treat them with respect. Politicians such as Dick Spring and John Bruton could not be imagined treating the loyalists with the sort of informal affability that is 'the essence of Ahernism', Rabbitte said. The ending of the violence and the achievement of a political accord 'lifted a huge pall of gloom that had been over the island for almost four decades and fed into the optimism concerning Ireland's economic future. Bertie saw that.'

As the 1990s came to a close, few could remember the doubts that people had had a few years earlier about Ahern's suitability for high office. Concerns about his ability were buried by his success in the North, by photo-calls and reported phone calls with his friends Tony Blair and Bill Clinton and, most of all, by the ubiquitous signs of increasing national wealth. As the economy grew, house prices rose steadily and became a staple of media reporting and general conversation. Those who owned property were buoyed up by thoughts of the increase in their nominal wealth. The number of unemployed was rapidly decreasing, emigration by young people in search of employment was coming to an end, and former emigrants were beginning to return. The international press and economic monitoring agencies were writing about Ireland and its transformation from 'the poorest of the rich' to being at the top of the European economic league table. A great sense of confidence spread through the country, and the Government made every effort to claim the credit. Ahern maintained a very high profile in the media but at the same time tightly controlled his exposure. He was a master of delivering sound-bites as he entered or left a building for an official function, which would then be used to top news reports on whatever the story of the day was. He rarely gave extended media interviews. His Dáil performances continued to be workmanlike, and he organised it so that he had to spend less time there than previous Taoisigh.

His great political achievement was to create the impression that he and his Government had delivered economic prosperity. For Richard Bruton, Ahern was lucky in his political career and lucky in the timing of his first appointment to the position of Taoiseach. The tax cuts introduced in 1998 and subsequent years boosted an already growing economy and the increasing amount of money available for personal expenditure. Given the long lead-in to the conditions of the boom it was self-evident that the tax cuts were not the reason for the economic prosperity; yet, by constant references to tax cuts, increases in public expenditure and economic statistics, the Government and Ahern in particular managed to associate themselves in the public mind with the country's evident good fortune. To claim responsibility for positive developments, and to disown unwanted developments, is a constant of politics; but the creation by Ahern and his Government of an association between the tax cuts and the boom was to prove a particularly important one.

Ahern worked hard at capitalising on the hugely positive economic conditions within which his Government was operating. Arguably the Government was poor at anything for which it had direct responsibility— reform of the public service, upgrading water-delivery systems, urban planning, transport, health—but it successfully trumped all these failings by assuming responsibility for economic growth. Ahern, according to

Richard Bruton, simply avoided difficult questions when they were put to him in the Dáil.

> If you asked him four or five hard questions, or a question that had four or five parts, he would pick up the part of the question that he could most use, and waffle. Pat Rabbitte tried very hard to question him forensically, and at times he succeeded, but other times Pat Rabbitte just ended up in a rage. I found it, when trying to question him about tax stuff or about the economy, Bertie's first tactic would be to agree with you. And agree with you extensively, worry about it, empathise about it, and by the time he'd finished with that, sure [there was no time left].

Miriam Lord, in her Dáil sketches, noted Ahern's delivery of answers and speeches that were lists of statistics, and how, when unquestionable Government failures were being discussed, Ahern might chew on his fist and then express sympathy with the views of the Government critic and bafflement as to how those who were in charge could be so inept.

Getting the public to associate the economic success a country is experiencing with your government, and with you yourself, is far from being an inconsiderable achievement for a politician, and it is one that is recognised by Ahern's political opponents. 'He had marvellous insights,' said Rabbitte.

> Bertie had a great capacity to see around corners. He must have had some very good people behind him too, because he captured the *zeitgeist* of the times very well. That period from 1994 to 2000 was a period of tremendous achievement and hope for this country. It is not a partisan point to make to say that when the rainbow Government handed over it was generally regarded as a good government and a fair government, and Bertie didn't much alter that when he took over, it seemed, initially. He was going to maintain an equilibrium, and the extraordinary growth continued right through to the wobble in 2001, and he did manage virtually to obliterate the role of the previous Government, and to have ascribed to himself the extraordinary economic expansion that continued, and to have attributed to Fianna Fáil the period of the boom. People believed that on the high street, associated it with him, and unlike Brian Cowen [his successor as Taoiseach] he was always positive, upbeat, optimistic. It coincided with the Northern Ireland settlement. That added a great deal of lustre to Bertie. He became a statesman. His skills were very suited to that.

Ahern was far from being the type of public representative who suddenly begins appearing on people's doorsteps once an election has been called. A Friday evening knock on the door on a winter's night, with election day years away, was not at all an unusual event, even when Ahern was Taoiseach. One Friday evening he knocked on this writer's door, looking particularly well dressed. The next day's newspapers featured photographs of him attending a meeting of EU leaders in Bonn.

As well as recognising the importance of canvassing in winning votes, Ahern appeared to like it and to draw encouragement and energy from it. Once in the Taoiseach's office he transferred his practice in Dublin Central to the national stage. For the entire period of his first Government he devoted all the Thursdays and Fridays he could to canvassing, subjecting himself to schedules that would exhaust a younger man.

Opposition is always a difficult task, but in the late 1990s the circumstances confronting Fine Gael and the Labour Party were particularly challenging. Pat Rabbitte cites the halving of the capital gains tax rate as an example of the difficulties his party faced. The Labour Party opposed the cut, arguing that it was an inequitable measure and one that meant that labour was being taxed at a much higher rate than dealing in assets. However, a result of the cut was that capital gains tax receipts to the exchequer shot up. When the Labour Party complained, Ahern and McCreevy would cite the improved exchequer figures for the tax, trumping the equity issue with the size of the figures. For Rabbitte,

> it was perfectly logical that the yield would shoot up, because there was so much pent-up demand in a growing economy and so many guys prepared to cash in their chips. So there was an initial flood of money. And, you know, it made it difficult.

Attacking the cut should have been an easy one for the Labour Party, but, 'confronted with the reality of dollops of cash coming in,' the criticism failed to find traction.

For Rabbitte the cut in the tax was the beginning of the property boom. 'That flood of money, and the property speculation that would henceforward only be taxed at the lower rate—that was the beginning of the property, speculative boom that took off.' Ruairí Quinn agreed. He believed that the 40 per cent rate may have been too high and contributed to a building up of capital that people did not want to release. The sudden halving of the tax, however, 'just triggered an avalanche of cash into the economy.' The problem for the opposition was that—even though, for a country dependent on exports, a sharp rise in the cost of housing is a negative development—this wasn't how it felt to the general public. Most, even if they were still on very modest salaries, were dazzled by the increase in value of their homes.

The partnership agreements also created a difficulty for the Labour Party. Sometimes when Rabbitte adopted positions in the Dáil concerning the Government's tax cuts, he found himself at odds with positions taken up by the unions. On occasion he was contacted by trade union leaders, who complained that his party was embarrassing them in front of their members. On balance, according to Rabbitte, social partnership was good for the trade union movement but bad for the Labour Party. Trade union leaders' speeches included repeated attacks on the 'PD wing' of the Ahern Government and calls for that wing to be driven out, Rabbitte said. 'They never attacked Bertie.'

For Richard Bruton the problem for the opposition was that it had to criticise the Government's economic policies when those same policies were putting more money into people's pockets and supplying increased services to members of the public. 'Nobody likes a Jeremiah.' In his opinion, the cut in capital gains tax was not the core cause of the later property bubble, though it was a contributory factor. The real error was the unleashing of public expenditure in the latter stage of Ahern's first Government.

> McCreevy went in the face of the election for having a grossly irresponsible growth in public expenditure. I remember looking at 24 months, and he had increased spending by about 45 per cent. The notion that you could increase public spending by 45 per cent over 24 months was just incredible, but that's what he did. There seemed to have been a sudden decision, 'It's party time, the election is coming up.' He went for this homespun notion: when we have money we spend it. I think it was then the cost base started to go seriously awry. This massive increase in public expenditure, into the teeth of a strong economy already close to capacity, definitely set the environment for [public-sector] benchmarking which followed quickly on its tail. You had a huge increase in the pay bill. It put pressure on the construction sector. It started the whole rot.

One of the threats that Ahern faced during his first term of office was the possibility that his public image would be dented by what was emerging from the Dublin Castle tribunals, both in his association with the past actions of people such as Haughey and, more directly, because of his own activities. When he appeared before the Moriarty Tribunal to give evidence in July 1999 and June 2000, the intensity with which he fielded questions from tribunal counsel John Coughlan sc was striking. There was an atmosphere of tension in the room that few other witnesses who appeared there over the years managed to create and that bordered on being menacing.

The tribunal's inquiries into Haughey disclosed that he had made personal use of the Fianna Fáil party leader's account. Not only had he lodged to the account money given to him by others but he had also dipped into funds that had been raised to pay for medical treatment in the United States for his long-time friend and political colleague Brian Lenihan and which had been lodged to the account. Withdrawals were by way of cheque. Two signatures were needed, and the main signatory after Haughey was Ahern.

Ahern had become a signatory at the time of his being appointed party chief whip. It was party practice for the chief whip to be assigned that role, though when Ahern moved on from that position he remained a signatory. Haughey had decided that he should do so. Ray MacSharry was also a signatory but was rarely involved. The account was first drawn to the attention of the tribunal by a cheque for £25,000 that was lodged to Guinness and Mahon Bank, the bank where Des Traynor ran his Ansbacher deposits operation. The cheque was dated 16 June 1989, the day after the general election of that year, and it was signed by Ahern and Haughey. The tribunal's inquiry into the use of the account proved labyrinthine, with no fewer than forty-five witnesses being called, some on more than one occasion.

A suggestion that Haughey had improperly used the party leader's account arose in 1997 after the McCracken Tribunal had reported and as the Oireachtas was in the process of establishing its successor. Spring raised the matter in the Dáil, but Ahern assured the chamber that the account had not been misused.

> I am satisfied, having spoken to the person who administered the account, that it was used for *bona fide* party purposes, that the cheques were prepared by that person and countersigned by another senior party member. There was no surplus and no misappropriation. The account, as far as her excellent recollection goes, was normally short, not the other way around. I have spoken to her at some length.

It was an extraordinary and misleading statement. The amount that went through the account in the period 1984–92 was more than £500,000 above what the exchequer gave the party. Ahern himself was the 'senior party member' who countersigned the cheques, and, as his subsequent evidence was to show, his performance of that function provided no safeguard against misuse of the account. The person who administered the account was Eileen Foy, Haughey's private secretary, who had previously worked for Jack Lynch when he was Taoiseach. Ahern obviously knew her well. During her evidence to the tribunal she frequently couldn't remember the most basic facts. When she was asked what she had said to Ahern that could have prompted him to give his reassurance to the Dáil, she said she couldn't remember.

Ahern would sign the cheques first, and then Haughey. Foy's evidence was that it was frequently difficult to contact Ahern once he became a minister. Ahern was sometimes referred to by the staff as the 'Pimpernel', so difficult was he to get hold of. When Ahern appeared at the tribunal he had to admit that, on occasion, for reasons of 'administrative convenience', he would sign a number of blank cheques so that Foy would have them available. In fact it emerged that he sometimes sat down and signed a whole book of blank cheques.

Miriam Lord was among the large number of political reporters who came from Leinster House to Dublin Castle in July 1999 to cover Ahern's appearance there.

His evidence was the evidence of a man who was extremely naïve and trusting and really a bit thick given the position he was in, and even at that stage everyone knew that he was anything but naïve and trusting and thick. But that was passed over and the legend grew.

Ahern's second visit to the tribunal, in June 2000, was to give evidence about a large payment given to Haughey during the 1989 election campaign. His involvement in this matter was not as straightforward as signing blank cheques which were then used by Haughey to, among other matters, buy tailored shirts from the Charvet shop in Paris, or pay for expensive lunches and dinners in the Coq Hardi restaurant in Ballsbridge. As a consequence it didn't register as deeply with the general public.

The tribunal was told that on the morning of the 1989 poll the wealthy businessman and property developer Mark Kavanagh left his home in Co. Wicklow and travelled across Dublin to Haughey's home in Kinsealy, where he handed over £100,000. The payment comprised a cheque for £25,000, made out to Fianna Fáil, and three bank drafts made out to cash. At the time, Kavanagh was part of a consortium, the Custom House Docks Development Company Ltd, that had won the contract to develop the Dublin docks site where the International Financial Services Centre is now. The money given to Haughey came from this company, with the consent of its directors. Kavanagh told the tribunal that he and his business colleagues wanted Fianna Fáil returned to power because of their interest in the docks project.

Haughey brought the £25,000 cheque to Fianna Fáil head office and handed it over. During that election he had made an unprecedented request of the party's financial controller, Seán Fleming, later a TD for Laois-Offaly. He asked that some of the receipts for sums he had delivered to the party be sent to him (Haughey) rather than to the donor. Furthermore, he asked that some of them be made out to 'anonymous'. In all, nineteen receipts were sent to Haughey during that election campaign, including a receipt for the cheque for £25,000 and another receipt for £100,000 received from a donor whom the tribunal did not identify. The receipt for the £25,000 cheque was made out to 'anonymous' and sent to Haughey's office; the three £25,000 drafts made out to cash Haughey apparently gave to his bagman, Des Traynor, as they ended up being lodged to Guinness and Mahon Bank.

In 1996, when Ahern was party leader and leader of the opposition, Fianna Fáil member Eoin Ryan Senior approached Kavanagh and requested a donation to Fianna Fáil. Kavanagh indicated that he was disposed towards giving money but was annoyed that he had not received a receipt for his contribution in 1989. Ryan's evidence was that he did not recall Kavanagh naming an amount but that he was clear that the donation for which he had not received any receipt had been a substantial one. Ryan told Kavanagh he would speak to Ahern about it.

Ryan did so, and Ahern said he would look into it. Ahern contacted Fleming. The £25,000 cheque Haughey had given him in 1989 had come from the Custom House Docks Development Company Ltd, so Fleming had known it was from Kavanagh, even though, as instructed, he had sent a receipt made out to 'anonymous' to Haughey's office. According to Fleming, he consulted his records and told Ahern that the party had received £25,000 from Kavanagh in 1989 and that the receipt had been sent to Haughey. Ahern told the tribunal that he could not recall the detail of what he had been told in 1996, but he accepted Fleming's evidence.

A short time later Ahern attended a function in Kavanagh's offices in Wellington Road, Dublin. There were a number of people there from the construction industry, and Ahern gave a short speech. Afterwards he spoke privately to Kavanagh and said he regretted what had occurred, and he assured him that his donation had been received and was appreciated by the party. Kavanagh was satisfied and made another contribution. What is extraordinary about the whole affair is that the evidence was that Ahern, Ryan and Kavanagh had not mentioned amounts during their various conversations and so were never confronted with the fact that, while £100,000 had been handed over to Haughey (a quarter of it was intended for the Lenihan fund), only £25,000 had been handed over to Fleming.

Opinion polls during this period showed that there was lingering public concern about Fianna Fáil and its potential for corruption; but the main focus for most people, understandably, was on their own immediate financial circumstances. McCreevy's early budgets all involved substantial tax-cutting measures in conjunction with transfer payment increases, significant capital spending and the reduction of the national debt. Especially for many younger people, Haughey and the evidence emerging at the tribunals were historical matters.

For politicians of Ahern's generation the positive trends with the economy and the public finances constituted an extraordinary *volte face*. For a man who liked to cite statistics it was heaven indeed. Ahern frequently peppered his speeches with figures such as the amounts allocated to various projects, increases in transfer payments and changes in data, such as in the number of people employed. Furthermore, in his Government's early years the rises in public spending that were introduced were broadly in line with economic growth. As the Government's term in office entered its second half, McCreevy decided to throw caution to the wind in an effort aimed at securing Fianna Fáil's re-election. The change in tack and the expansionary effects of the change soon prompted concern in the European Commission and the European Central Bank.

Ireland's spectacular economic growth in the mid-1990s was all the more impressive in that it had not led to a sharp rise in inflation. In 1997 inflation was 1.5 per cent. The following year it was 2.4 per cent, and the following year again 1.6 per cent. However, in 2000 it jumped to 5.6 per cent, and it fell by less than one percentage point in the following year. This was a very serious issue, since inflation levels that were persistently higher than those in the EU generally meant that Ireland was becoming a relatively expensive country—a disaster for an economy that depended on exports to pay its way in the world.

It was also an issue of general concern for the European Commission. In February 2000 the Commissioner for Economic and Monetary Affairs, Pedro Solbes, came to Dublin, where he met McCreevy to discuss the Commission's view that the Government should not go ahead with its intended tax cuts and pay increases. Solbes met other political leaders and spoke at the Institute of European Affairs. His message was clear: the Irish economy was overheating, and the Government's plan for further tax reductions would further stoke demand.

The debate rumbled on, with McCreevy and Harney in particular objecting to the Commission's views on Ireland's economic management. When, in December 2000, McCreevy announced another giveaway budget, the concern in Brussels mounted all the more. Irish officials who attended a meeting of senior EU civil servants in Brussels in mid-January 2001 were taken aback at the intensity of the criticism levelled against them. On 24 January the Commission 'sanctioned' Ireland—the first time a country had been singled out in this way. Quinn said McCreevy was stoking inflation.

> Minister McCreevy is in effect damned by his own figures. On Budget Day 2000 he announced a tax package of £942 million against a backdrop of inflation between 2 and 3 per cent. On Budget Day 2001 he announced a package of £1.2 billion against a backdrop of 7 per cent inflation. In the interim Minister McCreevy engaged in a campaign of vitriol against anybody who dared suggest we faced a significant inflationary threat, and that included the European Commission. This has come home to roost.

In general, however, Ireland appeared to be underwhelmed by the reprimand and the EU warning on economic policy. The *Irish Times*, in an editorial of 25 January 2001, said the Commission must recognise that the Irish economy has been the best-performing economy in the EU, by a distance, for some years. Ireland had a strong budget surplus and a sharply reducing ratio of national debt to GDP. The main cause of inflation was not budgetary policy but the weakness of the euro and the increase in oil prices in 2000. Greater demand in the domestic economy was only part of the picture.

The editorial also said that the initial draft of the Commission's reprimand, which suggested that the Government take corrective action by increasing taxes or reducing spending, was not likely to form part of the text that would be discussed by a coming meeting of finance ministers. David Byrne had intervened, as had others, to have the wording changed. Significant reversals in the budget tax cuts would be politically impossible, and there was a strong case for continuing to increase spending in order to improve public services and to invest in key infrastructure projects.

The editorial was certainly in line with the public mood. An opinion poll published in the *Irish Times* on 26 January showed that the Government had received a substantial boost from the budget and had enough support to be returned to power in the next general election. Satisfaction with the

Government was up 15 points, to 58 per cent, while dissatisfaction was down 11 points, to 35 per cent. The ratings for Ahern, Harney, Fianna Fáil and the PDs all increased. Fine Gael, on the other hand, was down 4 points, to 20 per cent, while John Bruton, at 37 per cent, scored his lowest personal satisfaction rating since November 1994.

The political correspondent Mark Brennock reported that the opinion poll

gives a substantial personal boost to the Minister for Finance, McCreevy, showing an overwhelming popular endorsement of the budget. The poll found that 71 per cent believed it was good for the country, 15 per cent believed it was bad for the country, and 14 per cent expressed no opinion. The poll was taken after it had been reported that the Commission was to censure the government for an inflationary budget.

The budgetary strategy being pursued by McCreevy was proving to be a political success. Perhaps it emboldened him. On the day the opinion poll was published, McCreevy, who was addressing a meeting of the Financial Services Industry Association, said Ireland's European critics were jealous of its economic success. The Commission's censure proposal was to be discussed at a meeting in February with his EU finance minister colleagues, but he would not be changing his budget, irrespective of what they said. He said Ireland's success in attracting foreign direct investment, through its low corporation tax regime, was a particular bone of contention for other member-states. 'We have no friends in Brussels regarding our corporation tax regime or in any EU capital, and this is creating the background music for what we are hearing now.' Green-eyed jealousy lay behind the criticisms that were coming from Brussels, McCreevy contended. 'The EU would like me to take money out of the Irish economy. It wants me to take a couple of hundred million pounds out of tax reductions and expenditure, but there is no question of rewriting the budget.' McCreevy said he was annoyed that the economy that had the highest European growth rate, the second-lowest national debt, a falling inflation rate and almost full employment was facing censure. Any censure by the EU would not be binding, because budgets were a matter for individual member-states to frame according to economic circumstances.

In early February the Brussels correspondent of the *Irish Times*, Denis Staunton, reported that diplomats there were warning that if McCreevy, in rejecting the Commission's criticism, was too strident, it would antagonise Ireland's EU partners. 'Within the complex political environment of the EU, small member-states such as Ireland depend on the goodwill of other states to achieve national objectives.' EU officials had responded with derision to McCreevy's suggestion that his European critics were motivated by envy, Staunton said.

The strong public reaction against the advice of Brussels sparked concern there. The process that had been put in train began with the Commission but would culminate in the meeting of the EU finance ministers, which would make the final decision in relation to any rebuke. Lobbying by Byrne and others, as well as concern in Brussels about stoking anti-EU sentiment in Ireland, led to demands for a reversal of the budget measures being changed to demands that restrictive measures be introduced during the course of the year. As the ministers' meeting neared, Staunton reported that the Commission 'has been surprised by the intensity of the public response in Ireland to its reprimand and is at pains to emphasise that its assessment of the Irish economy included praise as well as criticism.'

McCreevy met his fellow EU finance ministers on 12 February 2001. He remained defiant, but his remarks were met with silence. A formal recommendation criticising his December budget was adopted without a vote. No-one other than McCreevy spoke in Ireland's favour. He told his fellow-ministers that the censure was unjustified. 'Neither I nor the Government, and the majority of the economic commentators, believe that such a proposal is warranted. Nor is it, in my view, a proportionate or even-handed response.' Not only did he defend his budget but he also said he would defy the unprecedented rebuke and introduce another giveaway package later in the year. He told journalists after the meeting that he wanted to ensure that his next three budgets would be as successful as the previous three. He did not believe that his defiant stance would damage Ireland politically within the EU. 'Over the past five years we have received no favours or special treatment from the EU. What we got we've got on our merits.'

John Bruton wrote an extended piece on the row with Brussels in the wake of the rebuke. The fundamental difference between McCreevy and his EU finance minister colleagues, he wrote, was the European view that the Irish budget was 'pro-cyclical' and stoking inflation. While McCreevy responded to the Commission by saying that Ireland was producing large and prudent budget surpluses, and had measures to increase productivity and the labour supply, he did not, in Bruton's view, address the Commission's main concerns. 'McCreevy does not controvert them. He simply ignores them.'

Bruton argued that perhaps McCreevy had some argument that, in the modern world, what with technological change and an increased understanding of markets, business cycles were no longer an issue; but, if he had, he had not voiced it.

> If he did make such a contention he would have had to deal with the known fact that personal borrowing levels in Ireland are now at an unprecedented high level relative to personal incomes. He would also have to deal with the fact that recent rates of house-price increase have been higher than in any country which has escaped a subsequent house-price collapse.

The Government, he pointed out, had said 'it will have to bring in up to 300,000 immigrants to meet foreseeable labour demand.' McCreevy 'would have had to say where these immigrants would be housed, given the existing housing shortage,' if he was to deal frankly with the Commission's concerns.

The director of the European Institute in UCD, Prof. Brigid Laffan, also made clear her concerns. She pointed out that McCreevy had been isolated at the meeting of European finance ministers. 'His intervention was received by his fellow ministers with studied silence. Given that Ireland tends to position itself in the mainstream of most EU negotiations, was it wise of Ireland's representative to opt for isolation on this issue?' For Laffan, McCreevy, encouraged by Harney, had depleted scarce political capital with 'nothing to show for it.'

The former Fine Gael Taoiseach Garret FitzGerald was a particularly strong critic of McCreevy's and the PDs' economic policy. The tensions that had been introduced into Ireland's relationship with the European Commission and our EU partners were 'unnecessary and dangerous', he wrote in the wake of the meeting. Ireland's position in the EU had been damaged by McCreevy's budget and the way he had dealt with the Commission's criticisms. The row raised questions about Ahern's judgement both in his choice of ministers and in his execution of his co-ordinating role in the Government. McCreevy's combination of certainty and a strong ideological streak made him a dangerous choice for the position of Minister for Finance—one that Fianna Fáil might in time regret.

> He is an ideological PD rather than a Fianna Fáil pragmatist, and in a FF/PD government, which tends to be pulled dangerously to the right by the smaller party, there was bound to be a need for a counter-balance rather than to reinforce this pull in finance. There was also a danger in making the Minister for Finance a strong-minded accountant with a

gambling streak: the minds of some accountants can at times be resistant to economic considerations, and this is clearly so with our minister, who seems to be unable to accept even such obvious economic concepts as the need to pursue counter-cyclical rather than pro-cyclical policies.

The 2000 budget involved a package of more than €1 billion in pay cuts and spending increases. An analysis by the Economic and Social Research Institute confirmed the opposition position that the budget was skewed in favour of the better off, though such an analysis was not something that was as politically damaging as perhaps it should have been.

The budget included measures for the calculation of income tax (individualisation) that were designed to encourage more women into the work force. The initiative caused a furore, and what was designed as a giveaway budget turned into a political controversy. In a subsequent column in the *Irish Times*, Garret FitzGerald returned to criticising McCreevy. Economics was not an end in itself, he pointed out. 'Increased output is not an end in itself. It is, or at any rate ought to be, simply a means towards a better society.' As long as there had been a significant level of unemployment, seeking to maximise economic growth was reasonable; but, since full employment was now being reached, and as Ireland's income levels were now equal to those of its EU partners, maximising growth should no longer be a priority. 'Indeed, in our circumstances, growth maximisation can be a perverse policy, increasing unnecessarily the strains in our economy and pressure on our overburdened infrastructure.' McCreevy's policies were going in the opposite direction to what society required, he argued.

On New Year's Day 2002 Ahern went to his local newsagents in Drumcondra and bought sultana cake, milk and pears. He paid in Irish pounds and was given his change in euro. He came to the shop for newspapers and fruit regularly, according to the shopkeeper, Marion O'Neill, but this was different: it was a scheduled press event, and photographers and reporters were there to record the Taoiseach's first use of the new currency. Someone had even brought a bottle of champagne. It was election year, the reporters pointed out. Would Ahern still be Taoiseach after the poll? 'We'll keep trying,' he replied.

The circumstances facing the Government as it entered election year were not as they had been envisaged a year earlier. The dot-com boom, which had boosted the United States and the global economy, had come to an end, and the world economy was also suffering from the insecurities created by the attacks on the United States on 11 September 2001. The concerns that Brussels had about Irish and European inflation were no longer an issue, and, for the first time since its coming into power, the Ahern Government was having to deal with difficult economic circumstances. The change in the atmosphere, however, did not lead to any slowing in the rate of current and capital expenditure.

Ahern also found himself facing a new leader of the opposition. Poor poll results had prompted discontent in Fine Gael with the leadership of John Bruton, and, though he successfully resisted a number of efforts to shift him, he was eventually replaced in early 2001 by the Limerick TD and former schoolteacher Michael Noonan. According to Mark Brennock, nine months before Bruton was ousted, an unnamed Fianna Fáil minister had said to him, 'Fine Gael are going to dump Bruton and hand us the election.'

The shafting of Bruton certainly did little to improve the party's ratings or that of its leader, though Fianna Fáil was also having difficulties. An *Irish Times*/MRBI opinion poll of 25 January showed that satisfaction with the Government was down ten points since the previous poll, and support for Fianna Fáil had dropped one point. Ahern's personal satisfaction rating had climbed to 68 per cent, its highest level in eighteen months. A return to power of the Fianna Fáil-PD coalition was the preferred choice among those offered to respondents in the survey.

The final Fianna Fáil ard-fheis before the election took place in the second weekend in March, in the wake of an abortion referendum in which the electorate had voted against a Government proposal for constitutional change. In the opening remarks of his address Ahern hit the note that he and his party were privately hoping would not only return them to power but would provide them with an absolute majority. 'During the longest and most stable Government that this nation has seen in peacetime, during the longest and most spectacular economic growth that this nation has ever seen in our history, we have met the challenge with courage and with confidence,' he said. The speech was stuffed with figures. It also addressed the issue of political sleaze.

The uncovering of a previously hidden and unacceptable past in our political life undermined confidence in politics and politicians. This Government's response has been to initiate the most far-reaching inquiries not only in the history of this state but also in the recent history of most democratic societies. Through the tribunals the facts are being established and the truth is being found out.

Having praised his Government's achievements, Ahern turned to pouring derision on the Fine Gael-Labour Party alternative.

> Their vision is back to the bad old days. The bad old days called the 1980s. Their formula is to raise taxes! Raise taxes, reduce revenue, deter investment and destroy jobs.

The Rainbow's ideas would bring a dark cloud over the economy. 'They would take Ireland back to where they left it.' The record of the opposition parties was one of failure, he said.

Many observers of Bertie Ahern did not believe that he had strong political convictions, but there was general agreement that the desire he had to build a new sports stadium in Dublin, to be called Sports Campus Ireland, was a deeply held one. For Rabbitte, Ahern had a sincere interest in sport.

> The only time I ever saw Bertie being genuinely passionate about achieving something was the Bertie Bowl. I think he was furious with me for creating that term. He really identified with that project. Maybe he saw it in terms of it being his legacy.

The plan for the Bertie Bowl remained a matter for political and public debate, even though large amounts of public money were being put towards the redevelopment of Croke Park. By the time of the 2002 general election, work on Croke Park, which would see it accommodating close to eighty thousand spectators, was nearing completion. There was a second available stadium at Lansdowne Road. Ahern's stadium was initially costed at more than €400 million. The figure got larger as the project continued being debated, with the eventual estimated cost being raised to €1 billion.

Eventually Ahern's coalition partners came out against the project. As the election campaign got under way Harney spoke out about it and its cost. McDowell, Ahern's Attorney-General, had been tempted back into politics and was seeking to regain his seat in Dublin South-East. With characteristic rhetorical panache he referred to the stadium idea as a 'Ceauşescu-era Olympic project' that should be opposed as a matter of public morality. 'Campus Ireland is a potent symbol of all that has gone wrong in the past, and that will go wrong in the future, if the Irish people ever revert to the politics of one party, one leader, one voice.' He said the PDs were seeking a mandate to oppose the project. It was strong stuff from someone who was still the Government's Attorney-General. In response Ahern said, 'I am sure it is a tight situation in Dublin South-East.' The stadium was never built, and what appears to have been Ahern's pet project and his desired structural legacy never materialised.

Ahern called the election on 24 April, in odd circumstances. The 28th Dáil was the longest since the Second World War, and on the evening of the 24th a minister of state, Mary Hanafin, was in the chamber answering Pat Rabbitte's adjournment motion concerning cutbacks in funds for the intellectually disabled. Just before 9 p.m., and much to the surprise of the few who were there, Ahern came into the chamber and sent a note to the Ceann Comhairle, Séamus Pattison, saying that he wanted to speak. There was no-one in the public gallery, and two journalists who were out in the press rooms quickly ran to take their seats in the gallery when they saw him appear. Ahern had come down from his office in Government Buildings without telling anyone what he was doing. Hanafin stopped so that Ahern could speak. 'I wish to inform the house as a matter of courtesy that I intend to proceed to Áras an Uachtaráin at 9 a.m. tomorrow to advise the President, pursuant to article 13 of the Constitution, to dissolve Dáil Éireann.' Polling day would be 17 May. 'Let the battle begin,' said Rabbitte.

Fianna Fáil started planning for the 2002 general election campaign four years before it happened. The key figures in devising the campaign were Haughey's former press officer, P. J. Mara, and the general secretary, Martin Macken. They held their first meeting about the campaign in the autumn of 1998. They looked at the party's possible candidates and at constituency vote management. They commissioned research on a range of topics. Focus groups, in which a selection of people are asked for their views on current affairs, were organised, as were constituency opinion polls. All this, of course, cost a lot of money.

The day after Ahern unexpectedly called the election, the Fianna Fáil campaign was launched in the Shelbourne Hotel in Dublin, with Mara telling the assembled media, 'Okay, folks, it's show time!' The campaign was designed to come out of the traps with force. Each day had a master plan with a distinct message and a grid system to govern what was to be achieved. Ahern's contribution was to be on the road, doing what he did so well: canvassing. Des Richardson and Chris Wall were among the group that would meet Mara every morning at seven in the party head office to discuss the outcome of the previous day and the plans for the coming day. The centre of operations was on the first floor of Treasury Buildings, an office building on the site of the former Bolands Mill. The building is owned by the property developer Johnny Ronan, of Treasury Holdings, and the businessman Paddy McKillen.

The Treasury Holdings operation was in part modelled on the system run by the British Labour Party in its head office in London during the British general election. The assistance Fianna Fáil got from the British Labour Party rankled with Pat Rabbitte.

> I remember being in Millbank [the British Labour Party offices] expressing my displeasure to the general secretary that there were more Fianna Fáil people being housed there for the course of the British general election than there were Labour people, and the general secretary agreed with me. He told me privately afterwards that Blair personally phoned him and told him he was to facilitate Bertie. Bertie worked it very thoroughly with Blair.

The Treasury Holdings operation was so wound up that the passion with which it burst into action in the first week of the election campaign backfired, in that journalists began to resent its unrelenting and pushy efforts to manipulate the agenda.

Meanwhile Ahern was out canvassing, getting his picture taken and providing sound-bites. A piece by the political writer Deaglán de Bréadún in the *Irish Times* opened: 'They seek him here, they seek him there. Bertie is Fianna Fáil's Scarlet Pimpernel. Pity the poor media trying to keep track of him.' He quoted Mary Wilson of RTE, who was, with difficulty, following the Ahern canvass as it blitzed through Ireland.

> They like to go to shopping centres, press the flesh, in one door, out the other, hardly pausing for breath. Bertie Ahern shakes every hand. If he has missed a hand, a handler will have the hand waiting for him as he walks along. Nothing goes unnoticed by Ahern and his handlers as he walks around.

De Bréadún wrote that a handler had once explained the policy to him during a Donegal by-election. A man goes to a shopping centre to buy mince. He happens upon a crowd and, before he knows it, he has shaken the hand of the Taoiseach. When he goes home he tells his wife. When polling day comes around, he feels that same hand pulling his towards supporting the Fianna Fáil candidate.

> On our screens we see Bertie, barrelling along in his inimitable sailor's walk, seemingly determined to shake every hand of every non-journalist from

Malin Head to Mizen Head and Artane to Ahascragh ... Like some third world potentate, Bertie is reaching over the heads of the media to communicate directly with the voters. The ubiquitous Ahern posters contribute to the atmosphere of a benign and paternalistic African dictatorship.

On the businessman Denis O'Brien's 'Newstalk 106', Rabbitte complained of Ahern's image being 'more in evidence this month than Kylie Minogue's backside,' while on TV3 the broadcaster Damien Kiberd referred to Fianna Fáil as engaging in 'Joe Stalin-like hagiography'. Others, de Bréadún reported, were muttering comparisons with Ceauşescu. As we have already seen, Ahern had devoted a large part of his schedule over the previous five years touring the country, and the election campaign meant a full-time, as against a part-time, adoption of this practice.

The Fianna Fáil campaign was such a success that poll results, published on 15 May, two days before election day, showed that Ahern was almost certain to be re-elected Taoiseach and that there was a real prospect that he would be leading a single-party Government. The support for Ahern was spread right across the electorate, to the extent that for 39 per cent of Fine Gael voters he was the preferred choice for Taoiseach. Labour Party voters preferred Ahern to Noonan by a factor of three, and twice as many Labour Party voters indicated that they would transfer to Fianna Fáil as would transfer to Fine Gael.

It was at this late stage that McDowell made what many believe was a key intervention. He shimmied up a lamppost in Ranelagh with a new poster that attacked not the opposition but his coalition partner, Fianna Fáil. *One-party Government? No thanks!* shouted the poster, which received widespread media coverage, not least because McDowell was an Attorney-General inviting the electorate not to trust the majority party of the Government of which he was still a member.

Ahern came tantalisingly close to winning Fianna Fáil's first absolute majority since 1977. To do so required 83 seats, and in the 2002 election it won 81. It increased its representation by 8 seats, while the PDs doubled its representation to 8. Fine Gael performed disastrously, losing 23 seats, so that it held only 31; it changed leader again afterwards, replacing Noonan with Enda Kenny. The Labour Party trod water, at 20 seats, with the Green Party increasing its power threefold, to 6 deputies. Sinn Féin reaped the benefits of the peace process and grew from 1 to 5. Independents went from 11 to 14. They included Michael Lowry, who, despite having accepted money from businessmen while in office, having cheated on his taxes and having misled the Dáil in relation to possessing offshore accounts, continued to receive the support of his North Tipperary electorate. Joe Higgins of the Socialist Party was also re-elected.

A startling aspect of the election was that Fianna Fáil had come so close to winning a Dáil majority with only 41.5 per cent of the national vote. Dublin Central apart, successful vote management was part of the reason for this; but another was a breakdown in traditional voting patterns, with significant numbers voting for opposition or independent candidates and then giving their lower-preference votes to Fianna Fáil. Fewer voters held out-and-out anti-Fianna Fáil views, and the unusual number of transfers to the party gave it a significant boost in seats. 'The single most important factor in the broadening of the party's appeal has been Bertie Ahern,' wrote Mark Brennock in the wake of the election. 'Sold by the party during the campaign more as a charismatic celebrity than sober political leader, Mr Ahern's personal appeal and popularity went way beyond the confines of his own party.' It was an achievement, Brennock wrote, to win so many seats on such a national share of the vote, and an achievement to get that national share in the first place.

> The party has conducted extensive market research throughout the term of the Government and right through this campaign. Not for them the old-fashioned notion of writing a programme for government you believe in and selling it to the people. The scientific research was used to judge the public mood very accurately and then to devise a product that the public would be certain to buy. The research showed that enormous numbers of people felt better off now than they did five years ago, and would vote for someone who would keep things that way.

Fintan O'Toole wrote that it was time for critics to acknowledge Ahern's achievements. Ahern 'took over a demoralised, fractious party in the throes of a historic decline and turned it into a machine so slick that it can leave its traditional enemies at the starting line without even getting into second gear.' Attempts to emulate Ahern would be difficult for opposition leaders. 'If politics is framed as a contest to discover who is best at being Bertie, the winner will always be Bertie. Being Bertie is a hard trick, and it is time that his opponents acknowledged the Taoiseach's achievements.' Fianna Fáil's results in 1997 and 2002 would, under earlier leaders, have been seen as very poor, but Ahern had changed the view of the party, which no longer saw itself involved in a contest between it and the rest of the world. Ahern, the ultimate consensus man, did not treat non-Fianna Fáil politicians as the enemy. The old Civil War politics were being quietly dropped, and Fianna Fáil was benefiting from the resultant transfers, according to O'Toole.

The nature and result of the 2002 election was analysed in two books, *How Ireland Voted 2002* and *The Irish Voter*, written and edited by political scientists and commentators. The former said the electorate's concerns about the management of the health system, and the extent of the attention it was given during the election campaign, 'probably cost the party its first overall majority since 1977.' In general, however, it found that the data supported the argument that

> a feel-good factor favoured the incumbent government in general and Fianna Fáil in particular. This is hardly surprising. Governments that preside over good times are supposed to be rewarded. While the result for the Rainbow of 1994–1997 was inadequate to provide for its re-election, in 2002 the bonus was a little more generous.

What was more surprising was the weakness of the opposition in the face of new parties and independents, the authors wrote. In his contribution to the book, the political journalist Stephen Collins wrote that, even though the election took place as the economy was beginning to weaken, Fianna Fáil strategists had decided that there was an opportunity for them in this if they could convince the worried public that it was the best option available to manage the economic downturn.

The party's research, however, prompted it not to directly associate Ahern with the issue of economic management. The election posters all featured Ahern and the party's chosen slogan: 'A lot done. More to do.' Thought had been given to having Ahern's photograph alongside a slogan that referred to him directly—'Let Ahern lead'—but research and experience showed that this might not run so well with the electorate. Ahern had been put centre stage for the Nice Treaty referendum in 2001 and the abortion referendum in 2002, and both had been voted down. Ahern's popularity was a separate issue from the electorate's faith in his competence.

In his article on the background to the election, Gary Murphy, a politics academic, noted that there was little difference between the manifestos of the main parties. Health was recognised as a difficult subject by all, including the Government parties, but the range of solutions proposed failed to excite the electorate. Similarly there was little by way of real debate on taxation. Though the Government had been heavily criticised for the nature of its personal taxation cuts, no party was proposing undoing them.

Raising taxation for spending or to cope with any possible downturn in the economy was not an option [the parties] were willing to put into their manifestos. The Taoiseach provided the best evidence of this overlap in terms of macroeconomic policy when he stated that there was nothing in the manifesto of the PDs or Labour with which he fundamentally disagreed.

The Irish Voter was published in 2008 and so provided the authors with an extended period for assessing the 2002 election. Again they concluded that the governing parties, and Fianna Fáil in particular, were rewarded by the electorate for doing 'a good job'. Where there were negative assessments, such as with crime or with the quality of the health service, the Government was not held responsible, or was seen as, in any event, probably being better than the opposition parties would have been. Interestingly, however, the authors played down the importance of Ahern's popularity.

In the period before the 1997 poll, Ahern had enjoyed only a very small lead over Bruton and Spring. However, as that Government's period in office progressed, Ahern's lead over the Fine Gael and Labour Party leaders (later Noonan and Quinn) widened, so that by the time of the 2002 election Ahern's lead over Noonan was an unusually large one. What had happened was that, in the period since 1997, Ahern's star had ascended, while those of the opposition leaders had fallen. The authors looked at survey data on what it was that people liked about Ahern, Noonan and Quinn. Respondents were asked to rate the leaders in relation to honesty, competence and closeness to the people. Ahern won on all three counts, particularly in the last two. An analysis of the data, in conjunction with figures on popularity, found that in Ahern's case honesty had a particularly strong correlation with his general evaluation. 'Had the opposition been able to persuade more people that Ahern's character was more dubious, they might have damaged him, but they were unable to do so.'

Ahern's huge lead over Noonan in the popularity stakes had a limited impact on the performance of their parties, the authors said. 'It is clear that where the popularity of leaders and parties diverge, and they often do, voters follow parties rather than leaders. This is not to say that a popular leader is not an asset, but that the asset is one that makes only a marginal difference to vote totals.' However, they noted that a marginal change can make the difference between being returned to office and not. Fianna Fáil placed a huge emphasis on Ahern during the election campaign, but the conclusion of the authors' analysis was that the perception of the advantage this had conferred was exaggerated.

Ahern was back in office, but he was not happy with the election result. Micheál Martin met him in St Luke's soon after the poll, and they discussed the outcome.

He [Ahern] went through every constituency with me. It was extraordinary. The man was amazing in his detailed grasp of every constituency. He was really annoyed after 2002 in terms of not winning the overall majority, and he felt people had let him down in terms of telling him, We are going to win that seat, win this, and then they didn't. It was party organisation, ministers and TDs and so on that he was angry with, not Michael McDowell.

Chapter 9 ∾

| TAOISEACH, 2002–8

Charlie McCreevy nominated Bertie Ahern for the position of Taoiseach after the 2002 general election. McCreevy rose to address the Dáil just before noon on 6 June as Ahern's partner, Celia Larkin, looked on from the public gallery.

The Government leaving office today held it longer than any other in peacetime. At the end of five years it also became the first Government in thirty-three years to receive the people's mandate to continue in office and did so on the basis of increased representation in the House. Central to these unprecedented achievements has been the steady and clear leadership of Deputy Bertie Ahern. Although he has held high office for a significant period, he continues to be in touch with the people, and they continue to have faith in him. Over the past five years they saw a leader who helped deliver a historic breakthrough for peace, helped the largest sustained period of economic growth in our history and ensured economic growth meant real social progress throughout the country. He went before the people with a clear message of wanting to build on this peace, prosperity and progress, and they gave him a mandate.

Ahern was elected by 93 votes to 68. He got the support of his own party, the PDs and some independents. Accepting the result, Ahern spoke again of the honour involved. Politics was a noble calling, he said, and the justifiable pride those who had been returned to the Dáil could feel had to be matched by a sense of duty and by 'the determination to earn our place by hard work and with integrity.' He praised Michael Noonan, who had been replaced as leader of Fine Gael by Enda Kenny, and also spoke generously about Mary Harney, Ruairí Quinn, Trevor Sargent of the Green Party and the former party leaders Proinsias de Rossa, John Bruton and Dick Spring. 'I pledge to work ceaselessly . . . and never to give less than my very best.'

Ruairí Quinn congratulated Ahern on his political achievement and his return to office—a testimony to his extraordinary popularity and his dedication to politics and public life. He also spoke of the Lazarus party of Irish politics—the PDs—and noted that his constituency colleague, Michael McDowell, had on his third attempt managed to get into the Dáil at the same time as his party was going into government.

> For my part, the Labour Party will provide a critique of the politics of choice, this centre-right Government which has pursued a deliberate political ideological agenda masked in the cosy populism of a very popular man, who sincerely believes what he says but allowed his Minister for Finance to contradict him at every twist and turn in terms of the policy that was implemented.

At four in the afternoon Ahern was back in the Dáil chamber to announce his new Government. Harney was Tánaiste and Minister for Enterprise, Trade and Employment. The other members were Michael Smith (Defence), Joe Walsh (Agriculture and Food), Charlie McCreevy (Finance), Brian Cowen (Foreign Affairs), Noel Dempsey (Education and Science), Dermot Ahern (Communications, Marine and Natural Resources), John O'Donoghue (Arts, Sport and Tourism), Micheál Martin (Health and Children), Séamus Brennan (Transport), Michael McDowell (Justice, Equality and Law Reform), Martin Cullen (Environment and Local Government), Éamon Ó Cuív (Community, Rural and Gaeltacht Affairs) and Mary Coughlan (Social Affairs and Family). The Attorney-General was Rory Brady SC.

In his remarks to the Dáil after the announcement of the Government, Quinn touched on an issue that was going to define much of what was to come politically. He referred to the media debate over whether the public finances were out of control.

> We have seen a sustained splurge in public expenditure over the past eighteen months or two years. It was deliberate, considered and carefully

measured, down to the timing of its delivery. We are now about to get a reversal of that splurge.

Sure enough, as the summer progressed a range of announcements were made about efforts to cut back on the pace of increase in public expenditure. The isolated announcements on such matters as health, education and overseas aid were not, the public was told, part of an orchestrated programme of expenditure restraint; but for a society by then used to a continuous flow of new expenditure announcements, the application of the foot to the brake felt like cutbacks. It was also in conflict with the merry message from the Government parties that had seen them re-elected.

The change in tune caused a sharp fall in the Government's popularity and also created internal strains. Ahern was persisting with his plan for a new stadium and with the related bid for Ireland to host the Euro 2008 soccer finals; but the PDs, and even some of his Fianna Fáil colleagues, were resisting the plan, given the strain on the public finances.

On 16 September the then political editor of the *Sunday Tribune*, Stephen Collins, reported that McCreevy was contemplating introducing a tax on child benefit in his coming budget. The arrival of *de facto* full employment, and the movement of more women into the work force, had made child-care costs a major political issue. The Government had responded by granting significant increases in child benefit to everyone, regardless of their income or whether they worked in the home or not. Rates had increased dramatically in the two years before the election and had trebled since Ahern first become Taoiseach.

The pressures of full employment and wage and cost increases had also seen the Government creating the process whereby the pay of public-sector workers was to be benchmarked against those in the private sector. The INTO representative and senator Joe O'Toole famously referred to the process as an 'ATM for teachers'. Now the downturn in the Irish economy and the public finances threatened the promised pay rises under that process.

The discord between what the public had been told before polling day and what it was now being told was crystallised in a report by Rachel Andrews in the following week's *Sunday Tribune*. 'Exclusive!' shouted the headline over a genuinely great scoop. A lengthy and secret memorandum from McCreevy to his Government colleagues, drafted within weeks of the poll in May and days after Ahern's re-election as Taoiseach, set out the dire position of the public finances and the need to cut public expenditure in 2003 by €900 million. If a return of high unemployment and forced emigration was to be avoided, the proposals set out in the memorandum and its appendix would have to be introduced. Furthermore, the proposal for a reining in of public expenditure was based on a set of forecasts for the economy that were more likely to be over-optimistic. Ministers were told that if there were no cutbacks in expenditure there would be no money for benchmarking, no money for social welfare increases and no money for the Government's health strategy. Furthermore, a failure to implement the measures foreseen would lead to a reversal in the thrust of taxation policy of recent years.

The lengthy memorandum contained figures that dramatically illustrated the way in which public spending had been used as an electoral tool. Current spending had increased by an astonishing 27 per cent in the twelve months up to the election. Collins, in a piece forming part of the paper's four-page inside package on their scoop, said the document raised serious questions about the ability of the Government to run the country, and contended that its reputation was now 'in tatters'.

Matt Cooper, the paper's business editor, wrote of McCreevy's appearance on 'The Late Late Show' the previous Friday and of the way his usual confidence had wilted under the sustained hostility of the audience, many of whom were affected by the cutbacks that had already been introduced. McCreevy had been booed, and his syntax had become mangled as the audience laid into him. Yet the audience had not known about the memorandum, Cooper wrote, which illustrated in stark terms the scale of McCreevy's ineptitude.

Total Government spending had grown by 23 per cent in 2001, while tax revenue had increased by only 3.2 per cent. Yet in his budget for the following year, announced in December 2001, McCreevy had planned for a further 14.4 per cent in spending increases. Not only that: he hadn't been able to rein in his Government colleagues, and the actual level of spending had exceeded that figure. The public finances were in crisis, and it was evident, Cooper wrote, that McCreevy knew the full extent of the crisis during the election campaign. Yet the minister had told a press conference only a week before the poll that 'no cutbacks whatsoever are being planned, secretly or otherwise.' The scoop provided the material for the main news story of that day's and the following days' papers, many of which led with opposition calls for McCreevy's resignation. McCreevy, in his first public response to the report, confirmed that the economic circumstances facing the country were worse than had been envisaged in June.

The effect of the controversy was the creation of a lasting impression with most of the electorate that they had been cheated. In the first two years of the second Ahern Government, it argued unsuccessfully that no cutbacks were being implemented—that in fact public expenditure was growing: it was simply that it was not growing as quickly as it had hitherto. However, efforts by the Government to argue that what it was doing was a responsible reaction to changing circumstances did not wash with the public, who were not inclined to listen to a grouping in which they had lost trust. The first year and a half of Ahern's second Government was among the worst periods of his political career.

One of the great challenges faced by Ahern's first Government, according to Micheál Martin, was the resisting of the clamour for increased expenditure.

> The sense then was that we weren't getting the infrastructural work done fast enough. And efficiently enough. People wanted the road and railways done, because of all the wealth. The big political and psychological problem was how you could justify not spending the money when we were trumpeting that we have surpluses. The clarion call was 'Why don't you spend on this, on that?' The whole mindset of society was 'Gimme, gimme, gimme.'

But the political pressures changed dramatically after the second Government was formed. Martin was still Minister for Health.

> The first two-and-a-half years were covered by those cutbacks. The retrenchment regime led to some very tough meetings.

The tension grew in the Government as the local elections approached. McCreevy focused on arresting the growth in public expenditure, and his Government colleagues and their advisers focused on political popularity. But, for Martin, it was not so much the macro area of public expenditure management that created the tension as a certain perceived pig-headedness on McCreevy's part.

> There were crazy things that weren't done that wouldn't have affected the fiscal position dramatically. There was a big row coming up to the Special Olympics over spending on disabilities. Bertie was furious about that. I think it was €20 million. We had rows about whether it was in the budget or not. I had incredible rows over opening new hospital facilities which we had built and we couldn't get sanction to open them before the election. This was akin to having the ball in front of the goalposts and not

putting it into the net. You could have been opening these facilities that were going to be opened anyway—and guess what? They were opened after the election. Those sort of incidents really brassed off the Taoiseach, big time.

The opening ceremony of the Special Olympics in June 2003 was a huge event staged in Croke Park, in Ahern's own constituency. It was the first time the games had been held outside the United States, and they were impressively well organised. Participants came from around the globe, and towns and villages throughout the country hosted particular countries' teams and put on warm and impressive welcomes for them. The whole country appeared to be involved in a united effort and a sincere unleashing of good will, and the opening night was a genuine extravaganza, with fireworks and a parade of all the participating athletes. But Ahern was booed when he took to the stage during the opening night's festivities. His Government's stance on funding for the disabled was portrayed as being in marked contrast with the fund-raising and volunteerism of the organisers of the event. The public humiliation angered Ahern all the more because it was seen as owing more to pig-headedness on McCreevy's part than to a matter of responsible Government restraint.

Ahern in his memoirs wrote disparagingly about some backbench TDs, bitter about not being included in government, who got the jitters at about this time. He listed four TDs—Ned O'Keeffe, John McGuinness, Jim Glennon and Noel O'Flynn—as being 'unhelpful' to the party by giving negative comment to the media, while Michael Smith broke ranks on a controversial report that had implications for a hospital in his constituency. In December 2003 Ahern decided to reassert his leadership of the parliamentary party. According to his own account, he told the party that he was well used to party division and had been close to Haughey during the heaves against him. He knew every trick in the book. 'Anyone who wants to come after me, then I will come after you, one by fucking one, and I will rivet you.' He said that he deliberately used bad language, that everyone in the room was stunned and that it was 'good fun'. He also said he threw in the line that he would not tolerate 'kebabs' in the party, meaning cabals. In his memoirs he leaves it unclear as to whether his malapropism was intentional or not, but he notes that the fact that the media ran with the kebab issue, rather than the tearing strips off his colleagues issue, proved handy.

If the difficult economic circumstances of 2002 and 2003 meant that tax cuts and other forms of state largesse were no longer available for attempting to woo the electorate, Ahern's resourceful Minister for Finance was not without other ideas. The big story of the 2003 budget, announced in December 2002, was McCreevy's decision to go for a 'big bang' decentralisation of the public service. It had been Government policy for a number of years to decentralise so as to relieve pressure on the capital and to spread the economic benefits of Government activity more widely; but the budget announcement came as a shock. McCreevy had told his Cabinet colleagues that he would abandon the project if news leaked. The most senior civil servants were given only a few days' notice, and so McCreevy's Dáil announcement came as a great surprise to many who were at the heart of public infrastructure management.

> For the first time ever, decentralisation will involve the transfer of complete departments—including their ministers and senior management—to provincial locations. A total of eight departments and the Office of Public Works will move their headquarters from Dublin to provincial locations, leaving seven departments with their headquarters in Dublin. All departments and offices will be participating in the programme. Ministers with headquarters outside of Dublin will be provided with a centralised suite of offices close to the Houses of the Oireachtas for a small secretariat so they can conduct business while in Dublin and when the Dáil is in session. The previous decentralisation programme involved the relocation of some 4,000 public service jobs. The programme I am announcing today is far more radical. In total, it will involve the relocation of 10,300 civil and public service jobs to fifty-three centres in twenty-five counties.

It was the big-ticket item in the budget and went down well with non-Dublin Government deputies who had constituencies that were going to benefit from public investment. Given the scale of the project, that meant just about every non-Dublin constituency in the country.

Economically, things were beginning to look up for the Government. Introducing his budget, McCreevy said it came at a time when international economic conditions were on the mend. Ireland, he said, had come through the international downturn better than most, in no small part because of its sound budgetary policies. The budget did not include much by way of tax changes, though the minister did announce extensions to the tax relief schemes for film, seed capital schemes and property schemes. On the last he said:

A number of reliefs were due to expire at end 2004. I am aware that there is a range of construction projects either in the pipeline or under way which will be seriously affected by this termination date. As the end 2004 deadline approaches, pressure on construction resources will mount to deliver these projects. Accordingly, I propose to extend the termination date for all these area-based schemes until 31 July 2006.

The long run of the boom in Irish property prices had flagged as Ahern's first Government came to an end. However, by the time of McCreevy's decentralisation announcement, prices were beginning to rise again, for reasons that were not to become clear for quite some time. It was during this revival in property prices that the decentralisation programme was announced. The Government would be able to profit from the healthy price of property in Dublin and to use its windfall gains to finance the purchase of sites and properties and the construction of new properties around the country. Civil and public servants could voluntarily opt to move to the new locations, in part because of the lures of cheaper housing and of never again having to deal with the difficulties of commuting in the capital.

But the policy had many critics. Some pointed to the potential for disruption of the civil and public service through the increased need for travel within a dispersed service. Others spoke of the possible loss of corporate knowledge that would occur when some officials moved and when others, who chose to remain in Dublin, were allocated new roles, possibly in new departments or agencies. It emerged that the more senior grades, who tended to be older and have established roots in their communities, were less inclined to opt to move. There was a danger of a widespread loss of senior management. Dan Murphy of the Public Service Executive Union described the idea as a 'nonsense' that could not be implemented. It was a 'cynical political ploy'. Other critics were suspicious about a programme that involved expenditure of up to €1 billion on property deals being overseen by a Government that had such strong links with property developers and builders. According to Quinn,

no-one knows who was tipped off about what sites were going to be bought, what towns, what places would be chosen . . . And again this was McCreevy's criminal abuse, in my view, of the budgetary process, to prevent the civil service from knowing what was going on. The secretaries-general were only told about the decentralisation plan 48 hours before the budget was announced. And it was unsustainable. It didn't even adhere with the government's own spatial plan.

A Government sub-committee was set up, and in time Phil Flynn, a former trade unionist, Sinn Féin activist and then chairman of Bank of Scotland (Ireland), was appointed by Ahern to head the decentralisation process. Direct political responsibility was given to a new PD deputy, Tom Parlon, who was Minister of State at the Department of Finance.

However, if the hope had been that the decentralisation plan would revive Fianna Fáil's popularity, it was a forlorn one. The European and local elections were a disaster for the party. In the local elections it gained only 32 per cent of the national vote and lost 80 out of its 382 council seats. Fine Gael, by comparison, got 28 per cent of the poll, reversing the slide in its popularity in 2002. Sinn Féin saw a 150 per cent increase in its representation, to 54 seats. It also did well in the European elections, with Mary Lou McDonald being elected for Dublin. Royston Brady was the Fianna Fáil candidate in Dublin. His high-profile, well-funded campaign—Des Richardson was in charge of finance—collapsed spectacularly, and afterwards he had a row with Richardson over who had to pay his outstanding bills. Fianna Fáil got 4 seats, compared with 6 in 1999.

The first mention of the need for a Government reshuffle emerged on the very day of the election results. Soon afterwards, reports began to appear in the newspapers that McCreevy might be taking on the position of European commissioner—a surprising development considering the attitude he had displayed towards Europe during the row with the Commission over his budgets of 2000 and 2001. McCreevy consulted his advisers, and journalists were briefed against the idea; but the reports continued to appear. Most political observers believed that Ahern was behind it all. Nevertheless, when McCreevy yielded to the inevitable and went to Ahern saying he wanted the post, and Ahern nominated him for it, Ahern spoke publicly about his regret at losing his Minister for Finance.

With McCreevy despatched to Brussels (where he was to be hugely unpopular), Ahern reshuffled his Government. Brian Cowen was made Minister for Finance. Cowen made it clear when announcing his first budget that he was working in co-operation with his Taoiseach and his other Government colleagues. Harney surprised everyone, including her party colleagues, by requesting a move to the Department of Health. Her move away from Enterprise, combined with McCreevy's move to Brussels, meant that the PDs' view of economic policy was severely weakened within the Government. Séamus Brennan, another minister who was seen as having liberal economic views, was moved from Transport to Social Welfare. The move came only after two terse meetings between him and Ahern, during one of which Ahern said he might be moved from the Government altogether. Brennan managed to argue himself back into the Government, but not into an economic portfolio.

The new Government was Mary Harney (Tánaiste and Health and Children), Brian Cowen (Finance), Dermot Ahern (Foreign Affairs), Séamus Brennan (Social and Family Affairs), Micheál Martin (Enterprise, Trade and Employment), Mary Coughlan (Agriculture, Fisheries and Food), Michael McDowell (Justice, Equality and Law Reform), Mary Hanafin (Education and Science), John O'Donoghue (Arts, Sport and Tourism), Éamon Ó Cuív (Community, Rural and Gaeltacht Affairs), Willie O'Dea (Defence), Noel Dempsey (Communications, Marine and Natural Resources), Martin Cullen (Transport) and Dick Roche (Environment, Heritage and Local Government).

The absence of McCreevy from the Government table meant that Ahern could now assume control of his Government in a way he hadn't done before. The revival in economic growth from 2004 resulted in funds beginning to flow with force into the exchequer again, giving the Government the scope to authorise spending on increased employment and pay rates in the public service, as well as increases on a range of transfer payments. Once again, public expenditure was shooting up as Ahern set his sights on the next general election.

Martin, who was moved to Enterprise, Trade and Employment from Health, thinks Ahern took greater charge of his Government after the 2004 election. 'Seán Healy coming to Inchydoney and so on, and a social welfare focus in the budgets going into the election. That government consolidated things.'

Healy was a priest and leading light in the Conference of Religious of Ireland, who had throughout the boom years been a constant critic of the Government and of the effect of its policies on the distribution of income. Ahern invited him to address a gathering of the Fianna Fáil parliamentary party in Inchydoney in west Cork in the first week of September 2004, in an effort to alter the public's impression of Fianna Fáil as 'right wing' or uncaring. Healy's high-profile address called on the Government to focus more on the poor, who had been left behind despite the commendable economic growth of the previous decade. Ahern went for a walk on the beach with his jacket strung over his shoulder, accompanied by his new Minister for Finance and Minister for Education, Mary Hanafin, who walked barefoot, her sandals dangling from one hand. The relaxed trio were surrounded by a scrum of excited camera crews from the national media.

Reporters noted that McCreevy didn't attend Healy's address. They also noted that McCreevy, while up to then widely praised as an architect of the low-tax, high-growth Ireland, was now being spoken of within the party as the Minister for Finance who had failed to consult his party colleagues—or at times even his Taoiseach—before introducing the sort of policies that had led Fianna Fáil to the disaster that was the 2004 election. Ahern, in his memoirs, said it bothered him a great deal at the time that the party was seen as 'Thatcherite' and uncaring.

Before his move from Health, Martin oversaw the introduction of the world's first nationwide ban on smoking in the work-place. Ahern was noted for his view that decisions with a capacity to annoy someone, somewhere were best avoided. He was nervous about a measure that was heavily opposed by some—including the powerful publicans' lobby—and Martin was unsure about exactly what Ahern's stance on the matter was. According to Martin, Ahern would often keep his own views secret, and at times he even confused the Government as to what his real views on a matter were.

> You had to decode Bertie. John O'Donoghue told me that, way back. You never quite knew where he was at some times on a particular issue. There were some issues, not all issues, where he allowed the debate go around the cabinet, and I'd say it's plausible he would have started off with a proposition and ended up with a position he was quite comfortable with at the end of the day. He was quite a cunning politician.
>
> I was always trying to work out where he was on the smoking ban. He was always supportive of me in public and in the Cabinet. He never let the side down in Cabinet in front of other ministers, and he was brilliant when the Galway guy rebelled against it. So you were always wondering. I remember the day I announced it, he was downstairs to me afterwards. 'What are you doing? What are you doing?' He thought I was doing it immediately. Obviously some of the guys had got to him. I said, 'I'm doing it in twelve months' time,' and he said, 'Ah,' and you could see the relief, thinking obviously we could modify that by the time twelve months came.

According to Ahern himself in the 'Bertie' documentary, he would sometimes deliberately mislead his Government colleagues about what his position was on a certain subject in order to see what views they would express.

The makeover of the party's image after the 2004 election was dubbed a success by Mark Brennock in his end-of-year political review in the *Irish Times*. The new caring image had replaced the hard 'right-wing' image, with the shift being in part assisted by Brennock's own interview with Ahern, published in the paper in the period after Inchydoney. During that interview Brennock remarked on Ahern's apparent lack of interest in accumulating personal wealth, and the Taoiseach responded:

I don't. People might not believe this, but I have a very socialist view on life. I have it in my mind that I own the Phoenix Park. I own the Botanical Gardens. I own Dublin Zoo. And I don't feel I need to own any of these things. They are there. I don't feel I need to own a huge house with a huge glasshouse when I can go down the road ten minutes and do it [visit the Botanical Gardens]. It's just the way I think about things. What is the best form of equality? It's the fact that the richest family in this area can go on a Sunday afternoon to the Bots, and the poorest family can too. They can both share the same things.

According to Martin, it was in about 2004 that Ahern's attitude towards his role changed.

Bertie would have a few pints with his ministers two or three times a year. At Christmas and so on. But he did that less in the latter years. I think he got more presidential in the second half. I think some of his advisers said, Get more like Clinton, and I think that was a mistake. His first seven years he was more engaged with ministers, and I think he did better because of that.

Meanwhile, the planning tribunal was continuing with its confidential inquiries into allegations that concerned Ahern. From comments made during its proceedings it appears that as far back as 1999 the Luton-based Irish property developer Thomas Gilmartin had told it about allegations involving Ahern. Gilmartin said he had been told by the Cork developer Owen O'Callaghan that O'Callaghan had made payments to Ahern. It is not clear when exactly Ahern first found out what was going on, but on 15 October 2004 the tribunal wrote to tell him of Gilmartin's allegation that he had been told by O'Callaghan of two payments, one of £30,000 and one of £50,000. Ahern was being represented by Liam Guidera of Frank Ward and Company, the law firm that acted for Fianna Fáil. Guidera wrote back on Ahern's behalf and asked when the payments were supposed to have been made. On November 2004 the tribunal informed Ahern that Gilmartin said that he recalled O'Callaghan telling him in or around 1992 that he had given £50,000 to Ahern in 1989, and that the £30,000 was supposed to have been paid over between January 1989 and December 1992. Ahern was also told in

April 2005 that a claim had been made to the tribunal that he had received a cut of a €150,000 payment that O'Callaghan had made to Albert Reynolds. This payment related to tax designation being assigned to a site O'Callaghan owned at Golden Island, Athlone. The assignment of tax designation to the site was one of Ahern's last acts, if not his last, as Minister for Finance in the Reynolds Government. All the parties involved in these claims denied that any of the payments had ever been made.

This highly confidential correspondence between Ahern's solicitors and the tribunal that his Government had established was the beginning of a cat-and-mouse game for very high stakes which would ultimately bring Ahern's political career to a premature end. Its effect on his performance as Taoiseach during the period can only be imagined.

The issue of the tribunal and payments to Ahern involved a very bizarre prologue. The then *Sunday Business Post* journalist Frank Connolly was contacted in his office one day in 2000 by a Cork businessman and property dealer, Denis 'Starry' O'Brien. O'Brien claimed that he had handed over cash to Ahern in a Dublin car park after a major sporting fixture and that he had been acting for O'Callaghan. Ahern was Minister for Labour at the time of the alleged payment. Connolly did not know O'Brien, but the Corkman produced documents supposedly showing the money being lodged, and then withdrawn, from an Irish Nationwide account. Connolly eventually wrote a story saying that an alleged payment to a senior figure in Fianna Fáil was being investigated by the planning tribunal. The story was published on Easter Sunday, 2000.

Ahern had been contacted by the tribunal and told that O'Brien was claiming that Ahern had been given £50,000 by him in or around September 1989 and that the payment was on behalf of O'Callaghan. Ahern, in response, swore an affidavit in which he said that no such payment had been made. The tribunal in time dropped the matter.

On the day Connolly's story was published, Ahern was at the Fianna Fáil commemoration at Wolfe Tone's grave in Bodenstown, Co. Kildare, and was very exercised about the issue. Katie Hannon, a political reporter with the *Irish Examiner*, wrote a report on the matter for the following Monday's edition. She identified Ahern as the person being referred to, having been urged by a senior figure in Fianna Fáil to do so. She was assured that there would be no comeback—in the form of a libel action—against her or her newspaper if she named Ahern.

Ahern sued O'Brien in the Circuit Court. He did not sue the *Sunday Business Post*. The case went ahead despite O'Brien withdrawing his defence, and a number of witnesses were called who dismissed O'Brien's claim. The judge said the allegation against Ahern was 'utterly, completely and absolutely false and untrue.' Ahern was awarded £30,000 in damages—the maximum that could then be awarded by the Circuit Court—and his costs. But six years later it was reported that he had collected neither. In the wake of that report, Ahern's solicitors instructed the City Sheriff in Cork to collect the debt. The request was made only two days before the expiry of the six-year deadline.

The fact of the case was frequently referred to in the coming years by Ahern and his legal representatives, who said inadequate weight was given by the tribunal to the fact that it was obvious that some people were involved in a deliberate and malicious campaign to damage Ahern. The case also had the effect of dampening media interest in any rumours about payments to Ahern out of fear that they might again be sold a pup. What was motivating O'Brien in all this has never been disclosed.

One allegation that Gilmartin made concerning Ahern involved Joe Burke. According to this claim, Gilmartin had gone to Ahern in the late 1980s because he believed Ahern might help him. He was encountering difficulties in advancing his Quarryvale project because of the corruption of the Assistant City and County Manager, George Redmond, and Liam Lawlor TD. Ahern appears to have asked Burke, then a city councillor, to get in contact with Gilmartin. There is no dispute over the fact that Burke and Gilmartin met to discuss Gilmartin's difficulties in acquiring some county council land that was important to his Quarryvale project. Gilmartin, however, claimed that Burke asked him for €500,000, something Burke rejected as untrue. Ahern said he could not recall the conversation that he had had with Gilmartin; but he accepted the suggestion by the tribunal counsel Des O'Neill SC that he would have remembered it if Gilmartin had told him that the Assistant City and Council Manager, and one of his party colleagues, was 'on the take'. O'Neill said that Gilmartin had at about this time reported the matter to a number of others, including the Gardaí, and that it was implausible to suggest that he would not have mentioned the matter to Ahern. Ahern did not agree.

The planning tribunal organised itself into modules, each of which began with an opening statement outlining what the tribunal would be inquiring into. In November 2005 the opening statement of the Quarryvale module was made, and it included the allegations against Ahern; but they did not get much traction in the media, in part because similar allegations had been aired in the O'Brien article and had been shown to be mischievous.

Behind the scenes, the confidential correspondence between the tribunal and Ahern was failing to settle the tribunal's concerns. Ahern supplied a detailed statement in November 2004 in which he rejected the claims made against him.

It was standard practice for the tribunal to make orders of discovery against people whose affairs it was investigating, and in 2004 there was correspondence between Guidera and the tribunal regarding the scope of any such order. The tribunal wanted to examine Ahern's bank accounts to see if there were unexplained lodgements. If he could, in private, explain his finances, the tribunal would be inclined to let the Gilmartin allegations drop.

In November 2004 Guidera, on behalf of Ahern, suggested that the order covering bank accounts that had held money for Ahern be limited to the period 1 January 1989 to 31 December 1992—the period during which the O'Callaghan payments to Ahern were alleged to have been made. Guidera also suggested that discovery be limited to lodgements of £30,000 and more.

Later that month the tribunal issued an order that sought the identification, but not the production, of documents. The period covered by the order was January 1988 to December 1995, and it would in the first instance cover only lodgements that exceeded £30,000. The documents were to be produced by 11 January 2006. Ahern later agreed with tribunal counsel that, had his solicitor's request with regard to the period to be covered been agreed to, the order would not have captured most of the transactions that Ahern subsequently found difficult to explain.

He was asked about the matter by tribunal barrister Des O'Neill when he began to give evidence on 13 September 2007.

O'Neill: Now of course in hindsight, when we look at the submissions which were being made at that time, Mr Ahern, none of the matters which are the subject of our current inquiry today would have been caught by an order had it been limited to the period initially proposed by your solicitor, that is from January 1 1989 to December 31, 1992? Isn't that right?

Ahern: Yes.

O'Neill: And the reason for that, in the main, was that whilst these orders were directed towards accounts of yours, you in fact had no bank account that you were operating in your own name during that period. Isn't that right?

Ahern: Correct.

In February 2005 Ahern supplied an affidavit in response to the order of discovery. His solicitor said it was plain that there were no lodgements of £30,000 or £50,000. Ahern had no tax liability and had not availed of the 1993 tax amnesty, the tribunal was told. The solicitor's letter said that in early 1987 Ahern had separated from his wife and that from that period up to the end of 1993 he 'did not operate any bank account.' During the period 'each of his salary cheques was cashed either by himself or by one of his staff.' The letter also said: 'I am also instructed that in December 1994 our client transferred funds from his accounts at AIB Upper O'Connell Street, into the account of his then partner, Celia Larkin.' This sentence would later get Ahern into trouble. He had been instructed to inform the tribunal of every account into which money had been lodged to his benefit. The money that went to the Larkin account was money being held for his benefit. It hadn't been given to Larkin: it was still Ahern's. Yet he had not included it in the list of accounts that held funds for his benefit. Ahern subsequently told the tribunal that the transaction related to the renovation of his house in Beresford Avenue. If Ahern had listed this account, the tribunal's work would have proceeded more quickly than it did, as the account would in turn have led the tribunal to transactions concerning Beresford Avenue as well as to the alleged arrangement with Michael Wall concerning the house.

The first discovery did not include a lot of other transactions that Ahern later found difficult to explain, because they were for amounts of less than £30,000. In February 2005 the tribunal extended it to cover all amounts, giving Ahern until March to comply with the order.

In the main, Ahern was receiving the banking documents covered by the order a few days before the tribunal did. In March the tribunal decided to begin seeking not only bank statements that would have been issued to Ahern but also internal bank documents from its archives. In June 2005 Ahern provided the authority to the tribunal to do so. It would later emerge that two of the transactions being inquired into at this stage—from a total of sixty-six—involved foreign currency: lodgements of £24,838.49 and £19,142.92 in the O'Connell Street branch of the AIB. The bank provided the result of its searches to Ahern and the tribunal in October 2005. On 25 October the tribunal wrote again to the Taoiseach, by way of Guidera, this time asking questions about the source of identified lodgements and the purpose of certain withdrawals, as well as about some general questions, such as whether or not Ahern had sold any assets during the period at issue or if he had any other sources of income. The tribunal had no power to force Ahern to respond to its written questions, though it could, if he failed to respond, issue a summons for him to appear in public and put the questions to him in the witness box. The tribunal pointed out that if the matter could be resolved by way of private correspondence this would be in everyone's interest. No doubt by this time, if not since as far back as the late 1990s, Ahern knew he was dealing with a situation that had the potential to bring his political career to a sudden end.

The tribunal asked that Ahern respond by the end of November 2005. However, the end of the year came and went without the tribunal hearing from him. On 3 March 2006 the tribunal wrote to Ahern's solicitor saying it was anxious to conclude the information-gathering process, drawing attention to the correspondence that had already been exchanged and to Ahern's failure to respond to the letter of 25 October 2005. The tribunal solicitor, Susan Gilvarry, said a reply was now being sought by 24 March 2006. She asked Ahern to give priority to certain queries, listing five. They included questions concerning the two lodgements that the tribunal would eventually learn included foreign exchange. They also included cash lodgements.

On 7 March 2006 Guidera was informed that the tribunal intended to make orders of discovery against AIB in relation to Ahern's affairs. Ahern was asked the names of persons who were authorised to make lodgements on his behalf to AIB during the period 1991–8, as well as of those in AIB with whom he dealt. Furthermore the tribunal asked for Ahern's authority to allow it interview the bank officials who dealt with his affairs. They asked that the authority be returned within nine days. In late March 2006 Ahern supplied four books of documents in response to the order of October 2005.

Guidera asked the tribunal a number of questions, including what allegations exactly formed the basis for the request for Ahern's voluntary co-operation. 'The tribunal is engaged in a number of inquiries in which the payment of any money to your client could be of relevance,' it answered. 'The tribunal has decided to conduct public inquiries into tax designation, not limited to matters involving Mr O'Callaghan, and in this context payments received by your client which may be referable to the period during which he served as Minister for Finance may be inquired into.'

The tribunal expressed its concern that Ahern had still not furnished the information sought about the lodgements to his accounts, and it pointed out that what had been provided gave no information as to the source of the cash known to have been lodged. The letter of 30 March pointed out that the five cash lodgements that Ahern had been asked to give priority to totalled £108,981.41 and were made in the period December 1993 to December 1995, when Ahern was Minister for Finance.

Gilvarry told Guidera that his client had until 21 April 2006 to provide the information.

> I am to inform you that in the event that the tribunal does not receive the information requested by that date it will consider issuing a summons directed to your client requiring him to attend at a public session of the tribunal which will be listed to take place not earlier than Tuesday 2nd May 2006. At such hearing your client will be questioned in relation to the already mentioned five cash lodgements.

In political terms, the tribunal was threatening Ahern with a move that could in one fell swoop destroy the public image he had so successfully created over the previous decades.

On 6 April, Guidera told the tribunal that Ahern's lodgements were mostly made by Ahern himself or by his secretaries, Gráinne Carruth and Sandra Cullagh. Ahern identified, and gave the tribunal permission to speak to, the bank officials he sometimes dealt with.

When the deadline set by the tribunal for answers about the sources of certain lodgements and about the reasons for certain withdrawals arrived, Ahern supplied a document drafted by an accountant, Des Peelo. Peelo was a long-time friend of Charles Haughey who had featured in the Moriarty Tribunal. The Peelo document was dated the day before its receipt by the tribunal.

As O'Neill later put it to Ahern, 'the tribunal had invited your response; what it received was the response of Mr Peelo. Isn't that right?' Ahern replied, 'That's correct.' Peelo only had the documents that were already available to Ahern, as well as the information Ahern had given him orally.

In the document, Ahern said for the first time that he had been given sterling in cash after a dinner in Manchester. He said it was lodged along with £16,500 (Irish pounds) in cash that he had been given by four friends. They were Paddy Reilly (Paddy the Plasterer), £3,500; Joe Burke, £3,500; Barry English, £5,000; and Dermot Carew, £4,500. 'All of the above persons are personal friends of Mr Ahern. The amounts were entirely unsolicited and represented a goodwill loan from friends towards the building up of Mr Ahern's personal finances re possible purchase of a house.' The report said Ahern had lodged the money.

The document noted another goodwill loan in which Ahern received £22,500 from Paddy Reilly, Des Richardson, Padraic O'Connor, Jim Nugent, David McKenna and Fintan Gunne. It also revealed that Ahern had no bank account in the period from 1989, when he settled his separation agreement with his wife, to late 1993, when he began to lodge funds with AIB, O'Connell Street. By this time, the tribunal was told, Ahern had accumulated £50,000 in cash in safes in the Department of Finance and St Luke's.

Another lodgement that featured in the document—£19,142.92 to an account with AIB, O'Connell Street—had a complicated and tortuous explanation. Ahern had given money to Larkin, who had lodged it and then withdrawn it and had used some of it on the Beresford Avenue house before returning the remainder to Ahern, who then lodged it to the account. What the report failed to reveal was that the lodgement had been exactly £20,000 sterling in cash, which was exchanged in the bank for Irish pounds before being lodged. Ahern was later asked about this at the tribunal. He said:

> While I suspected that might have been either fully or partially sterling, when I had checked with the banks and tried to get the details behind that to clarify that, they had given me the information in Irish pounds. It was their view that it wasn't sterling.

Ahern was also later to agree that the Peelo document was not comprehensive and did not answer all the questions he had been asked. He accepted that he had known since October 2005 that there was a series of transactions in his accounts that would have to be explained before the tribunal would be able to rule out his having received the payments that Gilmartin had alleged.

While the Peelo document contained information on particular lodgements and transactions that the tribunal had wished to be given priority, the tribunal was still seeking responses to its original long list of queries. This information was supplied on 7 June 2006. Ahern's payments as a TD and those as a member of the Government came in different cheques: one was posted to him at home and the other to his office in Government Buildings. The lodgements being inquired into included a number of round-figure amounts. Ahern said the lodgements all came from his income as a politician. In some cases they were lodgements of two or more cheques; in other cases, the round-figure ones, they were the result of cheques being cashed and round-figure amounts being lodged. Not one lodgement was for an amount exactly the same as an individual cheque issued to Ahern. In a letter of August 2006 it was made clear that the inquiry into Ahern's finances still had a number of motivations.

Bank statements of your client show lodgements which are in excess of your client's gross salary at that time. The tribunal believes that this issue requires to be resolved in the context of its inquiry into tax designations during the period in which Mr Ahern served as Minister for Finance.

The letter also pointed out that the sum of the lodgements dealt with in the Peelo document—£97,338.49—exceeded Ahern's salary for the period, which was 'approximately £42,000 per annum gross.'

Meanwhile, as a result of the narrative in the Peelo document concerning the Beresford Avenue house and Larkin's dealings with AIB, O'Connell Street—as well as the goodwill loans from an identified list of people, most of whom were still alive—the tribunal's inquiry was spreading. All these highly confidential dealings with the tribunal were taking place during a period when Ahern's image as an international statesman was continuing to grow.

There were extended and difficult negotiations in the wake of the Belfast Agreement about policing, decommissioning and other matters. They involved Ahern continuing to work closely with Blair and also with the White House. As if that wasn't enough, on January 2004 Ireland took over the Presidency of the European Union. The EU, in the wake of the collapse of the Soviet Union and the unrest in the Balkans, was expanding to the east, bringing in tens of millions of new citizens from ten new member-states. This unenvisaged expansion led to the need for a reformed institutional framework. As Ahern took on his new role, the efforts to agree a constitution for the EU under Silvio Berlusconi were seen as having been unsuccessful, and few had an expectation that there would be any change now that the European leadership had shifted to Dublin. They hadn't reckoned with Ahern's negotiating ability, patience and drive.

He decided to mark the entry of the ten new states on 1 May 2004 in a special way. It was the largest expansion of population and territory in the EU's history, and many of the states that were joining had spent the previous decades under the yoke of Soviet control. Ireland and Britain were exceptional in their approach to the enlargement in that they opened their borders immediately to workers who wished to travel from the new member-states. Multinational companies that had set up in Ireland had been complaining for years about the difficulty of finding employees—something that had led Mary Harney, as Minister for Enterprise, Trade and Employment, and others to begin a programme of trying to lure workers to Ireland. The campaign began by urging Irish emigrants to return, then identifying members of the wider Irish diaspora and, lastly, seeking out non-Irish skilled workers throughout Europe and farther afield. Lavish expenditure during this period by FÁS, which was spearheading the effort, would later be the cause of political scandal. FÁS ran a Jobs Ireland campaign during the period 1998–2002 that included targeted advertisements in foreign media, as well as a roadshow that visited, among other cities, London, Brussels, Cologne, Hamburg, Hannover, Prague, Moscow and Mumbai. Cities in Canada, Britain, Australia, New Zealand and the United States were targeted.

Not all the workers who moved to Ireland, some with families, were returned emigrants or persons of Irish descent, and, in a significant change of policy, the state began to issue thousands of work permits. The downturn that hit the Irish and global economies in 2002 lessened the demand for workers from abroad, but the enlargement of the EU occurred as the Irish economy returned to growth, and it meant that a population of tens of millions of potential workers was now available to feed the once-again growing demand for labour. The number of young people leaving countries such as Lithuania and Poland for Ireland became a political issue in those countries. *The Mushroom Covenant*, a book by Laima Muktupāvela, a Latvian mother of four, became a best-seller in her home country. In it she wrote about her experience of working long hours on a mushroom farm in Co. Meath and sharing a three-bedroom house with eleven other Latvians. 'There is hardly a family left in this country who hasn't lost a son or daughter or mother or father to the mushroom farms of Ireland,' she told the *International Herald Tribune* when it carried a report on the phenomenon in 2005. 'During the Cold War we all dreamed of leaving but the risk is that if everyone leaves, our country will disappear.'

According to Micheál Martin, the contribution made by the growth in population to the overheating of the Irish economy has yet to be analysed.

It was Bertie who signed the 2004 agreement [on the accession countries] because at that time it made sense economically: all the multinationals were saying we don't have the skills sets. The IDA [Industrial Development Authority] too. Most multinationals would have said to us at the time, 'Where are you going to get the skills sets?' And we would say, 'Actually, our skill base now is Europe. We have access to here, there and the other.'

I was Minister for Health, and the effect was dramatic, not just on maternity hospitals but on accident and emergency services. And the demand on infrastructure, housing. It was part of the boom in housing. You were employing Lithuanians and Poles to build houses that were rented to Lithuanians and Poles who were coming in, and so it was a sort of circular thing.

I remember discussing the Green Card thing with Bruce Morrison [American senator], and he said he could not think of any country in the world, ever, that had such a volume of inward migration in such a short period of time—that it was the largest ever, per capita. After 2004 people did not expect the volume that came subsequently, but it was kind of virtuous at the time. There was full employment, virtually, even with all the numbers coming in, and the argument was coming from the Dells and the Hewlett Packards that they needed these people, to keep the expansion going.

I don't think the effect on expenditure on health and education was ever quantified in any systemic way. I'm not saying it has been a negative impact. I think in the longer term it will have a beneficial impact—even in the short term it had a good impact—but I think it did have an impact on the boom thing, on the bubble economy. Because remember we went from about a million people at work fourteen years ago to maybe 2.1 million. I remember telling international audiences this, and they thought it was absolutely incredible.

Ireland held the Presidency of the EU, and the expansion ceremony was held in Áras an Uachtaráin, with the heads of state from the existing and new states all in attendance, their flags flying, a choir singing the chorus from Beethoven's Ninth Symphony, the hugely popular Taoiseach Bertie Ahern playing host. The fact that Ireland was immediately welcoming in workers from the new member-states added to the positive atmosphere.

But it was Ahern's work on the negotiation of a constitution for the European Union that really made his mark on the EU stage. He threw himself into the project. He created a team of Irish civil servants and advisers and began to work the European capitals. His Minister for Foreign Affairs, Brian Cowen, and his Minister of State for European Affairs, Dick Roche, were the key politicians involved. It was an exceptional period in Ahern's political career in that his focus shifted to outside Ireland. At an intergovernmental conference in Brussels at the end of June he worked in the same way that he had in Castle Buildings in Belfast when persuading the parties to agree the Belfast Agreement. Issues and objections were dealt with one after the other with patience and determination, as Ahern moved the wide range of parties closer and closer to a deal to which they could not object. By the end of the meeting, and to most people's surprise, a final document was agreed. It was an enormous coup for the Irish presidency and for Ahern. When he got back to Dublin he gave an interview to Charlie Bird of RTE, selecting All Hallows as the location.

One of the matters the leaders had not been able to agree on was who the next president of the European Commission would be. Ahern was by this time the second most experienced prime minister on the EU stage—only Jean-Claude Juncker of Luxembourg had been in power for a longer period —and his achievement in relation to the constitution increased his status hugely. In his memoirs he said that it was at this time that other leaders began to suggest that he should become president of the Commission. He weighed up the matter and in the end decided against it because of his dislike of being abroad, his view of the job itself and his desire to challenge the record of the founder of Fianna Fáil, Éamon de Valera, and go to a third successful election in a row.

In June 2004 Ahern also met the President of the United States, George W. Bush, in Dromoland Castle for an EU-US summit in which they discussed items of geopolitical importance. During his presidency Ahern attended summits with the governments of Japan, Canada, Russia and some Latin American and Caribbean states. He also attended a G8 summit on an island off the coast of the American state of Georgia, where, much as he would later do in Inchydoney, he went for a 'relaxed' walk on the beach with the heads of state of the major powers, surrounded by a mob of photographers and television cameras. The picture of Ahern wearing a cream jacket and banana-yellow trousers among the other more sober-suited world leaders became one of his best-known images at home. It contributed to the view of Ahern as a politician who had become an international statesman while remaining the same old familiar, slightly hapless Bertie. Many surmised that this was precisely the impression he had aimed to create.

As the world economy picked up again, Irish property prices soared, and media reports about individual Irish investors or groups of investors buying iconic commercial buildings in London and elsewhere became a staple. Foreign observers began to refer to Irish property developers as oligarchs, a reference to the billionaire business figures who made so much money in post-Soviet Russia. Helicopters became a common form of transport for many of them as they rushed around Ireland and over and back to Britain, checking on their business projects. There were even reports of people being invited to children's parties with co-ordinates being included on the invitations for those who would be arriving by helicopter. When the property developer Seán Dunne married the journalist Gayle Killilea they hosted an extended celebration on the *Christina O*, the former yacht of the Greek shipping magnate Aristotle Onassis. The yacht was by this time actually owned by an Irish syndicate, which had used a complicated tax structure that sheltered some of their income from Irish tax.

The rebound in the economy in the period after 2003 meant that Ahern was back dealing with the problems of expansion rather than contraction. An enormous National Development Plan was announced for modernising and expanding the state's infrastructure so that it would be better able to cope with a bigger economy and a larger population.

Brian Cowen, in his period as Minister for Finance, presided over budgets that tried to cope with the demands for transfer payments, the pressures on parents who had to pay for child care, and concerns about the management of the property market. In his first budget speech in December 2004 Cowen said he aimed to ensure that the benefits of economic growth 'permeate society as a whole.' He increased personal income tax credits while leaving rates alone, which meant that more lower-paid workers found themselves not being taxed at all. 'More than 650,000 of the 1.9 million income earners will be exempt from paying tax on their earnings,' he told the Dáil. He also widened the standard rate band so that fewer middle-income earners would find themselves paying tax at the higher rate.

In the weeks before the budget, and for some time previously, there had been media stories running about the number of very-high-income individuals who had reduced their effective income tax rate to low levels, and in some cases to nil, through the aggressive use of the tax reliefs that were available. Joan Burton had elicited figures from the Department of Finance that caused quite a scandal. Eleven people who had earned more than €1 million had paid no tax at all in 2001, while an astonishing 242 people who earned between €100,000 and €1 million during 2001 had paid no tax. Many of the measures that facilitated this tax avoidance, such as the urban renewal and hotel investment schemes, were themselves contributing to the buoyant property market that was such a feature of the period. In his budget speech Cowen noted that the Revenue Commissioners had recently estimated that the annual cost of these more controversial reliefs was in the region of €200 million per year.

Because of the complex nature of this issue, the interaction of such reliefs with economic activity and the unintended consequences that untimely action may have for investment, I want to take the time necessary to strike a careful and considered balance in what I do.

Cowen said he had decided to ask his department to study the issue with the Revenue Commissioners and come up with proposals that struck a proper balance between the needs of the investor and the well-being of the community.

> I am now making it clear that I intend to include appropriate follow-up measures in next year's budget. Those using this particular group of reliefs should therefore realise that the concept of unlimited or unrestricted reliefs is no longer viable or acceptable to the general tax-paying public in current-day economic circumstances. I want to ensure that everyone makes an appropriate contribution to the state.

Nine property-based reliefs were already due to be abolished in July 2006, having been given a stay of execution in McCreevy's final budget, and the termination date for these schemes remained in place. However, the strategy adopted had an unforeseen consequence in that it acted as an incentive to those contemplating such investments to hurry on with them. Local authorities around the country were being flooded with planning applications for hotels, multi-storey car parks and other developments that qualified under existing tax schemes.

Ahern, speaking on RTE radio about the budget, said 'the game is up' for rich people who used tax schemes to significantly lower their tax bills, echoing a claim he had made at the time of McCreevy's first budget six years earlier.

Cowen returned to the subject with his second budget. There were 'more than 250,000 jobs in the construction sector, and the building industry accounts for approximately 20 per cent of the economy.' It was a percentage that was well out of line with the historical and international average. 'We should not do anything that disrupts unnecessarily an industry that is such an important driver of jobs,' he said.

He announced that a number of schemes were being terminated, 'subject to certain transitional provisions': the urban renewal, town renewal and rural renewal schemes and the special reliefs for hotels, holiday cottages, student accommodation, multi-storey car parks, third-level educational buildings, sports-injuries clinics, developments associated with park-and-ride facilities and the general rental refurbishment scheme. The transitional provisions for projects already in the pipeline gave an additional five months of 100 per cent relief on expenditure on approved projects, bringing the scheme forward to the end of 2006. A sliding scale of relief levels then covered the period of the following two years. He said that the design chosen for transitional measures was half way between the two schemes suggested by two sets of consultants who had examined the matter. He also retained some reliefs, including those applying to nursing homes, child-care facilities and private hospitals.

However, Cowen introduced a minimum rate of income tax. By reducing the amount of income that could qualify for certain tax reliefs, he in effect introduced a minimum rate of 20 per cent on those with high incomes. 'This phenomenon will help eliminate the phenomenon of tax-free millionaires.' Interestingly, Cowen's department, Finance, had been wary of introducing a minimum rate of tax for fear that those high-net-worth individuals who availed of tax schemes would consider it a target to be achieved by their accountants.

In this budget Cowen introduced a cap on the size of personal pension funds that could be built up by the wealthy while they availed of the income tax relief that accompanies pension contributions. People who owned their own companies in particular were paying themselves huge amounts of income, as pension payments, into their personal approved pension funds and so misusing a measure aimed at encouraging provision for pensions. Cowen's move had been well flagged, and the financial accounts for such companies, as they were filed in the months following the budget, showed large amounts of money being paid to owner-directors by way of pension contributions, with these payments having been made before the budget cap. In time it would emerge that many rich people used their approved retirement funds to invest in property, using the fund as an equity investment and borrowing the bulk of the price they paid for their office or retail building. When the crash came, they ended up with personal retirement funds that were in negative equity.

The consultants' reports into the tax relief schemes were published in February 2006. A review by Goodbodys for the Department of Finance concluded that a relatively small group of high-income individuals had avoided approximately €3 billion in tax over recent years through the use of Government-promoted relief schemes. Pride of place went to the urban renewal schemes, which the department now estimated had cost something in the region of €1.43 billion in tax forgone. During the more recent boom years the scheme had benefited the developers of projects that would have been built anyway, yet the tax breaks involved could represent up to 43 per cent of the value of the projects concerned. As the consultants put it, the measures had 'strong negative distributional effects', could no longer be justified and were an expensive way of achieving the objectives for which they were designed. Incredibly, the scheme, just like all the others reviewed, had been established without any cost-benefit study being conducted. In their report on a number of property-based schemes, Indecon consultants recommended that schemes promoting investment in private hospitals, nursing homes and child-care facilities should be continued, even though they would cost the exchequer an estimated €850 million in taxes forgone over the coming years.

As well as the cost of €3 billion to the state of the various property-associated relief schemes, an additional €1.4 billion in taxes was lost to the exchequer in 2001 alone as a result of the relief from taxes of pension payments. While such benefits were widely spread, some very high-net-worth individuals were using the relief to shelter huge amounts of income. The report cited two unidentified individuals with seven-figure incomes who had built up personal retirement funds of €100 million each.

While Cowen implemented many of the report's recommendations, opposition politicians criticised him for allowing the extension of existing schemes without their being subjected to a rigorous cost-benefit analysis. 'This is a key recommendation,' Richard Bruton said in response to Cowen's reaction to the report. 'It is regrettable that Minister Cowen chose not to implement this recommendation. Tax relief is a very blunt instrument for achieving social or economic objectives.'

Joan Burton, the Labour Party's finance spokesperson, pointed out that people with pension funds of €100 million were able to draw down a quarter of that amount upon retirement, entirely tax-free.

> It seems from this report that the beneficiaries of property-based tax schemes, such as builders and developers, not alone avoid paying tax as a consequence of schemes such as park-and-ride and private car parks, but as retirement approaches they have ready-made channels for setting up extraordinarily lucrative pension schemes funded by even more tax breaks by the state.

By the time of Cowen's third budget speech in December 2006, economic growth was running at 5 per cent, and the number of people employed exceeded two million. Ireland's unemployment and inflation rates were among the lowest in the EU, and the Government expected growth of 5¼ per cent during 2007, when more than seventy thousand new jobs were expected to be created. An unprecedented level of infrastructural investment was being made, the public services were being expanded and there were more gardaí, doctors, nurses and teachers employed than ever before.

Again, there were no cuts in income tax rates, but increases in tax credits and the standard rate band were announced. These changes meant that 'two out of almost every five earners will be outside the tax net in 2007, compared to one-third in 2004 and one-quarter when we took office in 1997.'

By the time Cowen had introduced his third budget, the *Irish Times* had broken the story about the Mahon Tribunal's inquiries into Ahern's personal finances, and the Government had been through one of the most difficult and intense political crises of his period as Taoiseach. The strength of the economy and the belief of many that it was Ahern's Governments that had delivered this level of prosperity were key factors in his ability to survive the huge controversy. He was an enormously popular political figure, and his Government was riding the crest of an economic wave.

However, the disclosure, and Ahern's interview with Bryan Dobson on RTE's television news, had used up much of Ahern's political capital and meant that he had indirectly supplied answers to the tribunal earlier than he would otherwise have done.

Following on from the Peelo document given in confidence to the tribunal in April 2006, a wider number of people were drawn into the developing inquiry. The tribunal was considering whether there were foreign-currency aspects to some of the lodgements it was examining. Celia Larkin, in her private interview with the tribunal's legal team, confirmed that she had been given £50,000 in December 1994 for use in the fitting out of the Beresford Avenue house, but she revealed that she had handed the money back to Ahern, in cash, the following month. The tribunal had also discovered another AIB account in Larkin's name into which £28,772.90 had been lodged in December 1994. It began asking about this money. In time it would learn that this was cash—mostly sterling, according to Ahern—that had been given to him in a briefcase on a Saturday afternoon when he had been fully expecting to form his first Government, with the Labour Party, the following week.

Guidera was busy answering questions on his client's behalf. In early February 2007—election year—he told the tribunal that the £50,000 had been sought back from Larkin when 'it became more apparent to Mr Ahern at around this time that it would be more convenient for the monies to be held in cash.' The cash had been held in Ahern's safe in St Luke's, the tribunal was told. On 2 March 2007 the tribunal again wrote to Guidera, informing him that it was 'of the opinion that the information so far provided via correspondence does not resolve the tribunal's inquiries as to the source of the following payments to Mr Ahern and subsequently lodged as set out hereunder or the purposes for which such payments were made to him.' Ahern was invited to meet the tribunal's legal team in private 'at the earliest possible opportunity suitable to him.'

On 5 April 2007 Ahern went to the offices of his solicitors, Frank Ward and Company, to be interviewed by the tribunal's legal team. A transcript of the interview was later leaked to a number of reporters, and its contents caused enormous controversy during the 2007 general election. In fact it is widely believed that Frank Connolly's reports in the *Mail on Sunday*, based on the transcripts, led directly to Ahern's panicked calling of that election.

When one reads the transcript it is obvious that Ahern was at times very uncomfortable. The tribunal lawyers revealed that they had compared some uneven amounts—lodgements of pounds and pence—with the exchange rates that had been in operation on the days of these lodgements. It emerged that a number of lodgements that Ahern had made had been in sterling—something he had not stated in the Peelo document or in other dealings with the tribunal. It also emerged that he was now saying that the £50,000 in cash that Larkin gave him in January 2005 had been used by him to buy £30,000 sterling, some of which was then later relodged to AIB, accounting for the sterling lodgements. It was a convoluted and bizarre story. Furthermore, the tribunal confronted him with its discovery that the lodgement made in October 1994—which Ahern said was £16,500 given to him by four friends, and sterling cash given to him in Manchester—equated with exactly £25,000 sterling, using the exchange rate of the day. Also, a lodgement by Larkin on 5 December 1994, which the tribunal had been told was sterling given to Ahern in cash by Michael Wall, did not convert into a round-figure sum of sterling; it did, however, convert into a round-figure dollar sum: $45,000. 'No way,' Ahern responded when this was put to him. He was emphatic about the matter, returning to it at the end of the interview to state again that he had not lodged dollars to his accounts.

The tribunal would later retrieve foreign-currency records from AIB that showed that only approximately £2,000 in sterling was exchanged in AIB, O'Connell Street, on the date Larkin supposedly lodged the Michael Wall cash. However, an unusually large amount of non-sterling foreign currency had been exchanged—enough to accommodate $45,000.

During his later examination in public sittings, O'Neill asked Ahern about inquiries Ahern had made of AIB during Chistmas 2004. Ahern had asked what information it had about a number of particular transactions, including the 'dig-out' lodgements and lodgements of cash. AIB documents show that he had at that point identified as meriting particular attention all the transactions that were to be highlighted by the tribunal twenty-seven months later, in the letter of March 2007, in which it suggested that Ahern should agree to a private interview.

All the transactions concerned were large cash transactions with which Ahern was personally involved, but they were for amounts of less than £30,000 and so would not have been covered by the restricted order of discovery that the tribunal was dealing with at that time (Christmas 2004). Ahern, it appeared, had isolated these transactions from all those through his accounts during the period at issue. It would, however, take the tribunal two years and three months to come to a position where it was concentrating on them. Ahern said he had focused on these cash payments because of their size and the fact that he had no documentary evidence to show where the money had come from; but O'Neill said this could not be the case, since there were other large cash transactions that he had not asked the bank about back in 2004.

O'Neill read into the record one internal AIB memo showing that Ahern had been looking for information about these cash lodgements on New Year's Eve 2004. O'Neill also displayed a bank memo, dated 3 February 2005, that recorded Ahern as looking for information about seven transactions on his accounts in 1993 and 1994. The transactions were ones that featured in the tribunal's letter of March 2007. The information Ahern had sought, and which was described in the memo of February 2005, had been collected for him by one of his secretaries, Sandra Cullagh, in January 2005 and brought to him. From that period on he had known that the bank's archives did not contain information that showed that the lodgements were foreign-currency transactions. At the same time Ahern had contacted Larkin, and she had in response sought whatever information the bank had in relation to transactions on accounts in her name that much later became the focus of the tribunal's public inquiries. Again, internal AIB memos documented what had occurred.

Although Ahern had asked Larkin in 2004–5 to obtain information from the bank, he had not disclosed her involvement in his banking affairs to the tribunal until the Peelo document was presented in April 2006. Nor had he listed these accounts when he had responded to the tribunal's original order of discovery. When Ahern appeared at public sittings, O'Neill asked him whether or not Larkin had supplied him with the documents she had been given by the bank in January 2005. Ahern said he didn't think so; he said he thought she had briefed him on what she had been given. It also emerged that it had not been until the tribunal had made an order of discovery against the bank that it learnt that it had much earlier given Ahern documents that had only later been discovered to the tribunal.

The pressure on Ahern as the general election neared, and as the tribunal was discovering more and more material about his finances, must have been immense. He was still working in a sustained way with Blair to achieve progress in Northern Ireland while Sinn Féin and the DUP were playing hardball in relation to their respective positions. The election for the Northern Ireland Assembly in March led in time to the formation of the first devolved government, with Paisley as its head, working with Gerry Adams and Sinn Féin. The following month Paisley came south, where he met Ahern in Farmleigh, the former Guinness residence in the Phoenix Park. Paisley stepped out of his car and walked towards Ahern, with the cameras recording his every word and move. 'I have to shake hands with this man,' Paisley said, smiling warmly at the Taoiseach. The two men also visited the site of the Battle of the Boyne. Adams's Sinn Féin colleague Martin McGuinness became Deputy First Minister to Paisley's First Minister, and the two men astonished everyone by how well they got on. Once again, historical developments in Northern Ireland were the focus of the domestic and world media, and Ahern was at the heart of them.

Soon after the establishment of the Northern Ireland Executive, Blair announced that he was stepping down as Prime Minister. Before doing so he extended the honour to Ahern of addressing a joint session of the Houses of Parliament. The 15th of May 2007 was a truly historic occasion, with the former British Prime Minister John Major, a number of former Secretaries of State for Northern Ireland, the former British Labour Party leader Neil Kinnock and all the major sitting figures in Britain's political system—including, of course, Blair—in attendance. Irish writers, actors, sports figures and fashion designers were in attendance, as were Des Richardson and his wife and the property developer Seán Dunne and his wife. Miriam Lord, in her report for the *Irish Times*, noted 'something' about Ahern 'sitting pensively in the gilded surrounds of the Royal Gallery as the illustrious assembly stood and applauded him. Him, Bertie, the boy from the northside.' Blair's glowing, heartfelt address introducing Ahern went far beyond the normal call of commendation, she said. When the moment came for Ahern to stand and make his address, he had stalled, she noted, and when he did stand he was not smiling, though he must have been delighted—the proudest man in the room. 'Yesterday evening he was back in his Dublin Central constituency, knocking on doors, looking after business. People on the Navan Road, who had been watching the Taoiseach on the six o'clock news in the Houses of Parliament, opened their doors to find Bertie on the step.' Lord wondered whether the pensive, worried air that seemed to surround Ahern was prompted by a general understanding that what was being marked was the closing of his political career. He was in the middle of a general election campaign, and he was fighting for his political skin.

In the weeks before Ahern's visit to London the tribunal was preparing for a module of public sittings that would be mostly about Ahern's personal finances. He had not been able to adequately explain the source of the large lodgements to his accounts, the tribunal was fed up trying to deal with the matter by way of correspondence and it had taken the highly charged decision to complete its inquiries by way of public sittings. The module was due to open on Monday 30 April, and the tribunal had said it would sit until two weeks before the election. The decision to hold public sittings meant that confidential papers would have to be circulated to interested parties before the sittings. It was at this stage that leaks to the media usually occurred. Ahern could have defused the matter by calling the general election earlier, as the tribunal would have had to stall matters until it was over and the papers would not be circulated. Privately he continued to urge the tribunal to wait, but he was reluctant to call the election. Perhaps he felt that if he held on, some unexpected development would set him free.

The tribunal papers were circulated in the last weeks of April. On the night of Saturday 28 April, Ahern learnt that Frank Connolly of the *Mail on Sunday* had them. Clearly panicked, he decided that he would call the election. Journalists were shocked on the Sunday morning to receive text messages at about 6 a.m. telling them that the Taoiseach was about to visit the President to hand in his resignation. He would be there at 8 a.m. Reporters and television crews raced to cover the unusual end of Ahern's second Government. His visit lasted only ten minutes. He said nothing to the assembled media. A statement issued to the press revealed that the general election was to be held on Thursday 24 May. Ahern later had a press conference at Treasury Buildings, where Fianna Fáil was again being accommodated for its election campaign. Ahern made a lacklustre address to the assembled media, then turned and walked away without taking questions. He appeared to be in meltdown. For Micheál Martin,

> that was a bizarre enough election . . . I think he called it at six in the morning. I don't think he was confiding much with colleagues at that stage in terms of what was happening. Most ministers found out about one o'clock in the morning that an election was being called at six. My only observation is that he may have been playing cat and mouse with the *Mail*. Maybe he wanted them to throw everything at him and then he could go to war.

Within the Fianna Fáil camp there was a disagreement over whether it should present itself during the election campaign as the party of fiscal responsibility or whether it should try again to woo the electorate with optimistic views of the future and of the decisions about public expenditure that would be made. Cowen was seen as being in favour of the fiscal responsibility message, with Ahern being nervous and tempted to unleash new, expensive promises. According to Martin,

> going into the 2007 election we were actually quite moderate . . . I think Brian Cowen was responsible for that. He said 5 per cent growth, everything is based on that; if we don't get it everything else is off the table. All the other parties were presuming 5 per cent growth. We actually were a bit more responsible going into 2007 compared with 2002. In fact when you look at 2007 you see Pat Rabbitte beating everyone else in terms of saying there would be tax cuts. There was a debate about cutting taxes again in 2007. I actually thought tax cuts were a bit over the top at that stage, given what we'd done already.
>
> Brian Cowen wanted conservative economic management to be our pitch. The fear in the party was, and it must have been Bertie, was that it was too conservative and that it was kind of dour stuff and wouldn't match the bidding war from the others, the kind of stuff that goes on in elections. There was nothing dramatic in the manifesto in terms of spending. There were no iconic issues compared to previous elections.

The campaign was dominated by Ahern and his inability to explain his personal finances. The present writer began to get access to leaked material, and other information, which appeared in the *Irish Times*. Every time Ahern emerged in public he was surrounded by reporters who wanted to quiz him about his money; every time he sought to explain himself his answers were evaluated, and more questions emerged. It was not until after the campaign that the media noted that during the first two weeks of the campaign he was emerging for only one photo-call each day. The party's main vote-getter, the crazed canvasser and sound-bite expert without equal, was in hiding.

Michael McDowell eventually responded to the leaks by calling on Ahern to explain what was going on—something that Ahern obviously had great difficulty in doing. By Sunday 6 May a number of the most senior figures in Fianna Fáil felt that the matter had to be confronted head-on. Brian Cowen, Micheál Martin and Dermot Ahern were due to give a press conference at

Treasury Buildings, but it was delayed. Behind the scenes the three Government heavyweights had sought a meeting with their Taoiseach.

'It was an incredible day,' according to Martin. The press conference was meant to be at midday, but there was fresh information in the *Mail on Sunday*. The ministers spoke to P. J. Mara, and Cowen said the press conference was being put back to three o'clock. Martin recalls that it was agreed that Ahern would come to meet him and Martin's cabinet colleagues, Cowen and Dermot Ahern.

> We couldn't have the media mob following us over to St Luke's. Looking back on it, it's really quite funny in a way. So Ahern came to us, in through a back way. He's very genial, as you know. He went through everything, relaxed and calm. He literally went through all his expenditures. I remember taking notes. I said, 'If that's all it is, why don't you go out and say this, issue a statement, deal with all these issues?' We thought he would issue a statement. He didn't think he should issue a statement yet. Then we thought he would. We had a no-holds-barred meeting. We were saying, 'This is serious, politically', but he went through everything in a plausible way, in terms of the issue that day, where all the money had gone in terms of the spending on the house . . . We were urging him to make a statement to settle nerves. He said he would, but he didn't want us to say when. For some reason he didn't want to do it before the following weekend. A spokesman said that after he'd left the building.

Cowen told the media afterwards that Ahern would be directly confronting the issues that were being raised in the media. While the party said the issue was not really of concern to people 'on the doorsteps', it was damaging morale within the party, damaging its ability to get its message across and threatening to leave it without any prospective coalition partner. Martin thought Ahern may have decided on an unusually long election campaign so that the matter could play itself out.

> He does think way ahead of most people. I was always curious as to why he gave a four-week campaign against the usual three. I think he gave himself enough time to recover.

On one occasion when a reporter from the *Daily Mail* asked Ahern a question the Taoiseach was lost for words. The question was met with an unusual response for a politician in a media scrum in the midst of an election campaign: silence. It lasted for a number of seconds. Ahern appeared to be crumbling. 'Next question,' a party handler said, bringing the silence to a close. The moment was shown on the six o'clock and nine o'clock news. Ahern appeared to have another moment of near-collapse later in the campaign at a press conference at which he was confronted from the floor by the journalist Vincent Browne. His story about his house just wasn't credible, Browne said. Ahern let his head droop and didn't speak, but then he picked himself up again and began to fight back. For many in Fianna Fáil, including Martin, this was a key moment in the campaign.

It was a fairly robust press conference which many journalists thought was a turning-point for us. And then we had the Westminster speech, which was a huge success. And then there was the debate [on RTE with Enda Kenny], and he won the debate, hands down, and you could feel it on the ground, and Brian Cowen had a powerful week on the economy, with Richard Bruton. These were the turning-points, but he [Ahern] had the two weeks to recover. It was only the last two weeks that he came out of his shell. He wasn't campaigning at all in the first two weeks. He seemed to be personally down about the whole thing. He played a blinder in the last two weeks; the first two weeks were a disaster. It was paralysis. It was meltdown territory.

Astonishingly, Fianna Fáil survived and the PDs didn't. The party of rectitude was seen as having lost its focus, and it collapsed. McDowell lost his seat and resigned as party leader on election night. Not long afterwards the party shut up shop.

But Ahern was still in business. Soon after the election, he announced that he thought Brian Cowen was the most suitable person to succeed him. It wasn't his decision to make, and his comments angered other senior party figures who had an interest in the leadership. And Ahern didn't indicate that he was going any time soon. However, the comments served as a disincentive to anyone else who might be considering a leadership heave, and Cowen was famously loyal. Ahern managed to put together a stable Government using support from the Green Party and a number of independent TDs, including Michael Lowry, who topped the poll once again in North Tipperary.

Ahern's last period in government was dominated by the proceedings of the Mahon Tribunal and his inability to explain his finances. Every time he or any of the other parties involved appeared at the tribunal it fed immediately into political debate, with TDs and ministers being asked for their view of the latest development. It is fair to say that many members of his Government continued to support him despite the evidence of large lodgements of cash to his accounts that he could not explain.

Matters crystallised around the appearance of a former secretary in St Luke's, Gráinne Carruth, though the true damage came, as always, from bank archives. Irish Permanent had produced what it believed was all the relevant documents it had about transactions on Ahern's accounts in its Drumcondra branch, and Ahern had given testimony that accommodated the available material. However, the bank discovered fresh archive material in or around March 2008 which showed sterling being exchanged for Irish currency before lodgements were made to Ahern's accounts. Carruth's name appeared on the lodgement dockets. Ahern and Carruth had already given their evidence about lodgements to the accounts, which Carruth frequently did for Ahern. Carruth had already said she had not lodged sterling, and on 19 March she was asked to explain that evidence. She was represented at the tribunal by the solicitor Hugh Millar, who had also represented Celia Larkin.

Ahern had travelled to Washington and the White House for the St Patrick's Day celebrations, but he was back in Dublin and fully informed of matters when the tribunal decided to recall Carruth. She was obviously in a spot, and the tribunal piled on the pressure. On her first day in the witness box her misery and her desire to be anywhere but where she was were painfully evident. 'I just want to go home,' she said in a low moan when asked to explain the conflict between her former evidence and the new archive material. She did not accept that she must have lodged sterling for Ahern. She was told to go home and ponder her position overnight. On the next day when she took the stand she again looked miserable. She said, as a matter of probability, she now accepted that she must have lodged sterling, though she couldn't recall doing so. Carruth, who lived close to St Luke's, said she hadn't contacted Ahern or his legal team in the period since she had first been informed of the new material coming to light. Asked why, she said, 'Because my first priority was to get my children sorted, and then, with his schedule, he was away or that, so I never thought of it.' She was, she said, hurt and upset. She was not asked to explain herself further.

There had been nothing to prevent Ahern contacting the tribunal or the legal team speaking on his behalf so that they could accept that sterling had been lodged and explain where it had come from. Ahern's legal team did not appear for Carruth's second day in the witness box. The acceptance that sterling had been lodged to an account that Ahern had said contained income from his political work was a huge blow to his already weakened hold on power. The way Carruth had been left to deal with the controversy on her own was also damaging to him. Miriam Lord laid into Ahern in the *Irish Times*.

> Bertie Ahern must be a proud man today. His ministers must be so proud of him too. It's such a pity none of them could make it to Dublin Castle to watch Gráinne Carruth give her evidence.

Lord wrote about Carruth

> alone and trembling in the witness box, battling back tears as she whispered in tones so anguished they were barely audible: 'I just want to go home.' It was so pitiful, it's just a pity Bertie wasn't there to see it. He might have stood up and shouted like a man: 'Let the girl go. It's me you want!' But that only happens in the movies.

Ahern later gave an explanation for the origins of the sterling and so could have short-circuited the whole affair at the outset and saved Carruth from having to give evidence. He chose not to do so and put off his response until the last possible moment. He was clinging by his fingernails to power, and Carruth's distress was the price that had to be paid.

The new evidence about sterling required a political response. Mary Harney and the Green Party leader, John Gormley, both said Ahern would have to give an explanation. The Dáil was on holiday and was due to resume on 2 April. On that morning there was a sitting in the High Court in a case in which Ahern had challenged aspects of the tribunal's work. The sitting was delayed when news broke that Ahern, surrounded by his Government colleagues, was making an unexpected public announcement on the steps of Government Buildings. The barristers, solicitors and journalists who were gathered in Court 6 for the sitting found themselves crowding around an RTE reporter's mobile phone as she played the live report. Ahern spoke of his life in politics, saying he had always been motivated solely by what was best for the people and had never put his personal interest ahead of the public good. The barrage of commentary about his finances was distracting the Government from its work. 'I have never received a corrupt payment . . . I have done no wrong and wronged no-one.' He said he was dealing comprehensively at the tribunal with the issues that had arisen. He announced that he would be standing down as Taoiseach and leader of Fianna Fáil on

6 May 2008. This would give him time to take up an invitation to speak to the joint houses of Congress in Washington as well as at other engagements. Power was being wrenched from him, but first he was to have a sort of last hurrah. In the emotions of the moment, no-one pressed him to explain where the sterling had come from.

Ahern's last official function was at the newly created Battle of the Boyne Centre in Co. Meath. Paisley attended, and the choice of venue was no doubt a pointer to the importance of developments in Northern Ireland during Ahern's years as Taoiseach. But it was also fitting in that the centre had been privately investigated by the Mahon Tribunal and others.

Before the decision to build the centre, Ahern's friend Tim Collins, acting in his role as land scout, had sourced the site for the McCann family, the controllers of the Fyffes Group. Two years later it was sold to the state at a considerable profit, and Collins made a personal profit from the deal of €600,000. Liam Moran, a solicitor and part-owner of the building firm Walsh Maguire, worked with Collins on the deal. The transaction was scrutinised by the Comptroller and Auditor-General, because the Office of Public Works had bought the company that owned the land, not the land itself, thereby saving the vendors a lot of tax. The Comptroller's report was later discussed by the Dáil Committee on Public Accounts. The tribunal never held public hearings into the deal.

After Ahern announced his intention to resign, Stephen Collins in the *Irish Times* said Ahern had had an outstanding political career, winning three elections in a row, presiding over three harmonious coalitions, the Celtic Tiger and, most importantly, the peace process. He was Fianna Fáil's most successful electoral leader since Éamon de Valera. However, within weeks of Ahern making way for Brian Cowen the huge difficulties in the economy became apparent. A year later Collins wrote:

It is becoming clearer by the day that Ahern was probably the worst leader the country ever had and people in all walks of life are now suffering because of his incompetent management of the economy.

Chapter 10 ～

| THE REAL BERTIE AHERN

It would be foolish to believe that the public persona of such a successful populist politician as Bertie Ahern was a true or full reflection of what the man was actually like. On the other hand, Ahern during his years in government had such a strong image as an ordinary man of the people, and one who was famously present in the media and in the public arena, that it was easy to believe that his public and his private persona were one and the same. Mary O'Rourke famously remarked that everyone in Ireland had met him.

The first time the present writer met him was outside a deserted count centre near Sheriff Street, in his constituency, during the 1989 general election. I had long hair and was wearing jeans and runners, standing beside my bicycle. A black Mercedes pulled up, and out got a tousle-haired Minister for Labour, wearing an anorak or car coat. I explained that I was a reporter from the *Irish Press,* and we discussed the extraordinary level of deprivation that was visible all around us. He spoke fondly of the local constituents and appeared to have all the time in the world to stop and chat. When I got back to the office I told colleagues about the meeting, about what an attractive character he was, entirely lacking in arrogance.

My first view of a less attractive aspect of his character came when he gave evidence to the Moriarty Tribunal in 1999. In the witness box he gave an impression of barely contained anger. He eyeballed John Coughlan, the tribunal barrister who was questioning him, and my impression was that he filled the large, high-ceilinged room with an air of menace. I thought how I wouldn't like to meet him in a dark lane at night, and how, if I did, I might just turn and run.

The tension surrounding his second appearance at the tribunal, in June 2000, followed him out to the castle yard afterwards, where the jostling by the photographers as they sought to get their pictures threatened to turn ugly. Ahern intervened to calm the situation. 'Ah, lads, lads,' he said, in his familiar, friendly way, urging everyone to relax. 'Someone will get hurt.' He was a completely different person from the one who had appeared in the witness box. The tribunal, of course, did not allow the broadcasting of its proceedings.

A number of political reporters came to Dublin Castle to watch Ahern give his evidence that day, and I remarked to some of them afterwards that Ahern in the witness box had not been at all like the politician I knew through the media. 'He's not a nice man at all,' one of the political correspondents replied definitively. None of his colleagues demurred. What struck me was how Ahern had so successfully created his powerful public image using the media, while those in the media who had the most dealings with him had a view of him that was entirely at variance with the image they were involved in creating. Of course the wider media, who knew little at all about Ahern, also played a huge role in the creation and enforcement of the view the public had of him. His public persona was not only useful to him: it was also a gift to the media.

Miriam Lord said she often heard those who worked with Ahern talk about his aggression.

I always thought that he 'went home and kicked the cat' sort of thing. Because you would hear from people who worked with him who'd say they'd be afraid of their lives to cross the boss or who would say to you, 'Jaysus, don't do that, the boss will be very upset. [You would write it anyway] and then you would meet the boss and you would be his best friend in the whole wide world. And then after he left office I was amazed at the amount of people who worked in Government Buildings who didn't have a good word to say about him. I remember an adviser to one of the ministers saying, 'But sure you knew what he was like when he was angry,' and I didn't know what he was like, but apparently he had them terrorised. Absolutely terrorised. So he was a street angel, house devil, I suspect. It was a mark of the man that he didn't lose his temper in the Dáil or in public, but that doesn't mean he wasn't a bollocks.

Gerald Kenny, the party activist who ran a security company, studied psychology for two years in Trinity College in the late 1980s before leaving to study Jungian analysis. In time he began to work as a counsellor and psychotherapist, which is still his profession. He lives in the Dublin Central constituency and remains on friendly terms with Ahern. In his view Ahern, despite his public persona, is a man filled with an unusual level of anger, who has a 'natural fury' inside. 'On one or two occasions, when speaking to loyalists, I have seen him get into a mode of public speaking that was almost demagoguery.'

Kenny's view is that Ahern was sincere in his interest in religion. Ahern, he said, would make observations such as 'We are all only passing through life' and that in this life we should try to help others. Yet he had another side that was without mercy and devoted to the winning and holding of power. In Kenny's view, everyone in Fianna Fáil knew that Ahern was ruthless, and everyone was intimidated by him, including the Government.

For Kenny, Ahern is a shy, retiring man who forced himself to act as the 'hail, fellow, well met' character that he presents in public.

> I remember one occasion when I was in charge of finance in the cumann. We used to have chicken-and-chips functions, and we had one up at the Parkside Hotel. Bertie was invited as guest speaker. There were three or four of us sitting at the top, on a slightly elevated stage, and Bertie went out to speak. He had his hands behind his back, and he was sort of wrestling with his fingers behind his back all the way through the speech. From the front he appeared perfectly calm, but from the side I could see his hands in combat. I remember thinking, That's not just nervousness: that's interior conflict. I always felt that Bertie was a forced extrovert.

Royston Brady was unusual among Ahern's inner circle in that he had fallen out with him and would speak to the media when Ahern was still in power. In the period before Ahern left office, Brady mainly spoke off the record. When the controversy first began about Ahern and his personal finances I made contact with Brady. I found out that he was also speaking to one or two other reporters. Interestingly, he had information he said had come from Dominic Dillane before the tribunal's inquiries became public knowledge. He shared the information with reporters, off the record, before the issues ever arose at the tribunal. This fits in with his suggestion that Ahern may have engaged Dillane as a constituency official years earlier and have begun disclosing information to him in preparation for inquiries that had not yet materialised. Ahern was once again grooming a third party, who would then be presented as giving independent confirmation of matters about which in fact he had received all his information from him.

Brady told me at one point that he would not speak on the record, because he 'still had to work in this town.' As Brady saw it, Ahern and the Drumcondra Mafia had taken over the Fianna Fáil operation in Drumcondra, had then taken over Fianna Fáil itself, and now, with Ahern in the Department of the Taoiseach, had control of the country. 'They're not going to give it up easily,' he said, and he added that Ahern couldn't believe he had got control of the party. It was only when Ahern was gone from office that Brady began to speak on the record.

This view of Ahern taking control of Dublin Central *from* the party is shared by the long-time party activist Joe Tierney, who says that Ahern was 'no more a Fianna Fáil man than the man on the moon.' People appeared at the tribunal to discuss matters relating to the constituency whom he had never heard of, even though he was immersed in the constituency organisation all his life. He said the annual dinners in Kilmainham had nothing to do with Fianna Fáil in the constituency.

It was obvious to anyone who considered the matter that Ahern had to be a tough character to become leader of Fianna Fáil, though it was an aspect of his character that he mostly kept out of public view. By contrast, his attitude towards money was entirely hidden. Ahern created an image of a man who was unusual in his lack of interest in personal wealth. According to Brady, nothing could have been further from the truth.

Ahern would sometimes bed down in the apartment upstairs in St Luke's before getting the house in Beresford Avenue. According to Brady, it was not without its luxuries.

Ahern was the first person I'd ever seen with underfloor heating in the bathroom—for a man who said he had humble tastes! He said, 'Take your shoes off and feel it.' A man who liked to give the view that he sleeps on the couch with an anorak on.

According to Brady, Ahern was very interested in money, and very tight with money. 'I would describe him as being borderline eccentric when it comes to money and stuff like that.' St Luke's was packed with gewgaws that Ahern had been given when performing official functions over the years. A friend of Brady's once pocketed one, and there was consternation until it was returned.

I remember another incident on St Patrick's Day. There were four of us: myself, Dominic Dillane [and two other supporters]. We went to the Brian Boru [a pub near Phibsborough] . . . We went in, and I just said, 'What are you having?' and he [Ahern] said, 'No, I'll stay on my own.' So I brought drink for the three lads, and he bought his own drink. We had four drinks. So it would have been the sensible thing to do to buy a round each. But he bought himself the individual drink on each of the four occasions. So I just said to myself, coming away, I said to the lads— because we went into town and had a good few drinks, and he went off— I remember saying to the lads, 'Did you ever meet such a miserable bastard in all your life?' Here he is, the Taoiseach of the country, and you think he would have said—lookit, all the work we do, knocking on doors—that he would buy us a few drinks, but not a chance. It's examples like that you remember.

Ahern's long-time associate Paddy Duffy does not necessarily disagree with Brady's claim that Ahern was slow to put his hand in his pocket. He said it was something they'd noticed about Charles Haughey, who would never have any money in his pockets. As time went on, Bertie became a little like that as well. 'A bit of tapping the pocket, though he was obviously well known for buying his pint as well.' His view on Ahern's interest in his personal finances is that Ahern would have known about his own financial situation 'down to the last dot' at all times. It would be the same in most aspects of his life, he said. 'He is a man of great precision, and particularly in regard to statistics.'

It became clear during Ahern's evidence to the Mahon Tribunal that he had a keen interest in his own money. At times it was the tone he used, for instance when referring to not wanting to see his savings being exhausted by paying the legal bills that arose from his separation from his wife. Some observers wondered if Ahern had an interest in money that was similar to that of the disgraced former Assistant City and County Manager, George Redmond, who famously hoarded his money in his garage in boxes.

In September 2007 the Review Group on Higher Remuneration in the Public Sector issued a report that included a recommendation that the Taoiseach's salary be increased by 14 per cent, to €310,000 from €271,882. However, in December the Government decided that it would defer the implementation of the recommended increases for ministers and the Taoiseach. When Ahern resigned as Taoiseach he became entitled to an annual pension of €111,235.20. As the economic crisis gathered momentum it was decided that serving deputies who were receiving ministerial pensions should accept a cut of 25 per cent. Then, later again, Ahern agreed to forgo his pension while he was a serving TD. In December 2010 he announced that he would not be standing in the 2011 general election. Had he not made the announcement until February 2011, his pension entitlements would have been considerably less. In the event, his combined ministerial and TD pension entitlements came to approximately €135,000 per annum, or almost €2,600 per week.

Ahern was paid in the region of £300,000 for his memoirs—money he earned tax-free because he made a successful application under the artists' exemption scheme, this despite the fact that he had the assistance of a ghost writer. (The book did not sell as well as expected, and the publishers, Hutchinson, are believed to have lost heavily.) After his retirement as Taoiseach, Ahern earned an unknown amount from paid speaking engagements at which his fee was of the order of $50,000 per event, and the cost included first-class flights, accommodation in a top hotel and all expenses. It is standard for famous politicians—especially ones involved in historic events, such as the Belfast Agreement—to earn money in this way. However, Ahern did not get the number of company directorships that might have been expected, and one senior figure in the Dublin business world expressed the view privately to the present writer that companies did not want to be associated with him, pending the outcome of the Mahon Tribunal. In this way, Ahern's engagement with the tribunal not only brought about an end earlier than planned to his career but also hit him hard in the pocket.

Ahern's interest in, and capacity for, retaining numbers and statistics was another aspect of his character that became apparent during his time in the tribunal's witness box. At one point, while giving evidence about a dizzying array of transfers between his various bank accounts, he launched into a lengthy list of movements of particular stated amounts, pounds and pence—between different accounts, on stated dates—all without referring to his notes. It was an extraordinary performance. Judge Mahon put down his pen and stared at Ahern, apparently more interested in his ability to rattle off such a list than in the evidence he was giving.

His ability to make people laugh was another aspect of his character that was not generally known. During Ahern's latter period in office this writer covered a trade mission to Saudi Arabia and Dubai, which Ahern headed. One night the Irish group found itself at a party inside the high walls of a compound in Riyadh. There was a large number of Irish and foreign business

people and public servants there, and, despite Saudi Arabia's strict rules and
the presence of armed soldiers on the other side of the wall, the alcohol was
flowing. I recall standing at the bar watching people in long robes ordering
glasses of Paddy. When Ahern arrived he stood up on a chair and delivered
an impromptu address. He was absolutely hilarious and had the crowd—
myself included—in stitches. Some people had tears rolling down their cheeks
he was so funny.

He repeated the performance a few days later at a reception in a hotel in
Dubai. His delivery was astonishingly good. A large part of the humour came
from the fact that he was the Taoiseach and he was standing up on a chair
talking about the money the people in the room were earning from their
exploits, about how he wouldn't mind having some of it, how he was sure the
Revenue Commissioners would be very interested to know about it, and so
on. Making money and keeping it was the dominant theme, with the Revenue
Commissioners—and, by implication, the state—being seen as adversaries in
that enterprise. Shock at the attitude being revealed was a large part of the
comic formula.

The trust that many people had in Ahern during most of his political
career was attributable to the belief that he had no interest in money or
personal enrichment. Events during his ministerial career such as the row over
the 1993 tax amnesty, the discussion of tax breaks for the wealthy during the
Fianna Fáil-Labour Party coalition and the tribunal's concerns about tax
designation all sparked less suspicion than they might otherwise have done,
because people in Leinster House thought that Ahern, unlike Haughey, had
no interest in money. Ruairí Quinn, who was in government with Ahern when
Ahern was Minister for Finance, said his view that Ahern had no interest in
money meant that he tended not to wonder whether Ahern was corrupt.

> I never got a sense that he had a hunger for money. The revelations
> subsequently came as a big surprise to me. The only correlation that came
> to me was George Redmond. George would eat his lunch out of a drawer.
> He loved the comfort of having the money. You just don't know with
> Bertie what it was. The volume of money that was going through those
> accounts, when you place it in the context of the times, was enormous,
> and yet he didn't seem to be the beneficiary of it or to live a life-style
> remotely like Haughey—or anybody else, for that matter.

The tribunal sessions changed many people's views about Ahern in this
regard. Instead of being uninterested in money he was in fact very interested

in it and hugely impressed by—if not in awe of—those who had a lot of it. Furthermore, he appears to have had a sense of grievance that so many people were getting rich while he, in the Department of the Taoiseach, was merely being paid a few hundred thousand a year. Joan Burton believes this to be so and that it was a view shared by many of those involved in the running of the country during the boom years.

Both Burton and Brady make the point that from early on in his political career Ahern arrived at a point where most of his expenses were covered. He didn't have to run a car or buy his meals; even socialising and attending sports events could be paid for by others. Both believe that he must have accumulated a vast amount of money. (There is no evidence of his doing anything with it, and he may well have left it in deposit accounts.) Burton says Ahern would not be alone in Leinster House with regard to accumulating money. Miriam Lord thought she noticed in Ahern an interest in luxury that was at odds with his public persona.

Ahern appears to have particularly enjoyed the company of wealthy property developers and builders, many of whom came from modest backgrounds—something that must have influenced his views on the management of the economy, the construction sector, property-based tax breaks and so on. He was less comfortable in the presence of old money or of people who came from privileged backgrounds. There was a view in Leinster House that Ahern resented Fianna Fáil blue-bloods, such as members of the Lenihan and Andrews families, and was less inclined to promote them. In general, many people feel that Ahern suffered from a sense of insecurity and resentment. This may in part explain his enormous ambition and political drive. Lord, who herself came from close to where both Haughey and Ahern grew up, used to get irritated by the inferiority complex she felt that both men had.

I always thought there was something not quite believable about the whole image of the young fella from Dublin, the working-class hero. When he went abroad he always stayed in the best hotels. And he was always very dazzled by those who had money and by people who were in showbiz. For a guy who professed to only like the simple things in life he seemed, from the Galway tent [the hospitality tent at the Galway Races] onwards, to like to be among those who liked the opposite: the trappings of wealth.

I often wondered if that [his awe of people who had money] was an inferiority complex and was that what he had in common with Charlie

Haughey. There was a sort of uneasiness with people who didn't seem to have a problem with their position and with people who had money and seemed at ease with it, and you wondered did he want to be like that, and couldn't.

The Dublin Fianna Fáil activist Joe Tierney said this was something he raised with Ahern early on in his political career.

I said to him, 'What's wrong with you, Bertie, is you are too insecure.' He was the most insecure man that God ever put on this earth, and this is what drove him all the time. Whatever it was happened to him in his past life, I don't know.

He added that you could 'have fifteen conversations with him, and every one of them would be about Bertie.'

Gerald Kenny was struck by the similarities between Haughey and Ahern. They were both driven by a desire for power and were without mercy. He thinks Ahern understood Haughey from early on and modelled himself on him. 'He would talk about Haughey's shrewdness, his ability to do deals, his work ethic. Because Ahern was a workaholic, really.' Both were interested in money, though with Haughey it was used to buy the good things in life and to aggrandise himself. Ahern had different issues with money, but they were both really motivated by power. 'A lot of people I knew were in the party because they thought that was the best way to run the country and was in the interests of everybody. But once Haughey took over it all began to change. Bertie was a direct continuation of that.'

For Tierney and Kenny, Haughey and Ahern between them brought about the collapse of Fianna Fáil's dominance in Irish politics. According to Tierney, Haughey allowed corruption to flourish because this protected him from his own corrupt acts. The years of scandal were noticed by the electorate, but the effect was muted until the economy collapsed. Once the economy faltered, however, the result was the party's miserable performance in the 2011 general election.

On the day of the election, according to Tierney, he received a phone call from the candidate Mary Fitzpatrick that prompted him to go to Stoneybatter, where Ahern was standing on the street close to a polling station hoping that his presence would encourage people to vote for Fitzpatrick's competitor for party votes in the constituency, Cyprian Brady. Tierney flew into a temper when he saw Ahern's state car sitting nearby.

I said, 'Are you a fucking headcase? Is there something wrong with you? Your fucking state car! There are people in there [O'Devaney Gardens] who haven't a bit to eat this morning. And the fucking state car!' I said to him, 'You fucked up the whole country, you fucked the party up, and you have the state car in the most deprived area in the place.' He said, 'You don't know what you're talking about.'

During Ahern's period as Taoiseach he had an enormous media presence, and he became a type of presidential figure, almost above politics. His press operation was formidable. He avoided serious current-affairs programmes and forums where he could be subjected to any sort of sustained questioning. Reporters were told where he was due to be appearing that day and would assemble—most often outside—to get a few lines from him on the way in. This was particularly important for broadcast reporters. Whatever the issue of the moment was would be put to him, and he would give his prepared response and then go into whatever function he was attending. His response, therefore, would often be the first item on television and radio, as it gave a fresh opening to the broadcasters' reports. And so he managed to be prominent in the media without being subjected to questioning by it.

Over time his press-handlers developed a system whereby they would ask the reporters beforehand what they were going to ask him so that he could consider his response. Some reporters objected to this, but the broadcast reporters were under pressure to get hourly updates on the stories of the day, and a comment from the Taoiseach was important to them in that regard. There was pressure on them to play ball. According to Lord, who attended many of these 'doorsteps', Ahern developed a strong dislike for reporters who asked him hard questions, but he went to great lengths not to show it.

The reporters would ask the agreed questions, and then when they had something in the can they would ask the hard question. Some hacks were more liable to ask the hard questions than others, and it soon became known from sources close to him that he absolutely detested those particular journalists. And yet when he met those journalists it was always a matter of great hilarity that he would go out of his way to be particularly nice to them when everybody knew he hated them. Ursula Halligan [of TV3] was a case in point. He hated Ursula. She didn't care, and he knew that. His unique charm didn't work.

While Ahern gave the impression of being amiable and relaxed, his press agents were often under great pressure. When he had been questioned in a way he did not like, the press secretary would often get it in the neck afterwards. Likewise, the press secretary might try to lay into the journalist beforehand to try and stop him or her from asking a particularly awkward question. According to Lord, the press secretary 'would have no compunction about ringing up people and absolutely tearing the head off them, and then you'd meet the boss five minutes later and it was like nothing had ever happened.'

Lord says Ahern spent his Thursdays canvassing around the country and his Fridays canvassing in Dublin. The country visits received huge coverage in the local media. The party press office didn't want the Dublin media covering the country canvasses, because it didn't want the local media being told that Ahern's visit to whatever constituency it might be was a type of *pro forma* event that was being repeated every week. The Dublin media engaged to some extent in a cat-and-mouse game in which they would seek to find out where Ahern was going to be that Thursday and Ahern's press people would try to keep the venues secret. On occasion there were minor scandals when the Dublin media reported on the speed at which Ahern's convoys sped along country roads. According to Lord, 'he was on a permanent canvass around the state, and it worked really well for him—really pissed off the opposition.' After he resigned, a senior figure in the Cowen Government privately expressed the view that the country was paying dearly for having a Taoiseach who was so heavily involved in near-permanent canvassing.

Ahern had charm, drive, stamina and patience. Brady believed he was vain, liked publicity, liked having his picture in the newspapers, liked being popular. He spent the bulk of his adult life in the glare of the media, and he certainly gave the impression of enjoying it. After his public image was damaged by the revelations about his personal finances, he at times made his dislike of the media plain and lowered his guard to display sulkiness and self-pity. In an extended interview with Ursula Halligan on TV3 after he had left office, Ahern articulated a sense of grievance and failed to assert his political achievements. Asked at the end of the interview if it had all been worth it, he said he wasn't sure.

One can only imagine what it does to a person to be constantly in the public gaze, to have to assert *bonhomie* at all times, to pretend to be optimistic and outgoing and friendly when in fact you are insecure or worried or angry. Some in Leinster House came to dislike Ahern because of the endless succession of friendly greetings, comments about sports events and so on, which were false insofar as he had no real interest in the people he was greeting. However, others appreciated the effort, the short pauses for brief conversations, the ability to remember names. Greg Sparks was once at a race meeting and found himself near Ahern. He introduced his wife and daughter, and during the very brief encounter Ahern remarked to Sparks's daughter Alannah that she was nothing like her sister Billy. (They have different colour hair.) When Sparks got home he asked Billy if she'd ever met Ahern, and she said she hadn't. Then she remembered that she'd been at an official function in Na Fianna GAA club some months earlier and had been one of many who had shaken Ahern's hand as he worked the room. She had introduced herself; he had asked if she was related to Greg Sparks, and she had said she was his daughter. That was the extent of the encounter, and months later, during another brief encounter, Ahern had been able to recall her name and to note her sister's different hair colour.

Miriam Lord had covered Ahern as a reporter since his days in the Mansion House, and she never noticed any change in him over the years, despite the years in power, the civil servants seeking to please him and the fawning backbenchers and councillors hoping for advancement.

> I never saw any change in him. Even when he became Taoiseach he was always very accessible to us, always very affable. No matter what you wrote about him he never got annoyed. In fact he'd make a point of seeking you out when you were hiding because of something you'd written; he would go out of his way to find you and be nice to you, to make you feel even worse, which was actually a great trick, because you'd feel less inclined to go hard on him the next time.
>
> Up to the very end, when things got very bad at the tribunal, he remained very accessible, very affable. Even on the day he left government he came over to me, said, 'Thanks for everything, no hard feelings, you were only doing your job.' But there was another character there, whom we never got to see.

She pointed out that Ahern's daughters were bright and attractive children who managed being in the limelight with their famous father with great grace and skill. They were a credit to Ahern as a father.

No-one I spoke to had any suggestion to make as to why Bertie Ahern was such a driven politician or why he wanted to be in politics at all. Pat Rabbitte professed to having been always fascinated by Ahern.

He was single-mindedly focused on politics like nobody I ever encountered before. Everything he did was a political action. The much-vaunted Manchester United fan, the Dubs aficionado—it was all a political action; going to Parnell Park or Croker. I'm not saying he didn't enjoy seeing the Dubs, but it was a political action.

He believed that for Ahern being in politics, 'being Bertie and functioning as Bertie', became a type of addiction. He recalled one Christmas when there was nothing much happening and then Ahern popped up commentating on English soccer for Setanta Sports. 'Nothing for two days but Bertie in his jumper commenting on the Premiership. They showed it over and over again. How could you compete with that?'

The disclosures that came from the Mahon Tribunal changed people's view. Ruairí Quinn was shocked, in part because he had never noticed a hunger for money in Ahern. Lord felt angry when she heard the evidence. 'When you think that someone who was in charge of running the country ... was accepting money ... which is what happened from the very start.'

Ahern's performance in the witness box, and the evidence that emerged from it, drew a picture of a wary man constantly mulling over potential dangers, making preparations for dealing with these dangers should they ever arise. Yet even as he was giving his evidence, it was clear that the man in the witness box had presided over a bubble economy and had overseen a period of economic management so disastrous that western Europe's star economic performer was about to again become the dunce.

For Pat Rabbitte there is no paradox here, nothing to be explained. Ahern's wariness was about politics but also about self-protection, and it goes back to the corrosive influence of Haughey. A number of people around Haughey knew what was going on, according to Rabbitte.

Bertie's wariness in the witness box was a wariness about his own protection. I never recall him demonstrating a similar wariness about where the economy might go, and I rationalise that along the lines that very, very few politicians in Leinster House would have been able to carry around in their stomachs what Bertie Ahern carried around during his period as leader.

He never told the tribunal anything that he wasn't sure they knew already. That was the way he treated them: tease out what do they know, and, who knows, next weekend it might be different. A challenge in the High Court might be successful, something might happen, one of the beaks might tumble over and die—who knows? He played it right up to the wire, and that's why he finally became so disorientated during the 2007 election. He felt that it was catching up with him.

But in fact, of course, the people were still prepared to give him absolute licence. As I said—and I came in for a lot of criticism inside the party for saying it—in answer to a question on TV one night as to why I didn't pursue [the issue of Ahern's finances during the election], when I did pursue it after the original story in the *Irish Times* I lost five points [in the opinion polls] and he gained seven, and I never got them back. People did not like—whatever it is about Irish people—they did not believe Bertie was dishonest, and they didn't like the *Irish Times* story, and they didn't like the opposition pursuing it, and they showed that in the poll. And although he was quite crestfallen during the campaign, the Irish people were quite happy to give him the benefit of the doubt. And the Irish people, of course, were also quite happy that if it could maintain our individual prosperity, then a little nod and a wink on the direction of minor corruption in Fianna Fáil was always a price we were happy to pay for and joke about it afterwards in the pub.

Ahern had a phenomenal capacity to retain information. His frenetic canvassing around the country and the endless succession of meetings with politicians, developers, professional experts, business figures, party activists and ordinary members of the public meant that he had an ear to the country like no-one else. Everywhere he went he received praise and was subjected to lobbying. He appears not to have understood the need to listen more closely to critics—in particular to informed critics—than to supporters and to those who are prospering from his policies. Hearing only what you want to hear is a common and human failing, and one to which political minds are particularly susceptible.

For Joan Burton one of the great political tricks Ahern managed was to project himself and his party as the begetter of Irish prosperity and to persuade the public to perceive him as being credible.

That's a very valuable political asset for a politician to have—an enormous political asset. The opposite is deadly. They can be very good, but they are ruined if no-one finds what they say believable. So that confidence that emerged, that he managed to create, was a tremendous asset.

However, in time, in Burton's view, he came to believe this myth.

In Sparks's estimation the economy had lost international competitiveness by the end of Ahern's first Government. But Ahern and his colleagues were in awe of the economic numbers, the growth that had occurred and the increase in employment. 'They lost the run of themselves. The figures were phenomenal, and they believed their own propaganda.' The fact that most Irish people who are not from a farming background are only one or two generations away from the land may form part of the fascination with property that developed then and later. When Irish people began to buy trophy properties abroad, such as the Savoy Hotel in London, it fed into a type of nationalism. 'But from a government's point of view you have to step back from the propaganda and be a lot more analytical than that, but there is no evidence that they did.'

Lord believed that Ahern had a well-developed capacity to overlook his own failings and to use whatever material was available to seek advantage. When she agreed to be interviewed for this book, it had just been announced that there would be a commission of inquiry into the collapse of the banking sector. Lord recounted that when Ahern was asked about the idea he had said he would be willing to give evidence. He was a 'taskmaster' at giving evidence, he had told the media. In Ahern's own mind, Lord speculated, he was making a virtue out of his appearances at the tribunal, ignoring the devastating testimony that had emerged. Perhaps he was able to compartmentalise everything he encountered, putting the good bits in one part of his mind and the bad bits in another. 'The bad box is every so often jettisoned off the end of the pier, and then the good box is opened and there to be used.' After he had left office this aspect of his character began to get him into trouble when the blatant ignoring of the mistakes he had made began to rile people.

Lord did not believe that there was any mystery about how a man such as Ahern could have presided over such gross mismanagement of the economy. The interview with Ursula Halligan on TV3 some time after he had left office, in which he seemed to be self-obsessed and filled with resentment, illustrated that,

> in the heel of the hunt, everything came back to him. It explains the sort of obsession with being in the constituency all the time, and making sure that his majority was secure, pounding the streets of Cabra and the North Strand when he didn't have to. It was all about him. It all came back to him.

Micheál Martin has no doubt that Ahern's chief motivation in politics was 'to genuinely serve the public. I think he had a fierce sense of history, a fierce sense of his father, the old IRA. We used to have long chats about that.' Ahern had a great interest in people's personal situations and would look out for them. He had a lot of honourable traits. For Martin, the evidence that came from the tribunal was very disappointing. 'I don't know what's behind it.'

Paddy Duffy said 'the Ahern I knew' had no interest in money. Ahern for him was a person devoid of self-importance, someone who retained his sense of humility and modesty throughout his years in power. When asked to define the political ideology or vision that drove Ahern, Duffy had this to say:

> Bertie and all the rest of us would be driven by a broad, deep-seated Irish Christian democratic [view]: Catholic, not socialist, but doing the right thing in terms of promoting equality of opportunity and fairness. Bertie would have had that, and we all would have had that from our own background. My own feeling is that Bertie actually developed his views as he did things. He didn't come to the table with a set view of how things should be done, but the philosophy evolved through doing it, and at the end, when it was done, you could look back and say, 'Ah, my goodness me, look what he did with the Northern thing; he must have thought all that out from the beginning.' But in fact no: he developed that view as he went along with everybody else, as they went along together, and the philosophy was created, or the thought patterns or the objectives were brought together [in that way].

Ahern was the most able politician of his era in the sense of winning power, and yet he had little or nothing by way of political conviction in the sense of having views that would differentiate him from others. Every politician in Leinster House is in favour of peace, jobs and economic growth and wants a society that has time for sports, volunteerism, a sense of community and neighbourliness. Ahern had enormous drive but no particular vision. Arguably what was a political asset for him was a catastrophe for the state in which he won power. Success for him came at a time when Ireland had at last achieved economic success and, precisely for that reason, needed new direction, new objectives, a particular type of management. Because he had no particular political vision he had nothing to guide his decisions. He was easily influenced by those who had strong views. And whenever there wasn't anyone around to impress their vision on him he was inclined to let matters drift. Circumstances, chance, political calculation and the electorate swept him along until he, and then the country itself, crashed onto the rocks.

PART FOUR

Economy

Chapter 11 ~

| DESPAIR

In his acclaimed book *Ireland, 1912–1985* Prof. J. J. Lee reviewed the country's performance when compared with other European states and probed possible reasons for its relative failure. It was published in 1989, the year of the general election that was to feature most heavily a decade later during the tribunals in Dublin Castle. It was written without a knowledge of the relatively huge amounts of money that were swirling round those at the head of Fianna Fáil at a time when emigration was high, population growth low, and optimism about Ireland's future a scarce commodity. It was also written without the author knowing the extent of the tax evasion that existed in Ireland, with those in the cash economy hiding their money in bogus non-resident accounts in towns and cities throughout the land. A Dáil inquiry would later disclose the extent to which the main banks facilitated, promoted and engaged in this widespread criminality at a time when there was a genuine fear that the International Monetary Fund would have to move into Ireland. Likewise, Lee did not know that the Irish economy was about to begin a period of growth that would attract the attention of the entire world.

Nevertheless, from the viewpoint of post-Celtic Tiger Ireland, Lee's observations and comments make for riveting reading and provide an excellent introduction to the nature of the Irish economy, and indeed to Ireland itself.

While it is difficult to talk about the performance of a country over time, it is possible to look at measurable phenomenon like economic and population growth. Lee illustrated that population growth during the period he reviewed was weak by European standards, despite starting from a relatively low density. Irish population growth was limited because of low marriage rates, late marriages and emigration; but this in turn did not mean higher-than-average growth in income per capita relative to other European countries. Lee showed that in fact Ireland—North and South—was not particularly impoverished, by European standards, in 1910. For national income per capita Germany scored 70.3, France 69.6 and Ireland 62. Ireland ranked higher than Norway, Sweden, Italy and Finland, with the last scoring 34.6. However, in the period to 1970 the rate of economic growth in Ireland was such that it ended up being well below the European average. In relation to national income, Lee showed, no country in Europe for which reliable data existed had as low a rate of economic growth as Ireland in the twentieth century. Poorer countries in Europe rapidly narrowed the gap between them and their richer counterparts in the wake of the Second World War, but not Ireland.

A boost did occur in both economic activity and population in the 1970s, at about the time Ahern was entering politics. International data show that the Republic had the highest growth rate of any country in the OECD in 1978. But Lee argued that this was bogus. The growth was achieved only by plunging the state into debt. Up to 1970 Ireland had been a creditor country. This changed during the 1970s. By 1975 foreign debt was equal to £4 per head of population. By 1985 this figure had soared to £2,269. This disaster occurred during Ahern's early years in politics and in the formative years of many of those who would end up sharing the Government table with him.

The irresponsible splurge during the 1970s led to a slump in the 1980s, with both economic activity and population growth returning to more 'normal' Irish patterns. Loss of international competitiveness led to a devastating loss of jobs. The national finances got into a perilous state as those in the sheltered sectors and in state jobs fought to maintain their position. Interest payments on the foreign debt began to consume a growing proportion of the national income. The Government was forced to increase the amount of income it was taxing (though it would later emerge that those not in the PAYE system were hiding their income to an enormous extent). The main use of the funds borrowed abroad was to maintain and increase the wages of those in the sheltered sectors. As Lee puts it, the bulk of the borrowing was a covert conspiracy between politicians and the more advantageously placed groups at the expense of those in the vulnerable, exposed sectors. The politicians, in return, held on to power (and an income).

It was common when reviewing the dismal performance of independent Ireland to refer to the effects of the War of Independence, the Civil War and then the Economic War, but Lee rubbished such views. The damage inflicted on Ireland during the early 1920s was small compared with that inflicted on the countries of Continental Europe involved in the First World War. Serbia lost a quarter of its livestock. Poland lost two million cattle, one million horses and five million acres of forest. Its railway system was wrecked. Ireland suffered less from the great economic slump of 1929 than did most of its European neighbours. And then, of course, there was the Second World War. Lee took the example of Finland, which, with the same population as Ireland, lost 25,000 people in civil war in 1918 and nearly 100,000 people of a population of 3½ million in the Second World War. After the war it had to settle 400,000 Karelian refugees fleeing Stalin and had to pay substantial war reparations to his government. Yet, Lee pointed out, it recorded one of the most impressive post-war growth performances in Europe. He quoted Prof. John Kelleher from an essay of 1957, 'Ireland, where does she stand?'

> Any conversation on Ireland in Ireland is almost bound to produce some defensive mention of the terrible troubles the Irish have survived and the hard time of it the nation has had generally. Alas, the truth is that Ireland has had an almost fatally easy time of it, at least in this century.

For Lee, the solution to Ireland's mediocre performance had to be found at the human level. Its economic history involved a struggle to foster enterprise. The Minister for Agriculture, Paddy Hogan, had sought to encourage enterprise in farming in the 1920s; Seán Lemass had sought to nurture domestic industry in the 1950s and had later turned in desperation to importing it. For Lee the reason for the lack of enterprise had to do with how a culture chooses to perceive opportunity. A blend of historical factors, economic and psychological, helped explain the primacy of what Lee called the 'possessor over the performance' principle. And for this reason he suggested that the changes Lemass had sought in the 1950s, when Ireland abandoned de Valera's failed 'sinn féin' economic strategy, were an attempt to overturn the dominant ethos of the Irish state.

Lee suggested that the arbitrariness of the relationship between landlord and farmer, and between farmer and labourer, fortified a craving for security, which expressed itself most naturally in an attachment to land. Similarly, a strong cultural interest in fixity of occupational tenure emerged. Loss of land or job could see a family facing economic and social ruin. Risk-taking in such circumstances was considered highly foolish.

Lee also pointed to the weak relationship that existed between effort and reward during modern Irish history. The eldest son got the farm, and one daughter got a dowry. Performance did not dictate material success: no matter how hard a labourer worked he would not normally become a farmer. The two largest gains to farmers during the nineteenth century were from the Great Famine and the Land War: in the former the survivors could tack on vacated land to their holdings; in the latter it was political rather than economic effort that led to the windfall gain. Even in the basic work of farming, the raising and sale of livestock, the exchange rate with sterling and the haggling skill of the farmer at the fair had as much or more influence on the financial outcome than had the effort put into actual farming. In 1882 Michael Davitt's attempt to introduce a land tax that would operate as a performance tax fell on barren ground. The Limerick Rural Survey (Tipperary, 1962) found, nearly a century later, that little had changed. 'The prestige and social rank of the family as a whole depends on the ownership and not on the use of the property. Size of farm, not productivity, determines one's place on the class ladder.'

Outside agriculture it was trade and the professions that dominated, not industry. Those involved in trade and the professions sought, like the farmers, to protect their positions more as a way of life than as an occupation. Possession took precedence over performance. Even in industry, family firms predominated, and the same ethos prevailed as in the farming family. Often the most able son was sent for a career in the professions, and the business was left to less talented siblings. The protectionism of the 1930s guaranteed markets to the new firms that emerged, meaning that there was little pressure on them to perform if they wished to retain their markets.

Lee also pointed out that the marginal propensity to import was exceptionally high in Ireland because of its incorporation in the English sphere of influence. Irish agriculture provided only a small market for Irish industry. It did little to increase output in the century after 1850, and it relied on the export of raw rather than processed product. Irish business failed to develop an interest in exports and was unable adequately to defend its home market, leading to the shift in official policy towards attracting foreign direct investment in the hope that the foreign firms would in time assist in the fostering of native enterprise and industry. But while the IDA had success in persuading foreign firms to come to Ireland to establish low-skilled manufacturing operations, the growth in such employment during the 1970s ran alongside huge job losses elsewhere. The foreign firms supported by the IDA had few linkages with Irish business and conducted very little by way of research and development.

In 1980 the National Economic and Social Council commissioned the Telesis report. It was highly critical of economic policy and the emphasis on foreign investment. It made it clear that the much-trumpeted success of the IDA was not quite what the public had been led to believe. No country had ever succeeded in achieving sustained economic growth except on the basis of domestic industry, the report said, and it set out recommendations for how Ireland might foster indigenous success. Official dislike of the report's conclusions led to its publication being delayed for more than a year. The official response to it took three-and-a-half years. The IDA and official Ireland did not like the Telesis report but did not dispute its view that Ireland was failing to produce a native cadre of high-quality entrepreneurial business figures. Likewise, when the Labour Party proposed in the mid-1980s that a National Development Corporation be established to foster industrial activity, the idea was met with hostility, not least because of the widely held view that state companies had failed in the past, had tended to become captive to public-sector trade unions and were inherently inefficient. By the mid-1980s the public finances were in dire straits, emigration was the only option available for a large number of school-leavers and graduates, and faith in both the public and private sectors was as scarce as entrepreneurial zeal.

This is the background in which the political career of Bertie Ahern must be viewed, and in particular his management of the economic boom.

Chapter 12 〜

| OPPORTUNITY KNOCKS

By 1996 Ireland's economic circumstances had turned around in a way that J. J. Lee could not have envisaged seven years earlier. The economy was growing at more than 5 per cent per year. The term 'Celtic Tiger' had been coined and had taken hold, and studies of precisely how the great economic turnaround had occurred—and of what was continuing to drive it—were being conducted at both the national and the international level. One can only speculate that Bertie Ahern looked at this development from the opposition benches and wondered if he would ever get back into power.

At the most simplistic level the change in the economy occurred because a number of factors that had been holding back the economy had been dealt with or had dissipated, and it was now catching up with its European peers. Ireland was experiencing a corrective bounce.

The period of economic growth had begun in 1987 and continued through the first half of the 1990s but without an obvious impact on the lives of many. Ireland experienced an above-average level of economic growth while maintaining low inflation and an excellent balance of payments position and overseeing a huge improvement in its public finances. However, unemployment remained stubbornly high, with more than 20 per cent of the work force on the live register of unemployed. These were the years of so-called 'jobless growth'.

The reasons for the 'invisible' growth were outlined in a medium-term review (1994–2000) published in 1994 by the ESRI. (The establishment of the institute was part of the change in economic policy introduced by the former

Taoiseach Seán Lemass, which Lee said was an attempt to foster performance over possession. One of the glaring failures to emerge after the collapse of the boom was the paucity of professional analysis to which Irish society and Government policy are subjected.) The ESRI review included a chapter by John FitzGerald and Patrick Honohan entitled 'Where did all the growth go?' which examined the phenomenon of jobless growth. A principal reason for the lack of employment growth was that the greater economic resources being produced were being invested on slowing, and then turning around, Ireland's foreign debt. As the authors put it, in the early 1980s Ireland had lived far beyond its means and had almost bankrupted itself. By the early 1990s it was doing the opposite: its means had increased, but the money was being used to pay off its debts and wean its way off its borrowing habits. Consequently the average worker was not experiencing any great leap in personal income, and unemployment was remaining at a record level.

Spearheading Ireland's recovery from the late 1980s had been the growth in manufacturing exports. While some Irish firms had been involved, the size of the contribution from foreign-owned exporters was unique in Europe. The effect on Ireland of the foreign-owned firms was less than it would have been if they were indigenous or more embedded in their host economy. Meanwhile, Irish business had suffered intensely from the contraction in the economy in the early 1980s. Honohan and FitzGerald in part explained this by showing that Irish wage levels had risen *vis-à-vis* those in Britain in the twenty years previously, weakening the competitive capacity of domestic business so that when conditions became strained, many businesses quickly collapsed. However, in the period since the mid-1980s the competitive position of Ireland relative to its nearest neighbour had improved, and the competitive edge had been maintained. Agriculture, despite continuing to contribute to economic growth, was still witnessing a falling off in farm employment. On the other hand, a series of mergers and acquisitions had seen the emergence of a number of large agri-business firms that were using their size to invest in product development and the process of selling their products on international markets. However, labour-saving technologies had dampened the sector's effect on employment numbers. There had been a marked increase in employment in services, reflecting international trends in outsourcing and developments in technology, though the increase in Ireland had not quite tracked the international trend. The number of jobs in the Republic in 1994 was still less than in 1980.

Wage restraint, transfers from Europe and relatively low interest rates, and their effect on Irish debt payments, all played their part in the improvement in circumstances during the early 1990s. Irish interest rates were by the late 1980s already tracking Germany's, and the increase in German rates, brought about by its reunification, caused a delay in the recovery of Ireland's fiscal position (by increasing the cost of servicing Ireland's debt) and contributed to a general economic slump in Europe. The higher debt-servicing burden for Ireland, which meant that more money had to be raised in taxes, affected the country's ability to achieve wage restraint so as to boost Irish competitiveness. German reunification delayed the arrival of the Celtic Tiger. The effect of developments in Germany on Ireland's employment and emigration performance is an example of how Ireland exists and must manage its affairs in a European context. Arguably it was the failure to focus on the European context in which Ireland operates that was the biggest mistake made in economic management during the Ahern years.

The 1994 ESRI publication pointed out that as the Irish national debt fell, the pressure on the economy from servicing the debt would ease and there would be greater scope for increasing economic growth to lead to job creation and affect the material well-being of people generally. There were other factors feeding into the positive economic background. Demographic change meant that Ireland was about to experience a period where there would be a lower percentage of older people dependent on the working population to support them. With a greater proportion of the population in the work force, there would be higher per capita income on this basis alone and a reduced requirement for public services. An increased level of educational attainment would also provide a boost to the economy. For these and other reasons the review opted for a bullish forecast for the coming six years. While the figures were to prove incorrect, notably in the predictions for getting rid of unemployment (it eased more quickly than predicted), the trend was spot on. Europe was about to experience a recovery, and Ireland a boom. If it wanted to spread the benefits among all the population, wage restraint would have to continue so as to boost employment, and resources would have to be targeted at those in danger of leaving the educational system too early, so as to reduce the number of people entering long-term unemployment. Upskilling and training would have to be provided to those already unemployed. There would be an opportunity for reform of the tax system. As a set of challenges set out for those charged with the management of the state, they were not difficult to understand.

Three years after the review the economy had prospered at a rate that had taken everyone by surprise. Net emigration had ended, and former emigrants were returning. Confidence in Ireland and its prospects was commonplace.

The institute came out with a new review in the same year that Ahern had become Taoiseach for the first time. 'Who put the tiger in the tank?' was one of the questions asked, and, as the authors made clear, no single factor could explain the extraordinary developments then occurring in the economy.

According to the review a number of mutually reinforcing domestic forces with widely divergent time-scales had come together to provide the Republic with an unprecedented push into the first division of European wealth levels. Sustained public policy over a period of four decades had built up educational and training levels (human capital) and had proved successful in attracting foreign direct investment. The crises of the 1980s, which had almost led to a loss of economic sovereignty, had provoked a much-needed shake-up of institutional attitudes, not least in political, public service and trade union circles, and had forced the Government to remedy the public finances. Pay restraint and social partnership had restored Ireland's international competitiveness. A better level of education was driving the increase in female participation in the labour force, affecting migration and the marriage and birth rates and, through increasing earning power and productivity, boosting economic growth. There had been a sharp change in the dependence ratio, or the ratio of those outside the work force to those inside it, and Ireland was rapidly moving from having the highest dependence ratio in the EU to having the lowest. A demographic dividend would give the country an opportunity of about twenty years during which it could consolidate its position and prepare for a more difficult future.

International factors were also at play. The American and British economies were growing at a satisfactory pace, and the Continental European economies appeared to be recovering from recession. European monetary union was due to take place in 1999 and would ensure the continuation of relatively low interest rates.

The 1997 review, in making its forecasts for the coming six years, presumed fiscal responsibility, moderate wage demands, modest reductions in direct taxation and increased investment in infrastructure. The circumstances in which Ireland found itself were a 'historical opportunity for Irish society. It should not be wasted.' This was the context in which the 1997 general election, and indeed Ahern's career as Taoiseach, took place.

The ESRI envisaged that the 'current exceptional rate of growth in the economy is likely to continue into the next decade.' Maintenance of Ireland's competitive position would see the economy create jobs at a rate that would be exceptional in Ireland's history and in relation to the EU norms of the time.

Furthermore, and unlike previous spurts in employment, the growth in jobs would see a sustained falling off in the unemployment rate.

In the introduction to their review the authors referred to Lee's book and to the question it had posed as to the cause of the Republic's lack of economic success. 'Now the question posed by outsiders looking in is why it is such a success. To those of us living through the experience there is a certain sense of bemusement at this rapid reversal of fortunes.' The review put an emphasis on the changes to educational provision in the 1960s—twenty years later than most western European countries. Increased access to education was a key factor in explaining the transformation of the Irish performance, the authors said. Increased educational attainment explained many of the demographic changes that were now producing positive economic benefits as well as directly providing for increased productivity. Ireland had been a laggard at introducing educational reform after the Second World War, and its 'baby boom' was also taking place decades after that of most other Western societies.

In a chapter entitled 'Interpreting the recent Irish growth experience', John Bradley, John FitzGerald, Patrick Honohan and Ide Kearney probed the factors that had led to the sudden economic blossoming, making the obvious point that understanding the causes of the success was an essential first step to forecasting its future. It is also, of course, an essential first step in deciding how to manage that future.

Interestingly, the authors considered the existing literature on the link, if any, between the harsh cutbacks introduced by Haughey in 1987, with the support of Alan Dukes and Fine Gael, and the sustained period of economic growth that stretched from that year to the date of the review. The popular view was that the 1987 cutbacks had led to renewed confidence in Ireland's future and to a concomitant increase in private-sector investment and activity. However, the authors noted that the studies that had been carried out had come to an alternative view, namely that it had just so happened that the cuts had occurred at a time when international interest rates fell, when Britain introduced tax cuts and when there was unexpectedly strong global economic growth. Irish policy-makers, the authors said, had been 'lucky'.

In the chapter on the origins of, or explanations for, the Celtic Tiger, the authors noted the effect on individual and institutional attitudes of the pessimism that had developed during the 1980s. Because of the level of despair, everything was up for questioning. A greater spirit of self-reliance began to manifest itself among younger people, many of whom, even if they chose to emigrate, had a stronger determination than heretofore that they would return. Reforms were introduced in the semi-state and state sectors because the need for them was so evident. But the most dramatic change, according to the authors, came in the attitude of the leadership of the trade union movement, which convinced its membership of the need to focus less on local pay and conditions and more on the competitiveness and long-term sustainability of the economy.

These were the considered views of some of Ireland's most respected economists, published by the institute set up by one of Ahern's stated heroes, Seán Lemass, to encourage a higher standard of performance in Irish society. These were also the ideas that drove the partnership process with which Ahern was so closely involved. He had reason, therefore, to be more aware of the importance of these factors to the long-term health of the Irish economy than most senior figures in Irish politics.

| PARTNERSHIP

T he dire economic situation, as well as fears within the trade union movement that it would be sidelined, as was the case in Thatcher's Britain, was a contributing factor to the first partnership agreement, the Programme for National Recovery of 1987. The return of Charles Haughey and Fianna Fáil to power was also a factor. Alan Dukes, Minister for Finance in the 1980s' Fine Gael-Labour coalition headed by Garret FitzGerald, said he detected a view at the time that the labour movement preferred Fianna Fáil to the Labour Party, despite its formal links to the latter. Haughey was sympathetic to a desire for a deal that had emerged among the social partners and was willing to give it a go. Ahern was the man he appointed to steer the issue to a conclusion.

A report by the NESC, 'A Strategy for Development, 1986–90', set out what the social partners might agree in the year before Haughey's return to power. The council involved employer, trade union and civil service representatives and was a forum in which they could come together to discuss the nation's woes without having to commit themselves to any particular policy. The economist Jim O'Leary, who was working for the NESC at the time, is credited by some with coming up with the formula that led to the document. When Haughey was returned to power and appointed Ahern as Minister for Labour, the partnership approach was looked on favourably and was soon implemented.

A key aspect of the 1970s and 1980s, according to Blair Horan, general secretary of the Civil and Public Service Union, was that wage increases were contributing significantly to inflation and that the abnormally high income tax rates being imposed by the Government to redress the crisis in the public finances were feeding into the demand for wage hikes. This is a significant point worth bearing in mind when considering what happened during the Ahern years. According to Horan,

> the 1987 settlement was that we would go for low pay increases and the Government would reduce the tax take. It was a trade off. The abnormally high [income tax] rates that were the result of the 1970s were lowered.

The pay deal aspect of the agreement was a modest 2½ per cent annual increase over three years. The deal included general objectives aimed at the public good, such as maintaining social welfare levels, narrowing the Government deficit and reducing the ratio of the national debt to GNP (almost 130 per cent by 1987). The principal objective of the plan was to enhance Ireland's international competitiveness.

It was not envisaged initially that the Government would play a crucial role in the partnership arrangement; rather, it was thought that the structure would be a matter for the employers and the trade unions. However, the state became centrally involved, and over time the process became more complicated, with a fourth pillar, the voluntary sector, eventually being incorporated. There were three-year deals covering pay in 1990, 1994 and 1997. Then came Partnership 2000 (1997–2000), the Programme for Prosperity and Fairness (2000–3), Sustaining Progress (2003–5) and Towards 2016 (2007). During this period the ability of the structure to agree three-year pay deals that were adhered to came under great strain and arguably collapsed.

As has been seen, the external environment into which Ireland was exporting improved considerably at about the time Ray MacSharry began imposing his cutbacks and the partnership process began to deliver wage moderation, industrial peace and medium-term consensual plans for the management of the economy. Improved wage competitiveness *vis-à-vis* our competitors, especially Britain, boosted economic activity. The profitability of companies began to recover and turnovers grew, although the investment in new employment was not sufficient to create significant net job growth.

When Partnership 2000 was being negotiated in 1997 John Bruton was Taoiseach. He and his Government oversaw the acceptance of the new deal, even though the trade union movement found it more difficult than heretofore to get it past its members. The success of the process was creating a new challenge.

The economy was booming, and the media were reporting ever-greater company profits and windfall gains for the owners of capital. There was also frequent coverage of the growing daily fee rates being charged by professionals. Some of the latter were equal to or above the monthly average industrial wage. The relentless increase in the price of housing was putting pressure on the average worker. Some banks were beginning to shift from using multiples of a person's salary as a measure for mortgage purposes to affordability based on the person's take-home pay. Because of this, every tax cut became a boost to house prices. The significant tax cuts introduced by McCreevy in his first budget were a direct spur to an already-strong property market.

Horan, who studied for a degree in economics during the 1990s and took an objective as well as a professional interest in the Government's policies, was prompted to write to Ahern as early as April 1998. 'Dear Taoiseach,' he wrote,

> I am writing to express the serious concern of my executive council at the soaring house prices in Dublin, and also increasingly in provincial cities. This is such a serious problem and one that will affect the model for economic success developed under social partnership that I would like to set out our views on the matter.

His union represented young people on modest incomes, and they were now facing a situation where inflation in the price of housing was in the 30 per cent bracket, while the partnership agreements that their union had settled for involved 2 to 3 per cent increases in nominal wages per annum. Demographics, Horan said, indicated that house prices were about to become a very serious issue in the wage-bargaining arena.

> I have no doubt whatsoever that with the advent of the euro next year, a continuation of the economic model we have developed under social partnership is of even greater importance. The consequences for our economy if this problem is not successfully addressed will be very severe indeed.

Horan advocated Government intervention. The Government, in the wake of a report by the economist Peter Bacon, did intervene to try to suppress price growth but then reversed its stance and in the end opted to let the market, through supply, deal with the issue. The main point about this scenario is that price inflation was feeding into wage demand—the opposite of the situation in the 1970s and 1980s. Likewise, the various tax reliefs that were available to higher earners created an impulse in union circles to try and combat the growing gap between the income level of the most well off and the average worker.

In 2000 the country's largest union, SIPTU, announced that it was seeking increases from profitable companies that were in excess of what had been agreed in the local bargaining clause of the existing agreement.

The Programme for Prosperity and Fairness included a new structure, the National Implementation Body, that was there to oversee the agreement and intervene where it appeared to be flouted. Sustaining Progress saw another such mechanism introduced, again illustrating the pressures that economic growth and rising expectations were putting on the model. Such developments also demonstrated the capacity of the structure to bring new bodies into being. As time passed, 'the institutions of social partnership expanded, and little organisations were set up to keep everyone happy,' according to Brigid Laffan, a former NESC member.

By the early years of the new century Ireland was being confronted with skills and labour shortages. Much to most people's amazement, unemployment had dropped to 4 per cent—*de facto* full employment. Many companies were making satisfactory profits and were confident about future growth, and acquiesced in pay deals that were well in excess of what had been agreed in Sustaining Progress. Many companies felt it was in their interest to ensure that they kept good staff and secured suitable new employees, and were willing to pay to do so. Housing and other costs were continuing to rise, and they were again putting pressure on wages. Many in the highly unionised public sector felt that they were falling behind their counterparts in the private sector. A model that at the outset had been predicated on working together for mutual benefit was being transformed by the changed circumstances it had helped to bring about. Employers, unions and people generally were looking less to the maintenance of the common good and more to getting what they could from an increasingly rich cake. 'It became a monster,' said Laffan. 'It became who gets what. And everyone got something!'

The dip in economic growth that came in the wake of the attacks on the United States in 2001 and the bursting of the dot-com bubble in 2002 served to lift some of the pressures on wage demands. Likewise, the flood of new immigrants after the enlargement of the EU in 2004 served to ease the pressure on wages.

In the public sector, meanwhile, the benchmarking system was established in 2002. In return for pay increases the system was supposed to provide public-sector reform, but it failed to do so. In response to criticisms in this regard, the leaders of public-sector trade unions countered that the Ahern Governments never looked for reform. They said it was not fair in such circumstances to blame the public-sector unions for not leading the charge.

According to Horan, the spending splurge that occurred half way through Ahern's first Government made it difficult for the unions not to seek more than they might otherwise have sought. Tax reductions from McCreevy's first budget onwards were greater than the norms before that, when they had cost approximately €400 million per budget. In the 2000 budget Ahern noted that, while the unions had sought a package of about €600 million, the Government had delivered €1.2 billion. According to Horan, 'no more than wage negotiations adjusting to a higher rate of inflation, the next trade union tax demands responded to the higher norm set by the Government itself.'

No substantial reform of the public sector was attempted during the Ahern years, despite the resources that were available and the pay rises that were allocated. On the other hand, it is perhaps because of the fact that resources were available, and because a populist Taoiseach who disliked making decisions that might upset voters was in power, that no reform was attempted.

The history of the social partnership phenomenon was reviewed in *Saving the Future* (2007) by Tim Hastings, Brian Sheehan and Pádraig Yeates, in which many of the key participants are interviewed. It makes it clear that it was the depth of the crisis in the 1980s that led to the seriousness of purpose that in turn produced social partnership. When the process began to produce fruit the seriousness of purpose collapsed.

Another feature worth noting about the social partnership process is the effect it had on the Department of Finance. Partnership was run from the Department of the Taoiseach. It involved huge multi-year commitments affecting the national finances, and part of the role of the Department of Finance in scrutinising expenditure plans and arguing against what it believed could not be afforded was thereby diluted. Power shifted to Ahern's department. Likewise, the Programmes for Government he negotiated with the PDs involved tax-cutting and expenditure commitments that the Department of Finance was presented with as a *fait accompli*. After Ahern's departure from politics, the performance of the Department of Finance during his period as Taoiseach was the subject of an independent study that identified these two factors and said that the department's repeated warnings about the dangers of the budgetary policies pursued during the Ahern years were ignored. It criticised the department for not shouting louder as the years passed.

Chapter 14 ～

| COMPETITION

S ome economists question the proposition that countries compete against each other in the same way that companies involved in the same sector might. Countries trade with each other, and so innovations and cost reductions in any one country benefit them all, they argue. However, the argument is not seen as being applicable to Ireland, owing to its nature as a small and very open trading economy highly dependent on foreign investment. Modern global industries such as biotechnology, software and aerospace tend to converge or cluster in particular places around the world, and therefore countries are indeed involved in an intense competition to have them choose to operate within their borders. Ireland's achievement in wooing Intel in the late 1990s was seen as a cornerstone of the country's subsequent success in boosting its electronics sector. Ireland's gain constituted a loss for countries such as Wales and Scotland that had also sought to woo the semi-conductor fabrication project. The increasing globalisation of the world's economy during the Ahern years made this issue of competitiveness all the more important.

As part of the first partnership agreement, the Programme for Prosperity and Fairness, a council was set up to monitor Ireland's competitiveness. As Ahern himself put it in his foreword to its annual report in 2000, the economy's ability to compete in international markets was a key component of the prosperity that the society was then experiencing, and 'it is vital that we maintain and develop the competitiveness of the economy.' The chairperson of the council was Brian Patterson, a senior business figure who was later the first chairperson of the Financial Regulatory Authority. Other members included people from the private sector, the public sector, the trade union movement and the employers' group, IBEC.

Measuring competitiveness is a complicated and inexact process because it involves so many variables as well as decisions about the relative importance of the factors selected. When those studying the matter thought about Ireland there was even a consideration that such factors as the national personality—if there is such a thing—and the Irish ability to form relationships might be important elements in particular business sectors. Such matters, of course, cannot be measured. On the other hand, exchange rates and the cost of making a phone call to the United States are easily measurable.

In his foreword to the report Ahern referred to the National Development Plan and its intention to invest heavily in infrastructure in the period 2000–6, while Patterson referred to the need for speed in reacting to competitive challenges as they emerged. The development plan needed to alleviate the bottlenecks that were being created by the combination of rapid growth and historically under-resourced infrastructure. These were the problems of success.

Ireland's unemployment rate was falling below 5 per cent, and there was even positive change in what was the main repository of deprivation: long-term unemployment. Given this falling off in those not at work and the continued growth of the economy, Ireland was experiencing skills and labour shortages, which in turn were contributing to growing inflationary pressures. The shortage of labour was also affecting the infrastructural investment projects outlined in the development plan. The distribution of the increased prosperity that Ireland was experiencing was particularly unequal, though the extent to which the Government, and the bulk of society, considered this to be a serious problem did not seem significant. Michael McDowell, whose views were influential within the PDs, even argued that income differential was a good thing, saying that it had positive benefits for the economy. As the new century began, Ireland's richest 20 per cent earned six times as much as the poorest 20 per cent. This put Ireland at 20 per cent below the EU average and was twice the ratio of the best-performing country, Finland. McDowell's argument was contested by many economic analysts, who argued that there was a correlation between high inequality and poorly functioning economies.

In its earlier period the Competitiveness Council ranked Ireland's performance annually, monitoring whether the changes in a range of indicators were positive or negative. In its report of 2000 it found that Ireland had improved its ranking in 24 indicators (for example marginal tax rate for a single person, interest rates and percentage of small and medium-sized businesses that exported), worsened in 29 (telecom line-rental charges, compensation per employee, unit labour costs, research and development expenditure) and remained constant in 14. According to the report, 'due to the strong improvement in employment growth and the reduction of the number of unemployed, Ireland's position in terms of compensation per employee and unit labour costs is among the worst performing indicators.'

In his foreword Ahern said that the Government greatly appreciated the work of the council and that the relevant ministers should give careful consideration to its recommendations. But against the backdrop of the situation described in the report and that of the expansion in Government expenditure, over which Charlie McCreevy was presiding, it is hard to take Ahern's statement seriously.

One of the effects of these expansionary budgets at a time of strong economic growth was the boosting of inflation and the domestic economy at the expense of Ireland's international competitiveness. For Horan the crucial issue was that the policy dampened the exporting sector, which, as he pointed out, was predominantly based on manufacturing as against services during this period. It did so by boosting domestic activity such as consumerism and the property sector. (The increase in prices caused by the latter had a stifling effect on the competitiveness of the exporting sector.) This analysis in turn led Horan to a particularly stark view that is not widely voiced.

The expansion of the domestic economy in the period after 1997 was not sustainable. Up to this point unemployment had remained quite high and we probably needed to develop indigenous exports more in order to get it down. [After the expansionary budgets] unemployment dropped to 4 or 5 per cent, but probably a lot of it was [because of] an overheating economy, fuelled by debt. It was probably all a bubble. We have probably had a bubble for the last ten years [since 2000].

This view fed into the stance Horan took within the Irish Congress of Trade Unions in the wake of the economy's later collapse, when the ICTU was arguing that the Government should put more money into the economy to protect jobs that, in Horan's analysis, had been produced by unsustainable economic conditions in the first place. We will look at matters concerning the euro later, but it is worth having a brief look at the matter in the context of competitiveness.

Fig. 1: Growth in employment, 1997–2010

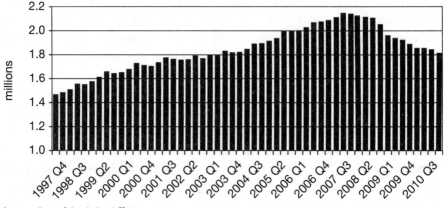

Source: Central Statistics Office.

As part of the preparation for the new currency, those countries that wanted to participate had to fulfil certain criteria relating to the size of their public debt relative to their economy, their inflation rates and so on. Ireland maintained low inflation rates in the years before qualifying for membership, but the McCreevy budgets in the second half of Ahern's first Government contributed to a level of inflation that caused alarm in Europe. By way of the currency project, Ireland was now locked into a low-interest environment and so would have to find other ways to stop asset price bubbles and other undesirable phenomena. But Ahern and McCreevy had ignored this, and the expansionary budgets boosted an already-strong economy, encouraging the 'domestic' side of the economy: housing, retail and so on. This occurred at the expense of the manufacturing and exporting part of the economy.

By the time the Competitiveness Council produced its report in 2001 the world that Ireland was operating in had changed considerably. Ireland's dramatic loss of competitiveness had occurred at a very bad time. Patterson, in a press statement in October of that year, put the matter succinctly.

> The dramatic change in global economic conditions, the heightened uncertainty following the terrorist attacks in the US on September 11th and the fact that Irish wage rates are now growing at the fastest rate in the OECD are all serving to undermine Ireland's competitive position.

Wage rates were growing at twice the rate of productivity. (Wage increases that lag behind productivity do not put pressure on competitiveness.) Taxation and insurance had risen, as had electricity prices. There were continuing problems with telecommunications and in particular with broadband access and telecommunications costs. 'We have started to take our competitiveness for granted, and this can have very serious consequences in a scenario where global demand is slack, particularly since we no longer have domestic control of exchange rates and interest rates,' Patterson said.

Ireland's nominal wage costs were rising at about three times the EU average. (A nominal wage increase is when your pay goes from €100 a week to €105 a week. A real wage increase is when you take inflation into account. If inflation was at 5 per cent the real wage increase would be nil.) The EU believed that Ireland's average wage level had been 3.6 per cent above the euro-zone average in 2001 and would increase to 13 per cent above that average in 2003, that is, 13 per cent above the average rates in the richest countries in the world if the trend continued. Irish productivity was falling, not rising. In its report of November 2002 the Competitiveness Council warned about rising costs, increasing wages, an inflation rate higher than acceptable and inadequate investment in infrastructure. In a review of projected increases in unit labour costs in sixteen countries it had found that Ireland came second-highest in 2002 and 2003.

It is interesting to look at where the inflation was centred. 'Competitiveness: Costs and Inflation', a report in 2003 by Forfás, the state body charged with fostering indigenous industry, concluded that approximately 73 per cent of inflation in the period 2000–2 originated in the services sector. The biggest engine of inflation was the non-traded services sector. Professionals such as lawyers, accountants, doctors, surgeons, dentists, architects, bankers and insurance providers were taking advantage of the weak competitive environment in which they operated to increase their share of the pie. Many opted to invest their increased level of wealth in property and, when the economy eventually collapsed, were left with debts to the banks that wiped out all they had gained.

A report of the Competitiveness Council in 2003 found that Ireland ranked thirteenth of the sixteen countries it examined on the issue of domestic competition, where coming first would mean the greatest intensity of competition. Transport, distribution, wholesaling, private refuse collection, communications and energy were among the areas cited. An important aspect of this issue is that it was capable of being reformed through domestic effort. Furthermore, the state was very often by far the largest purchaser of the services the council considered to be overpriced. To tackle the problem would have required the Government to go up against a succession of vested interests, but this was precisely the sort of challenge that Ahern tended to avoid.

Chapter 15 ~

WHAT GOVERNMENTS CAN DO

Governments influence economic growth and social direction, but the effects of their actions have a wide range of time-scales. The unexpected proclamation of free secondary education in 1966 by Donogh O'Malley was seen as a key factor in the economic boom enjoyed a quarter of a century later. On the other hand, changes to tax rates and to transfer payments can have an almost immediate effect on an economy. There can often be a tension between what is fiscally prudent and what is politically tempting, and a review of the economy since independence reveals a tendency to succumb to temptation.

For certain areas of the economy the Government has direct and often monopolistic influence. Transport, planning, health services, education and of course the running of the civil and public services themselves are matters on which politicians have direct influence and for which they have responsibility. While the Ahern Governments made great political use of the buoyant economic backdrop in which they operated, their record in managing aspects of society for which they had direct responsibility was generally recognised as being very poor. Yet efforts by opposition politicians such as Richard Bruton to draw attention to the waste of money and the lack of reform created little by way of political return for him or his party.

––––

Bruton believes that the idea of public-sector reform 'collapsed' when Ahern came to power because his Governments used the public service as part of its electoral strategies. Ahern's instinctive response when confronted with any difficulty, according to Bruton, was to pretend it wasn't there and, if that didn't work, to throw public money at it.

In the five years to 2006 the public-sector pay bill rose by 59 per cent, and the staff increased by 38,000. The largest increases were in health, education, security and the civil service. Government politicians, when challenged, asked which nurses, gardaí or teachers the critics would want to let go. It was a reasonable riposte from a political point of view, but the plain fact of the matter was that the scale of the increase was not sustainable and was, as we shall see later, funded not only by boom-time taxation receipts but by foreign borrowings as well.

Salaries increased greatly, according to Bruton, 'but there has been no *quid pro quo* for the taxpayer because ministers did not build the necessary reforms into the benchmarking structure.'

It is worth noting that the benchmarking process led to salary increases for Ahern himself, his ministers, his senior civil servants and such figures as High Court judges. The master of the art was overseeing the biggest patronage scheme of them all. According to Joan Burton, the trend in top-level remuneration among the social partners reflected a view that they had presided over the creation of one of the richest countries in the world and deserved something for their achievement.

Apart from pay and the increase in its size, the other major initiative on public-sector management during the Ahern years was the unexpected announcement by McCreevy in December 2003 that the Government was going to move a large proportion of the public sector out of the capital. Arguably this was the most cynical use of the public service since the foundation of the state.

There were fifty-three sites involved, and electoral considerations appeared paramount. Tom Parlon of the PDs assumed responsibility for the effort in his position as Minister of State at the Department of Finance in charge of the OPW. FÁS was to move its head office to his constituency as part of the plan—something he sought to use for electoral gain.

The head office of the Central Fisheries Board was in Ahern's own constituency, in an unusual 1930s' building on a lane off Mobhí Road. Speaking of his continued commitment to the decentralisation policy after his party's disappointing results in the 2004 local elections, Ahern told the Dáil: 'The Central Fisheries Board were on the banks of the Tolka for years, protecting the pinkeens.'

A huge amount of money was wasted on the project before it was eventually called to a halt. The planned move of FÁS to Co. Offaly never went ahead. It bought a landlocked site outside Birr, Co. Offaly, in 2006 for €1½ million. At about the same time it rented office space in a converted mill in Birr that had been developed by some local business people, a tax inspector and two accountants as part of a public-private partnership with the Shannon Development Authority. The office space was to be used as the FÁS head office, pending the construction of a new building in the field outside the town. The premises were upgraded at a cost of €1 million, with the contract for doing so being awarded to a building company belonging to one of the landlords and without the matter being put out to tender. However, the head office was never moved to the well-fitted spanking-new offices. The former director-general, Rody Molloy, who is a native of Birr, retired in November 2008 because of a scandal over spending controls at the authority. His replacement, Paul O'Toole, had only visited the FÁS premises once, as part of a courtesy visit, when he was asked about the matter in September 2010. The lease on the offices costs approximately €100,000 a year. Tom Parlon, who trumpeted the move to Birr during the 2007 election campaign, lost his seat and almost immediately took up a post with the Construction Industry Federation.

Richard Bruton is very harsh on Ahern in relation to reform.

The big decisions his Governments made were disastrous. The damage they did to the ethic of performance in the public service is a big legacy: paying out benchmarking without regard to what was achieved; having decentralisation without any cabinet papers, without any consultancy. They just pushed it through under the secrecy of the budget and then pushed civil servants around like pawns on a board. When amalgamating the health boards into the Health Service Executive, the one advantage was that you could rationalise your administration, and then Bertie goes in and says there will be no rationalisation.

All those things were saying to ambitious people who wanted to work in a high-performance organisation that our political leaders don't care about a high performance. All they care about is a quiet life. It was about satisfying short-term political needs in the case of decentralisation; avoiding a row in the case of benchmarking. All of that now has to be massively undone, unfortunately at a time when there is no money to pay public servants, and you are going to be cutting the pay bill while saying to them we now have to have a performance culture. There has been a wasted decade.

They spent heaps of money, but the system was undermined. And I think that's another legacy that he has. He bought out problems instead of confronting them. That is his instinct. I don't think history will be that kind to him.

The explosion in economic activity that occurred during the Ahern years was facilitated by the availability of labour. The huge numbers of unemployed and the number of women who did not take part in the work force constituted a huge resource for the early years of the Celtic Tiger.

The increased participation of women in the work force was seen by many in the Government as a positive development, even if it entailed an increasing number of mothers leaving young children in care. The explosion in the price of housing also put pressure on young parents. It was difficult for one salary to support an entire household, including mortgage repayments. The rising cost of child care increased the pressure on young families.

The issue of child care had been a subject of discussion for more than two decades, as was evidenced by the number of reports commissioned on the subject. However, subsidising those who wanted to put their children into child care so that they could work was perceived by some as an assault on mothers who wanted to remain in the home—even on traditional family life and Catholic sexual morality. By the late 1990s the matter of how best to raise children had become a subset of the drive towards economic growth. The strains on families caused the matter to become politically charged.

The Partnership 2000 'Report of the Expert Working Group on Childcare' pointed out that quality child care can have both social and economic benefits. Ireland's child-care policy was characterised by a lack of co-ordination and a lack of state support, despite the wide range of international studies showing the beneficial effects of pre-school education, particularly for children from disadvantaged backgrounds. The returns were huge, the report pointed out.

One widely reported longitudinal study from the United States found that children who attended a carefully designed programme, known as the High/Scope Programme, were more likely to stay on into third-level training and education, were less likely to get in trouble with the law, and were more likely to be supporting themselves when compared to a control group who had not experienced the programme. When reviewed in terms of cost benefit analysis, the researchers found that for every $1 invested in this type of early education programme, the State saved $7 per child by age 27 years.

There had been severe pressure on the Government in the period before the 1998 and 1999 budgets to provide tax relief on child-care costs, but the issue had not been grasped because of the political sensitivities involved. This changed in the two expansionary budgets that preceded the 2002 general election. In his budget speech in December 1999 McCreevy announced a range of measures to support the existing system of child care. He also announced an increase in child benefit. In the budget speech of a year later he announced what he called the largest package ever of support for children and their parents. Again, grants and other support for the existing system were a major element of the announcement, but so too were universal transfer payments to all mothers. McCreevy increased child benefit by £25 per month for first and second children, to £67.50 per month. For third and subsequent children the increase was £30 per month, to £86. These were huge increases, but more was to come, he said.

> This increase of over 50 per cent in current payment rates marks the first step in a three-year programme. At the end of this process, an additional one billion pounds will have been invested directly in our children's well-being. Child benefit monthly payments will stand at over £117.50 and £146, well beyond [partnership] commitments. This will mean up to £90 per month extra for each child at the end of three years. By then, a family with four children will be receiving the equivalent of over £120 per week in Child Benefit support. This unprecedented increase will help all parents with the costs of caring for their children and will represent a major move towards achieving the goal of ending child poverty in this country.

The striking increase in payments delighted all types of parents around the country. However, the announcement constituted something of a rejection of the expert working group's reports and of other reports. A very detailed study of the issue and of all the previous studies and reports that had been carried out was initiated by the National Economic and Social Forum, chaired by the psychologist Maureen Gaffney.

As already noted, Ahern and his party held a meeting in Inchydoney, Co. Cork, in September 2004 which received extensive media coverage. The following year the equivalent meeting was held in Ballyconnell, Co. Cavan. This time they invited an American academic, Robert Putnam, author of *Bowling Alone: The Collapse and Revival of American Community* (2000). Ahern let it be known that he had read the book twice. 'He's a fascinating guy,' he told the *Irish Times*. 'He was a big adviser to Clinton, who has huge, huge regard for him. He continued on that road with Bush and Blair as well. I'm glad to say we were talking to him before either of them, since the early 1990s.'

Another invitee to the Ballyconnell get-together was Maureen Gaffney, who was asked to speak on the child-care issue, which continued to be a political challenge. She put her heart and soul into her address.

> The entire issue during the Celtic Tiger years had been about labour supply and the need for more creches. I argued that this was a golden moment. I tried to re-orientate the debate towards the big issue: children and their future. I wanted money spent on early child care and education. There was absolutely no argument about the benefits. There is a boomerang effect, with a return for every euro invested.
>
> It is particularly beneficial to the disadvantaged, but I argued that it should be universal. It can help support communities and [with a universal system] the most resourceful parents in the community become a resource to the service. I spoke with as much passion as I could muster.
>
> The Government did take up some of the recommendations, but I was looking for a 'big bang' moment, something like the introduction of free secondary education. It could be a moment like that, a great legacy of the Celtic Tiger era.
>
> I argued against giving money to everyone, which I suppose was a brave thing to do. I said there was no guarantee that it would be spent on children's welfare. It might be spent on a foreign holiday, or to put in a deck.

Gaffney thought the politicians had a concern that giving money to early child care and education would be seen as discriminating against the stay-at-home mother, especially in the wake of the row over Charlie McCreevy's introduction of individualisation for income tax assessments in his 2000 budget. She felt that the stay-at-home mother was something of a myth. Rich mothers didn't work, but they put their children into creches so that they could pursue other activities. Extremely poor mothers didn't work because they couldn't afford child care.

> Politics overshadowed the longer-term view. There was a very strong idea or ideology at the time that people should be given their money back. How receptive was Bertie? He invited me there. But I didn't get the impression it was a eureka moment for him. I think he thought in a very political way.

Brian Cowen in his first budget speech in December 2004 announced another increase in child benefit rates and pointed out that they had increased by a whopping 270 per cent since 1997. But throwing vast amounts of money at the problem hadn't made it go away. Indeed, it might even have fed into the issue. Just as there is a correlation between house prices and the amount of credit available, there is a correlation between the number of households where both parents are working and house prices. The greater the household income, the more a couple can afford to pay for a house, and the more house prices rise. The more expensive housing became, the greater became the pressure on young parents to both have jobs. Encouraging female participation in the work force created a positive-loop system, with one factor influencing the other in an upwards spiral.

In his budget speech of December 2005 Cowen announced the Government's new child-care strategy. He said the Government wanted to help all parents by widening their options. 'Having carefully considered all the complex issues involved, the Government has developed a five-year strategy to tackle the problem.' The Government had decided to support the provision of more child-care places and to assist in the care in the home of children in their first year through extended maternity leave. It was going to address 'cost pressures' by providing an entirely new payment: an early child-care supplement for all children of less than six years of age. When announcing the measure, Cowen pointed out that child benefit that year would cost €2 billion. This compared with €500 million only five years earlier. He had decided that the most effective way of dealing with the continuing pressures being felt by the parents of young children was to introduce another payment. Everyone, regardless of whether the parents were both working or not, would receive €1,000 per annum per child until the child reached six years of age. The new scheme would cost €353 million a year. The Government was going to spend more on giving out money than it would have cost to establish a system of pre-school education, even though the world by then knew of its benefits.

In March 2009 the Competitiveness Council published a statement on competitiveness and training, which spoke about the need for a state-run system of pre-primary schooling for children of three years of age and more. Despite the recession that was by then well entrenched, the development of a universal pre-primary system was seen as a 'key long-term priority' mirroring the steps taken over past decades in primary, secondary, tertiary and 'fourth-level' education, it said.

Pre-primary education is considered the most important level of education in an individual's cognitive development, as educational progress is cumulative for most individuals. Participation rates in state-funded pre-primary are extremely low in Ireland by international standards. The percentage of Irish three-year-olds in state-funded education in 2005 was 1.7 per cent compared to an EU average of 82.2 per cent.

A month later, when introducing an emergency supplementary budget, the Minister for Finance, Brian Lenihan, announced the decision to scrap the early child-care payment introduced by Cowen in 2006.

It is of course true that what experts suggest should be done and what politicians believe to be politically achievable are two different matters. Nevertheless, the gulf between what many believed to be important requirements for the future development of Irish society and what the Ahern Governments chose to do was noticeably wide. This in turn, it should be noted, set an unfortunate example for people in all walks of life.

Chapter 16 ∿

| BOIL AND BUBBLE

T he short version of Irish economic history during the Ahern years
breaks into halves to such an extent that it bolsters the case that it was
the circumstances and management of the first half that led to the
catastrophic events of the second. Indeed, in a speech to the Institute of
International Finance in Washington in October 2010 the Governor of the
Central Bank, Prof. Patrick Honohan, described what had happened to
Ireland in exactly such terms. He referred to the American economist
Robert Schiller, whose book *Irrational Exuberance* (2000) predicted the
collapse of the dot-com bubble, which ended in March 2002. (The second
edition, published in 2005, waved a warning flag about real-estate prices in
the United States, which peaked in October 2007.) Schiller examined why
markets can run wild and why bubbles occur. Included in his analysis were
such non-economic issues as hype in the media, herd behaviour, the nature
of optimism, and how people listen to others' messages despite their better
judgement.

Honohan told his audience that it was the half-truths of the late 1990s that
had led to the myths of the 2000s. In a speech concerned with how Ireland's
banks could have lost so much money, he linked Schiller's views and the Irish
experience.

A pulse of optimism, built on a faulty analysis of the potential from some
new technological or institutional development, starts a wave of
optimism, reinforced by processes of collective psychology that build a

myth on this half-truth. For Ireland, the combination of rapid but solid and sustainable convergence to full employment and high income in the 1990s—the period known as the Celtic Tiger—with the low interest rates promised by euro membership formed the basis of the myth or half-truth which triggered the bubble.

Fig. 2: Foreign borrowing by Irish banks, 1999–2007 (€ billion)

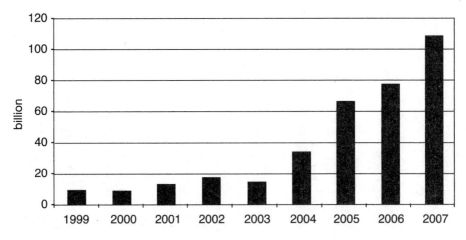

Source: Central Bank of Ireland.

The first-half, second-half analysis of the Ahern era can be divided in a number of ways. There is the first and the second Governments. There is the treatment of income tax: rates were reduced significantly during the period to 2001, while credits and bands were extended significantly in the period thereafter. McCreevy was Minister for Finance for the first half, Cowen for the second. The banks' reliance on funds from abroad was modest during the first half but grew rapidly during the second. The wealth of the country was earned during the first half but borrowed during the second. Ireland had its own currency in the first half but was part of the euro for the second.

Half time does not fall at exactly the same moment for all these factors, but the structure of the narrative is fairly clear. It is not the intention here to go through all the factors in any detail, though one point deserves to be made: despite what Ahern would say later, he and his Government colleagues were warned about the dangers of the pro-cyclical budgetary stance they adopted for almost the entire Ahern period. Ahern did not respond to those warnings by having second thoughts about strategy or even by taking a breather and worrying for a bit before deciding to press on. Rather, he ignored what was being said and, if that didn't work, reacted as if the warnings were threats to his political position, sometimes verbally assaulting those who had dared to speak. There is little evidence that any of his Government colleagues were opponents of what was going on.

Fig. 3: Budget packages, 1999–2008

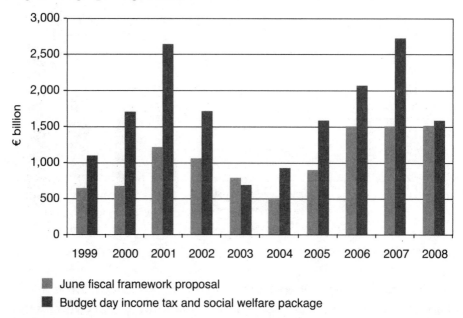

June fiscal framework proposal
Budget day income tax and social welfare package

Annual budgets exceeded the advice of the Department of Finance. Note the spikes just before the two general elections.

Source: Rob Wright, report on performance of Department of Finance. Reproduced with permission.

Growth rates such as 10.1 per cent and 8.7 per cent are phenomenal for a developed Western economy and are well above what economists would describe as sustainable. The collapse of the Irish economy at the end of the Ahern era was the largest for a Western economy in the period after the Second World War.

In money terms, the growth equated to a gross national product of €83 billion in 1996, €161½ billion in 2007 and €139½ billion by 2010. GNP is a measure that tends to exclude the activities of multinationals, which export their profits.

Fig. 4: GNP, annual change, 1996–2010

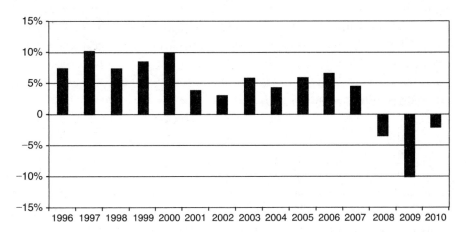

Source: Central Statistics Office.

As can be seen, the spectacular growth began before Ahern's period in power and McCreevy's cuts in tax rates and continued towards—but did not quite reach—the May 2002 general election. The economy then trod water until, at the first sign of green shoots, confidence returned. When the property market revived, reckless lending by the banks became a distorting factor in economic growth.

The revived property boom soon turned into a bubble. House prices soared, and land prices soared even more. Property developers and speculators began to factor future expected increases in property prices into the price they were willing to pay for land. In other words, when estimating how much a field outside a town in Co. Leitrim might be worth, they would calculate how much could be made from selling houses built on that field in a year-and-a-half's time, when house prices in the area would be a certain percentage higher than they were when the field was bought. Speculators in the main urban centres made similar calculations, and the banks issued loans based on these calculations. Builders turned into speculators and developers. Bankers, accountants, architects, doctors, dentists, gardaí, teachers and others joined in. At times it seemed that the whole state was involved, not least politicians such as the former Government minister Frank Fahey, from Galway, and the Fianna Fáil senator Francie O'Brien, from Monaghan. Behind the boom in asset prices was a wave of credit issued by the banks, who were in turn borrowing the money abroad. No-one outside the world of banking appears to have noticed; inside the world of banking regulation, no concerns arose that we know of, and no effort was made to clamp down on what was happening.

One effect of the bubble was that the construction sector began to take over, or to account for more and more of the economy. At its peak it employed 13 per cent of the work force. Elements of the economy outside the construction sector suffered. Much of the multinational exporting sector has very high productivity and so is not so sensitive to wage increases; but for the Irish exporting sector this did not apply. Whereas the domestic and exporting parts of the economy were roughly equal in 2001, by 2006 exports were less than 15 per cent of the economy.

In November 2008, when it was beginning to dawn on everyone what a hames had been made of the economy, the Society of Chartered Surveyors held its annual conference in UCD. Prof. John FitzGerald delivered an address, 'Blowing Bubbles and Bursting Them'. He presented some astonishing figures: Ireland had about 570 dwellings per thousand of population, but only 477 of these per thousand were occupied (only Spain had a similar gulf between existing and occupied dwellings); in Ireland in 2005 housing had comprised 13.9 per cent of GDP, compared with 4.6 per cent for France and 3.9 per cent for Britain. The average for Ireland over the period 1970 to 2005 was 6.1 per cent.

Before Honohan became governor of the Irish Central Bank, he said in a paper called 'What Went Wrong in Ireland?' (written for the World Bank in May 2009), that growth in Ireland up to 2000 had been on a secure, export-led basis, underpinned by wage restraint. However, from about then a property price and construction bubble took hold, which sustained employment and output growth until 2007. Property booms and easy credit were an international phenomenon in the first half of the new century, but Honohan pointed out that the Irish property boom had started much earlier, and lasted longer, than those in surrounding jurisdictions. The three-fold increase in prices in the period 1994–2006 was the highest boom in any advanced economy in recent times. 'Long before it peaked, it looked unsustainable to most commentary.' Nevertheless, from 2003 the banks continued to ease loan conditions such as loan-to-value ratios.

Competitive pressure on the leading banks to protect market share came especially from reckless expansion by one bank, Anglo Irish Bank (whose market share among Irish-controlled retail banks jumped from 3 per cent to 18 per cent in a decade, as it increased its total portfolio by an average of 36 per cent real). Foreign-controlled banks, especially the local subsidiary of HBOS [Bank of Scotland (Ireland)], also contributed.

For some reason, bank regulation was 'complacent and permissive'. It failed to impede the growth of Anglo-Irish Bank and allowed the reckless lending practices to spread. By 2006 two-thirds of loans to first-time buyers had loan-to-value ratios of 90 per cent; one-third were getting 100 per cent loans. Banks funded the lending surge with huge borrowings of their own, and increasingly they got the money from abroad. By early 2008 net foreign borrowing by Irish banks had jumped to more than 60 per cent of GDP, having been just 10 per cent in 2003. Although many economists have pointed the finger at the euro as the cause of this, that argument does not stand up to examination, given that banks in many European countries that were not in the currency also borrowed wildly in the international markets. The international markets grew complacent about risk, and money was easily available.

Blair Horan pointed out that early in the Ahern period the banks began assessing mortgage applications in accordance with affordability and the applicant's take-home pay. The more conservative measure of two-and-a-half times salary was abandoned. This meant that each cut in income tax by the Government fed directly into house prices. It also meant that when tax rates had to be increased later, the borrowers were put under increased strain just as the economic circumstances they were operating in were deteriorating.

The huge borrowing abroad by the banks went largely unnoticed in public debate. However, the price of property, the scale of the construction sector and the loss of international competitiveness were all factors remarked on by serious domestic and international economists from 2004 on. Given that there was so much concern about the reality of the values being ascribed to housing and property generally, the banks' views on loan-to-value ratios are all the more bizarre. The combination of high property prices, high loan-to-value ratios and short-term foreign borrowing by the banks was to prove calamitous for the Irish public. During the boom years the Government had rapidly reduced the national debt and also put large amounts of money into the National Pension Reserve Fund, which was created by McCreevy in 2001 to help pay social welfare benefits and public-service pensions from 2025. However, in the first decade of the new century private-sector Ireland was creating a pile of foreign debt that would in time, through the Government's handling of the banking crisis, be converted into public debt and so undo the debt reduction that had occurred over the previous period.

The general Government debt as a percentage of GDP stood at 95 per cent in 1993 but dropped to 74 per cent by 1997, 36 per cent by 2001 and 25 per cent by 2006. This was well below the European average and was one of the indicators used at the time, when many commentators stated that Ireland was one of the euro zone's healthiest economies. By 2011 its debt-to-GDP ratio was back at the level of the late 1980s.

It was not just house-buyers who were finding it easy to get money. Money was being handed out with gay abandon to an increasing number of people involved in property investment, speculation and development. For example, Bernard McNamara, a developer and former Fianna Fáil councillor in Co. Clare, appears to have gone on a spending spree funded by the banks in the later, most overblown years of the property boom. Originally a builder, he became heavily involved in a range of deals, usually in partnerships with other developers and investors. McNamara was involved in the purchase of a €416 million site in Ringsend in 2006, one of the largest transactions of the boom and one that turned a cash-rich Dublin Docklands Development Authority into a financial basket case. With others he bought the Shelbourne, Conrad, Montrose and Burlington Hotels in Dublin, the Great Southern Hotel in Co. Kerry and the Radisson Hotel in Galway, as well as the Superquinn Group. He was also involved in an elaborate scheme of purchasing property between Grafton Street and South Great George's Street in Dublin with a view to building a new link between the two. A financial services firm that investigated McNamara's affairs in 2009 estimated that he had borrowed more than €1.4 billion in the period since 2005.

When the downturn came there was little surprise among those who were concerned with such matters that Anglo-Irish Bank and Irish Nationwide had been involved in a spectacular level of recklessness. Banking literature stipulates a limited number of classic reasons for bank failures, among which are the presence of a dominant individual within the institution and above-average rates of growth. Anglo-Irish had Seán FitzPatrick, a chief executive who went on to become chairman, against all rules of best practice. Nationwide had Michael Fingleton, a man who appears to have run the supposed building society as a personal fiefdom since the 1980s.

Among the professions that got involved in property investment were the bankers themselves. Some senior executives and members of bank boards invested heavily in property and property development at the height of the bubble. Fingleton and FitzPatrick were serial investors. Some senior executives in different banks went into business together. John Hughes, head of business banking with AIB in Eyre Square, Galway, developed a substantial property portfolio in Galway with Tom Browne, a one-time contender for the top job at Anglo-Irish Bank and the head of Irish operations with that bank up to 2007. The properties included a substantial Galway office property built by

McNamara where their tenants included the state. Hughes also had property dealings with Tommy Hopkins, a senior executive with AIB Bankcentre, Dublin. Their company, Banagher Investments Ltd, took out mortgages from Anglo-Irish on property in Stoneybatter, Dublin. Hughes was involved in property dealings in partnership with Galway businessmen who separately banked with AIB in Galway. When everything fell apart for McNamara he gave an interview to Mary Wilson on RTE radio's 'Drivetime' in which he said that during the boom years the banks 'sought out' people like him.

The level of reckless lending by AIB, one of the largest and most successful commercial institutions in Ireland, came as more of a shock to observers. It emerged that the bank, under the chairmanship of Dermot Gleeson SC, a former Attorney-General, had become concerned about the growth of Anglo-Irish and what it perceived to be the taking of its natural clients. A drive was initiated to win back many of the developers who had moved to Anglo-Irish, and in this effort to attract these customers the bank lowered its banking standards. It did so just as the bubble was about to burst, and the disastrous policies pursued resulted in the bank coming under majority state ownership. These developments involved an enormous loss of wealth for the banks' shareholders and, eventually, for the population generally.

At the core of the whole disaster was the astonishing failures of those who were charged with regulating the banks. Brian Patterson, who accepted a request from McCreevy and Harney to be the first chairperson of the Financial Regulatory Authority, which he chaired until 2008, later told RTE that the focus was very much on consumer protection and that insufficient attention was given to the robustness of the banks, because the idea that they might fail seemed outlandish. The chief executive of the authority during the bubble years was Pat Neary. What is clear is that the regulator knew about the reduction in lending standards, the greater reliance on property business and the increased borrowing from abroad.

An interesting aspect of the whole affair is the way Michael Fingleton was left in *de facto* sole control of a financial institution. It was known that people could approach him and that he could personally approve a loan. Many business journalists over the years did so, especially back in the 1980s and early 1990s when it was difficult to secure a mortgage. Fingleton usually charged a high rate. It appears that his powerful position within Irish Nationwide was generally recognised in the political world also. Michael Lowry gave evidence to the Moriarty Tribunal about going to Fingleton when he was a Government minister in the mid-1990s and getting immediate approval for a 100 per cent loan on a house in Blackrock, Co. Dublin. In September 2006 McCreevy and his wife, Noeleen, were given a €1.6 million loan to buy a property valued on the Irish Nationwide files at €1.5 million. The property was in the к Club golf resort in Co. Kildare. Irish Nationwide documents later seen by Simon Carswell of the *Irish Times* showed that the loan was an interest-only one and was granted nine days before the Ryder Cup competition on the club grounds. A Fianna Fáil senator and former chairperson of Monaghan County Council, Francie O'Brien, borrowed millions from Irish Nationwide for his investment dealings. Fingleton was involved in approving the loans even though he personally later got involved in business dealings with O'Brien. Fingleton and O'Brien, along with two others, borrowed €13 million from Ulster Bank to buy fifty acres in Co. Cavan, near the border with Co. Monaghan, on which they hoped to build houses. When the Mahon Tribunal began inquiring in 2008 into the house in Phibsborough that Celia Larkin had bought in 1993 using money from the в/т account, Fingleton personally authorised the fast-track loan for €40,000 that Larkin used to repay the money she had been given to buy the house.

One way of getting a handle on the scale of the economic mismanagement in the bubble years is to consider taxation. By 2007 stamp duty was accounting for €3.2 billion of the €47.3 billion taken in by the exchequer in taxes. A large amount of the VAT, income tax and capital gains tax going into the exchequer was also coming from the property sector. This inflow of tax money allowed for the reduction in income tax rates and the exclusion of many workers from the income tax system at the same time as the Government oversaw a rapid increase in public-sector expenditure. When the property bubble collapsed a lot of the tax take went with it. Stamp duty fell by two-thirds, to €1 billion by 2009. VAT, which was €14.5 billion in 2007, fell to €10.6 billion two years later. Capital gains fell from €3.1 billion to €500,000. A large amount of the fall in income tax also arose from the collapse of the construction and property sector. The state found itself trying to deal with the colossal losses of the banking sector while also facing the challenge created by a huge hole in the public finances.

People had borrowed from the banks to buy housing or invest in property development and, when doing so, had factored in the cost of stamp duty and other taxes. This meant that a significant amount of the tax take during the bubble years came from people who had borrowed the money from banks that in turn had borrowed it abroad. When the market collapsed and people found themselves with debts that exceeded the value of their assets, the strain of dealing with the situation was added to by the need of the state to increase taxation. The excesses of the bubble years were literally being paid for in its wake.

By late 2010 the state could no longer borrow abroad and had to seek recourse to the EU and the IMF. The mismanagement of the economy by the Ahern Governments was such that Ireland's economic sovereignty had to be in part conceded.

Prof. Laffan was on the board of the NESC during the period of the second Ahern Government.

> We produced a report on housing, and I sat through the discussions on housing week after week, because it takes months for a report to get through the system. Peter Bacon was there at the time. John FitzGerald. The whole issue was about affordability. No-one actually said, 'Is there something going wrong here?'

The report was published in December 2004. Laffan remained on the NESC board right through the heart of the bubble years. There was a lot of conversation about land speculation and what to do about windfall profits, but no-one mentioned the possibility that the size and rate of growth of the property sector might contain a danger for the banks.

> The first person who I heard raise really serious concerns was Morgan Kelly, down the corridor here. In fact at the time Morgan's office was [near Laffan's in UCD]. Our administrator, Mary Buckley, said, 'Would you keep him away from me? He's terrifying me.' He was the first. He looked at the history of housing bubbles and came to the obvious empirical conclusion that they always end the same.

The view within the NESC, according to Laffan, was that if the Irish economy imploded it would be because of a global implosion. In other words, domestic policy was fine. A commonly held view among economists and economic commentators, many of whom worked for financial institutions, was that there would be a soft landing. 'People convinced themselves that this time it is different,' said Laffan. 'It must be deep social psychology. It is not rational.'

Morgan Kelly's first powerful broadside appeared in the *Irish Times* in December 2006.

> Offering no evidence except wishful thinking, estate agents and politicians assure us that we have nothing to worry about: the Irish housing market can look forward to a soft landing. If, however, we look at what has

happened to other small economies where sudden prosperity and easy credit drove house prices to absurd levels, we should be very worried indeed. If experiences of economies like ours are anything to go by, we may be looking forward to large and prolonged falls in real house prices of the order of 40 to 50 per cent and a collapse of house building activity.

In July 2007 Kelly followed up his article with a paper published by the ESRI in which he said that up to 60 per cent could be wiped off the value of Irish housing over an eight-year period. Kelly had studied almost forty property booms and crashes that had occurred in the OECD countries since 1970. 'Typically real house prices give up 70 per cent of what they gained in a boom during the bust that follows,' he wrote. However, he pointed out that because of the strong growth in new houses built in recent years and the number of housing units lying empty, the housing bust in Ireland had the potential to be worse than the OECD average.

The paper was a serious contribution by a professor of economics published by Ireland's premier research institute—an institute founded by one of Ahern's predecessors in an effort to improve policy performance. Ahern gave his response to the article, and to other warnings that were by then emerging, in an aside to an address to the ICTU on the day the Kelly paper appeared.

Sitting on the sidelines or on the fence, cribbing and moaning, is a lost opportunity. In fact I don't know how people who engage in that don't commit suicide. The only thing that motivates me is to be able to actually change something.

Ahern's comment on suicide elicited laughter and clapping from his audience, though he later apologised and said it was well known that he was very involved with the Suicide Action Group. He said he had only meant to get at people who are 'always against things and looking around at things.'

It wasn't as if he changed his tone as the concerns about the housing sector grew more widespread. In September 2007, at the annual Fianna Fáil think-in, Ahern spoke out about people 'talking down the economy' and referred to recent comment that the economy was in danger of collapse. 'I don't know which wizard wrote it,' he said. 'How can you talk about an economy collapsing and it growing by 6 per cent?'

By this time Kelly had moved on to consider the effect of a sharp property downturn on the banking sector. 'Banking on very shaky foundations' was published in the *Irish Times* on 9 September 2007. Kelly pointed out that, while mortgage lending had been slowing since the middle of 2006, lending to builders and property developers was continuing to grow rapidly. In the previous year such lending had increased by €20 billion, to €100 billion, with €20 billion being the equivalent of the share capital of the Bank of Ireland. All the Irish banks' capital, and a substantial chunk of its depositors' cash, was now riding on these loans. Since 2000 lending to construction and real estate had risen from 8 per cent of Irish bank lending, a European norm, to 28 per cent. Just before the Japanese bubble burst in 1989, bank lending to the sector stood at 25 per cent. Japan had not yet recovered. International experience showed that when markets turned, developers tended to walk away, leaving the banks, and often the exchequer, to pick up the pieces. Since the beginning of the year, he said, sales of new homes had not slowed: they had collapsed. Yet 80,000 new 'units' were due to be completed in 2007, and a further 60,000 were on stream for the following year. The Government's decision to abolish stamp duty for all first-time buyers, intended as a fillip to the housing market, had meant that young people found buying second-hand houses as attractive as buying new ones. According to Kelly, it had put an unintended final nail in the coffin of the new homes market.

He raised the prospect of the state having to bail out the banks, as had happened in Japan and Finland in recent years. His estimate, €15 billion to €20 billion, was far short of what would eventually turn out to be the case. He then said:

> You probably think that the fact that Irish banks have given speculators €100 billion to gamble with, safe in the knowledge that taxpayers will cover most losses, is a cause for concern to the Irish Central Bank, but you would be quite wrong.

But Ahern wasn't listening to university professors or other disinterested observers. Just as he had an apparent dislike for blue-blood Fianna Fáil politicians, he had an aversion to academics and intellectuals. He and his party's fund-raising operations always had a close connection with the building sector, and during the property bubble years some of these people became enormously wealthy (or certainly appeared to be). They flew around in helicopters, had palatial homes, got married on yachts formerly owned by Greek shipping magnates. Many, if not most, were men who had finished their education after secondary school: self-made men. They crowded around Ahern at his annual dinner in the Kilmainham Castle and in the party's Galway tent fund-raiser.

The annual shindig at the Galway Races became a symbol during the Ahern years of the connection between the builders and his party. It was an in-your-face phenomenon, with the people who gathered to drink champagne with the country's political leaders the beneficiaries of the multiple tax schemes that continued to exist right through one of the most sustained property booms in the Western world since the end of the Second World War.

Ahern's character as revealed in the witness box of the Mahon Tribunal was that of a man who foresaw difficulties long before they bubbled to the surface and who devised strategies for dealing with them long before most others knew of their existence. He was an intelligence man, a man who sought information, studied it, absorbed it and linked it together. Yet he genuinely appears to have been unaware of the grave financial dangers that were created during his second Government. According to Rabbitte, Ahern's focus on the political aspect of everything is part of the explanation for this. He also believed that Ahern's habitual wariness and worry was more focused on his own personal situation, and on the financial skeletons in his personal cupboards, than it was on dangers to the well-being of the state.

> He had access to anyone in the country, but he didn't seek out the advice of people he didn't want to hear from. I was always immensely impressed by Bertie's grasp of detail, despite what people might think, and it came not just from doing his homework. No Irish politician ever, in the history of Ireland, including Daniel O'Connell, had such frequent interaction with so many people. You could see at ordinary, boring question time, as distinct from leader's question time, that Bertie had hoarded the detail that had been whispered in his ear when he was at a party event in Clonakilty and the local builder or businessman told him something, or when he was at an IBEC dinner and they told him something, or a trade union leader told him something.

Ahern had a tremendous facility to absorb and regurgitate data.

For every economist or ESRI paper that warned him of the dangers that existed, there were scores of bankers and property developers and local politicians telling him the opposite, said Pat Rabbitte.

> The builders were whispering in his ear, 'Don't listen to that bearded academic [economist John FitzGerald], sure he's fucking Garret's son, what do you expect? Let me tell you about the project I have, Bertie. I have this project in Chicago; I'm gone to Canary Wharf now. I'm going to do a marvellous job on the quays.' I mean they had direct access to him ... The show he ran out of Luke's is a temple to modern-day lobbying. I

mean the people who mattered got in there to tell him what they thought. Bertie was there for a long time, and all the evidence was around the place that those guys were right in the past, so why shouldn't they continue to be right?

For Rabbitte, the Galway tent, in the main treated lightly by the media and the general public during the boom years, was a terrific representation of how Ireland was governed during Ahern's tenure. Haughey, he said, would never have got away with anything so vulgar. 'There is no Calvinist tradition in Ireland,' according to Rabbitte. 'If people had a job and things were going well, they were willing to turn a blind eye.'

Miriam Lord used to attend the Galway races each year and report on who was in the tent. At first, she says, there were people such as the millionaire tax exiles Michael Smurfit and J. P. McManus there, but they drifted away, and it became the haunt mostly of builders, developers and auctioneers. She doesn't think many deals were done there. 'It was more like a dating agency for developers and politicians, an introduction service, where they can touch base and exchange numbers.' Later again some people decided it wasn't good for them to be seen there, and they began to stay away, though most didn't care. 'Near the end it got such a bad name, it was always oversubscribed, but it was a lot of PR companies bringing clients who wanted to be able to say they had been in the Galway tent, even though there was no-one of any great note there, apart from Bertie and the occasional minister.'

However, the lavish parties thrown by the developer Bernard McNamara for his guest of honour, the Taoiseach, continued to the end.

There would be a big party in Bernard McNamara's penthouse suite in the Radisson Hotel, I think on the Thursday night. Ahern was paraded around as the guest of honour. There was always a lot of vulgarity. One of the prime movers was always asking if I wanted a lift in the helicopter anywhere. There was a lot of them staying in Ashford Castle and places like that, and they would come up on the chopper.

At the McNamara parties you could have anything you wanted. There would be about sixty guests. Bollinger champagne was freely available. The penthouse had a panoramic view over Galway Bay.

Near the end the atmosphere was very strange. The final year he had that reception there was a strained atmosphere; people knew the good times were maybe coming to a close, and Bertie's troubles were beginning to emerge, so there was a feeling that things were maybe on an edge.

Chapter 17 ～

AHERN, EUROPE AND MONETARY UNION

In the wake of the Irish banking collapse—perhaps the greatest ever in relation to losses as a proportion of a country's economy—the Government commissioned an inquiry into how it could have happened. Prof. Patrick Honohan had been appointed Governor of the Central Bank, the first holder of the office in a long time who was not a former secretary-general of the Department of Finance. (Ireland's practice of appointing former secretaries-general was an exception in Europe, where it was seen as contrary to the fostering of independence.)

Seen from the Fianna Fáil backbenches, Honohan was an outsider. While the party, and Ahern in particular, had shown an aversion to informed public debate and analysis during the period 1997–2008, Honohan was the sort of man who was most happy in an economics workshop exploring the solidity of the arguments being put forward. His appointment, brought about by the depth of the crisis in which Ireland found itself, was part of a process whereby the dislike of data and argument that had marked the previous decade was swapped for the opposite.

As part of the inquiry, two outside experts, Klaus Regling and Max Watson, were appointed to draft a report on the international and domestic backdrop to the disastrous performance of the Irish banking sector. The report in turn led to a consideration of its contents by an all-party committee of the Oireachtas, the Committee on Finance and the Public Services, which received assistance from a professor of economics at Trinity College, Philip Lane. The committee reported in November 2010 and recommended such measures as multi-year budgets and the establishment of independent councils that would comment on the economy and the performance of budgetary policy so as to generate a more informed budgetary debate. (The distance between this idea and the practices of McCreevy is worth dwelling on.) The report recognised that during boom periods the public finances should be run in a counter-cyclical way. In other words, the public finances should be used to cool booms and counter economic slow-downs. A rainy-day fund would be created, into which money would be put during boom years, thereby dampening economic growth during the upswing in the economic cycle. The money could be used to stimulate the economy during slumps and would stop the state having to go to the markets to borrow. It also envisaged a lot more economic data being collected and analysed, and the boosting of the intellectual performance of the Department of Finance.

Almost everything in the report was an implicit criticism of the way the state was run during the Ahern Governments. 'The setting of formal fiscal frameworks forces government policy to avoid short-termism or "capture by elites".' In the press release accompanying the report it was stated that in a single European currency the state did not have all the tools it formerly had to control macroeconomic policy (devaluation of the currency and the setting of exchange rates), so the Government had to pay attention to the new environment in which it operated when considering its economic policies. Fiscal policy would have to be run in a 'new way', said the committee chairperson, Michael Ahern, in his introductory comments.

Considering the fact that the single currency was launched on 1 January 2002, and had a long lead-in, it was a surprising statement. It was the equivalent of saying, half way up a high mountain, that in future when setting out on a hike the family would put on appropriate clothes and bring something to drink. Debate had taken place in the period before the euro on how economic policy would have to accommodate the new circumstances, but it had not been absorbed by Ahern or his Governments. When I asked Micheál Martin to what extent the loss of the interest rate mechanism featured in the Government's consideration of fiscal policy, he was clear that the new currency was welcomed for providing low interest rates. That it required the introduction by the Government of fresh ways of dampening down economic activity when the economy was threatening to overheat appears not to have framed Government debate on fiscal policy.

According to Laffan, an element of 'soft Euroscepticism' emerged in the first Ahern Government as the 1990s drew to a close. Laffan, who is regularly turned to as an expert on EU affairs, recalled a comment made to her at a party.

> It was a very casual comment. Someone said to me, 'Ah, Brigid, Europe is over. You are going to have to find something else to do.' It was someone senior in Fianna Fáil, not a politician. And I felt immediately that something was happening, that that person wouldn't have said that to me if they weren't operating in a milieu where that was being said. It was 1999. We'd had a great roar of the Tiger, very high growth rates, so obviously there was a sense of arrogance.

At the time, she was with the Policy Institute in Trinity College and was working on a paper entitled 'Organising for a Changing Europe? Irish Central Government and the European Union'. She went around the system interviewing senior politicians and civil servants. 'I picked up on the fact that somehow or other Europe had gone down the hierarchy in terms of interest.' The state had just come through some budgetary talks with the EU and secured that issue for the coming period. At the end of her paper she wrote that Ireland was in danger of losing its moorings on Europe. 'And it did.'

Reviewing the change in Ireland's relationship with Europe, Laffan cited the row McCreevy had had with the European Commission and the European Council in early 2000 over budgets that the Europeans believed were unwise because they were pro-cyclical or were boosting rather than calming matters. Ireland's economy was booming, but interest rates, because of the currency project, remained low. (Normally interest rates are raised to cool a booming economy and lowered to boost a flagging one. Euro-zone interest rates are set to suit the needs of the entire currency area.) McCreevy 'put on the green shirt', according to Laffan. This began a period when, for the first time, the Commission was portrayed in Ireland as other than its 'best friend'.

In a speech to the American Bar Association in the Law Library in Dublin in July 2000, Mary Harney said the relationship of the Irish people with the United States and the European Union was complex. 'Geographically we are closer to Berlin than Boston. Spiritually we are probably a lot closer to Boston than Berlin.' Ireland, she said, was a country that believed in economic liberalisation, the incentive power of low taxation. Ireland had sought to steer a course between the European and American outlooks but had 'sailed closer to the American shore than the European one.' She didn't want key economic decisions being taken at the Brussels level. Ireland wanted regulation but not over-regulation. She repeated the views in a later article in the *Irish Times*, and the Boston v. Berlin idea entered popular debate on Ireland's EU membership.

In September 2000, in an address at Boston College, Massachusetts, the Minister for the Arts, Heritage, the Gaeltacht and the Islands, Síle de Valera, said she was frequently asked when abroad about the Celtic Tiger. A number of factors had helped create it, including 'our ability to take advantage of our membership of the European Union.' However, the development of the union in the period since Ireland joined had seen decisions other than economic ones being taken. 'We have found that directives and regulations agreed in Brussels can often seriously impinge on our identity, culture and traditions. The bureaucracy of Brussels does not always respect the complexities and sensitivities of member-states.' De Valera said she looked forward to a time when Ireland would 'exercise a more vigilant, a more questioning attitude to the European Union.' It was, according to Laffan, the most Euro-critical speech ever delivered by a serving Irish minister. She does not believe that such speeches would have been made when Ireland was receiving large budget transfers from Europe.

This developing tone of 'soft Euro-scepticism' fed into the Nice Referendum in June 2001, in which a low turn-out voted 54 to 46 per cent against, creating a dilemma not only for Ireland but also for the union on which it was so heavily dependent. According to Brigid Laffan,

> Suddenly we had a problem with the EU, and Ahern understood very quickly that he needed to get Ireland back onside. One thing about Ahern is that he recognised constraints pretty quickly. He responded very quickly . . . And that then dampened down that Euro-sceptic end of the cabinet.

While the tension between Dublin and Brussels created by McCreevy's expansionary budgets in the period before the 2002 election eased with the downturn of those years, Laffan believes that Europe continued to be concerned about Ireland's economic policies, the erosion of its tax base and its pro-cyclical budgetary policy.

However, Ireland was the poster boy of the Baltic and Eastern European countries that were lining up to join the EU. For them Europe had been a huge stabilising factor in the wake of the collapse of the Soviet Union, since it was clear that nationalist tendencies would have to be suppressed and parliamentary democracy developed if they were to gain entry to what they saw as the rich men's club. Acccording to Laffan, politicians and senior civil servants from these countries rolled in to Dublin wanting to talk about Ireland's experience of EU membership.

> Ireland had been a poor country and was now a rich country. And in the history of the EU, Ireland is the only country that came in a poor country, below 75 per cent of the average per capita income, and converged [with the average income]. No other country has ever converged except Ireland. It is an extraordinary achievement. Right up to before the Single European Act [1987], our per capita incomes were still way down, around 65 per cent of the EU average. We were still way off, until the single market came. I'm convinced structural funds helped, but it was the single market that drove it in the end, coupled with the devaluation in the early 1990s.

Fig. 5: Income per capita relative to EU average, 1991–2010

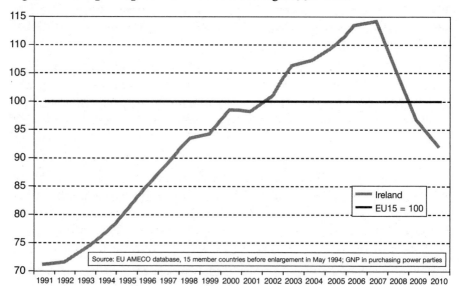

Source: Rob Wright, report on Department of Finance. Reproduced with permission.

There was another difficulty. The single currency had a set of rules governing borrowing and debt levels for member-states. Seen from the point of view of these rules, Ireland was again the star pupil. It was running government surpluses and paying off its national debt, driving it down to levels below the European average. How then could it be criticised as an errant member of the euro club?

The period when Ahern was in power was one of tectonic shifts in the global economy. Countries like China and India were selling ever-increasing amounts of manufactured products to the richer countries. The huge savings they amassed became available for the global financial system, and this in turn tempted many countries, companies and people to take on excessive debt. Western countries found themselves involved in a heavily globalised marketplace with competitor economies that had wage levels far below the Western norm. Technology boosted the capacity for outsourcing. Blue-collar income in many Western economies, including the United States, has fallen in real terms over recent decades, and the income level of the middle classes is treading water. Capital, meanwhile, has benefited from lower wage costs and access to the global marketplace.

The development of the European banking system saw banks moving into new markets. New entrants into the Irish market increased competition at the same time as money became more easily available in the international markets. This increased banking competition and new access to unlimited cheap money occurred as the Irish economy had just come through a period of exceptional economic growth. As Regling and Watson put it,

> this fostered expectations of a continued rise in living standards and in asset values. Another factor, with even deeper roots, was the strong and pervasive preference in Irish society for property as an asset, and the fact that Ireland never experienced a property crash.

Regling and Watson made it clear in their report that they were not saying that what occurred was inevitable. They pointed out that prudent Government policies aimed at mitigating the risks of the boom-bust cycle could have increased the chances of a soft landing. However, the opposite path was the one chosen.

> Fiscal policies heightened the vulnerability of the economy. Budgetary policy veered more towards spending money while revenues came in. In addition, the pattern of tax cuts left revenues increasingly fragile since they were dependent on taxes driven by the property sector and high consumer spending.

Ireland was also unusual in having so many property-related tax reliefs but no property tax. Regling and Watson pointed out that such was the level of tax reliefs available during the Ahern years that in 2005 the OECD calculated that the cost of giving these reliefs was greater than the actual amount of income tax collected.

The failure at the Government level was accompanied by the spectacular failure at the banking and supervisory level, as well as by that of the civil service generally. The performance of international bodies such as the OECD and the IMF was patchy. Although some did strike occasional warning notes about what was going on, in general the criticism was muted, and it was accompanied by other commentary of praise for, and even awe at, the Irish performance.

According to Greg Sparks, a Taoiseach and a Minister for Finance need to be 'apart from as well as a part of.' He meant that they should at all times be standing back from what is going on, even if it is their own work, and questioning its wisdom. He doesn't think that Ahern, McCreevy or Cowen did this during their periods in office. 'I think they listened to their own propaganda.' Criticism was not invited and was sometimes nastily repulsed. When John FitzGerald and some of his colleagues in the ESRI warned about the dangers of the Government's fiscal policies in 2000, McCreevy dismissed them as 'pinko-liberals'. A few days after the comment, Ahern, during a trip to a meeting of the Irish Management Institute in Cork, referred to a kind of 'creeping Jesus' who was always criticising Government policy but had been shown to be wrong. Some commentators

> always want the glass to be half empty ... Provided we maintain our discipline, we will have great pleasure in confounding the pundits in the City of London, Brussels and Frankfurt, who, blinkered by orthodoxy, still cannot quite understand how the Irish, of all people, have managed to get it right.

The nationalism involved in the response is interesting, but what is most important is that this was the Taoiseach and leader of Fianna Fáil responding to considered comment by senior members of the organisation set up by Lemass to provide continuing analysis of economic policy.

In March 2001 the ESRI published a paper by John FitzGerald entitled 'Fiscal Policy in a Monetary Union: The Case of Ireland', in which he said that in a monetary union the handling by a government of its finances—fiscal policy—can affect wage inflation and the allocation of resources within an economy. By the latter he meant that money and economic activity can be directed towards or away from particular sectors.

For example, fiscal policy can have a significant effect on the domestic housing market through changing household disposable income and through changing the cost of capital for homeowners. The tax treatment of interest payments on house loans can have a big effect on the cost of capital for homeowners. Because the legal instrument under which the mortgage lending takes place is country specific, the taxation or subsidisation of mortgage interest payments is not affected by the country of residence of the financial institution making the loan.

By the latter point FitzGerald was saying that, although banking was becoming more international, it was still possible to use the treatment of mortgages—which were specific to countries—to affect housing. Because of monetary union, the rate of interest charged was no longer under the control of the Central Bank. But, instead of the Central Bank raising interest rates to calm the housing market, the Government could alter its treatment of mortgage interest payments and have the same effect.

To date the fiscal policy instrument has not been used actively in Ireland to reduce demand for housing in the current boom. It remains possible for the government to eliminate interest relief on mortgage interest payments in the income tax code. In addition there are a range of other fiscal measures that could directly reduce demand pressures in the building sector.

FitzGerald's suggestions that taxation be used to calm the housing market and that special tax incentives for building be removed were of course not listened to.

For Laffan, the concern that was created within the European Commission about the management of the economy by McCreevy's policies in the period before the 2002 general election never went away. Asked for her view on how we managed the transition to becoming a member of a single currency, she gave a stark reply.

We didn't. We didn't take on board the fact that as a member of a single currency we had fewer instruments and levers in terms of our economy: we didn't have devaluation to regain competitiveness. Given the state of the German economy at the time, we were likely to have a low interest regime, and we had a booming economy, and we didn't understand [the consequences of this]; or if we did we ignored it because it made political sense to ignore it. We continued to behave as if we weren't in a single currency, and the consequences have been disastrous.

They didn't sit down and think. It would have required Finance to put on paper to the cabinet about what being in a single currency means. Did they do that? I suspect not. I doubt if McCreevy was in that mode. I don't think McCreevy saw a constraint. I think he saw: reduce taxes. He was very much at the liberal end in terms of his economic philosophy and outlook. I think he was [in favour of] less state, less regulation, and let the country fly. You know, capital gains tax, he really was very pro-enterprise in an extraordinary way. So I can't imagine he ever wanted something to go to cabinet saying 'Constraint, we need to tie our hands behind our backs.' I can't see it.

Laffan said that when interviewing senior civil servants throughout the departments in the late 1990s she formed the impression that there was something wrong with the Department of Finance, and she reported her view to the Department of the Taoiseach. She felt it was a department that was not performing as well as it should. One of the surprising aspects of the department that came into focus after the collapse of the economy was the absence of any serious research component. Laffan contrasted the department's brainpower with the finance ministries of other European states, where large numbers of economists at the PhD level and higher conduct research on the economy that their department is managing. Indeed, a number of economists and social researchers spoken to by the present writer in the period since the crash mentioned this failure to encourage research, and not only by the Department of Finance. Amazingly, industrial relations issues may in part be behind the phenomenon, as the grading structures that operate do not allow highly qualified economists and social scientists to be paid at rates approximating what they might get outside the public service.

However, it is difficult not to believe that there may have been political reasons for this failure of management, ones relating to not wanting a civil service that would challenge its political masters. Certainly there is a widely held view that independent views were not encouraged in the Department of Finance, or elsewhere in the public service, during the Ahern years.

Pat Rabbitte is of the view that the rapid increase in the rate of pay of the state's senior civil servants might have softened them and in an indirect way prompted them to acquiesce in the unwise economic policies being pursued by their political masters.

It worries me if you look at it now that Alan Aherne writes a few articles in the *Irish Times* and the next thing he's the chief economic adviser; Peter Bacon is in charge of banking; Colm McCarthy is in charge of public expenditure. You are almost driven to the conclusion that if you are an economist it's not safe to walk down Merrion Street or someone will grab you and drag you into Finance and give you a job. What the fuck were they doing before this?

Laffan, for her part, says that the Irish interaction with Europe has been mixed and that some aspects of how we engage with Europe are very successful. She does not believe that the performance-possessor explanation offered by Prof. Lee in *Ireland, 1912–1985* is an accurate or full one. 'It is too much of a silver bullet,' she said. The fact is that there has been excellent performance in some sectors, notably in relation to industrial policy and the attraction of foreign investment but also in relation to many of the ways in which Ireland has interacted with Europe.

What is clear is that Ahern's period as Taoiseach, and McCreevy's period as Minister for Finance, followed by his period as EU Commissioner, coincided with a change in the European view of Ireland as a 'good European'. In April 2011, during a visit to Dublin, the EU's most senior civil servant, the Irishwoman Catherine Day, who is the secretary-general of the EU Commission, said that the 'shine' had gone off Ireland in Europe and that it had lost the good will that had formerly existed. 'The perception is that the more prosperous Ireland became, the more arrogant it became, and the less it engaged. It shouldn't be a fair-weather engagement.'

Blair Horan said that when he is abroad meeting colleagues in European civil service trade unions, he encounters annoyance that Ireland, having been allowed into the euro club, went on to mismanage its affairs at a cost to the club generally.

Ahern and his Governments did not seem to understand that the management of a boom and the transition to a single currency involved a new and substantial challenge for political leadership. He did not seem to understand that because of the one-off and historic nature of what was occurring there was an onus on him to devise strategies that would make the most of the opportunity he had inherited. He appears to have been fixated on short to medium-term growth but to have had little by way of interest in how growth could be used to establish an optimum medium to long-term environment for maximising the well-being and potential of Irish society.

Laffan sees an explanation for this in the struggles that dominated public life during Ahern's early political career. When he became Taoiseach he did not see his role as bringing the country to the next stage.

I suspect he thought he *had* brought it somewhere. He had inherited an economy in very good nick in 1997. I mean the rainbow Government . . . Ruairí Quinn turns out to be the last good Minister for Finance we had. I think Ahern thought we had arrived.

KESHCARRIGAN

On the day I went from Dublin to Co. Leitrim to have a look at housing developments there, the Met Office was warning of an impending period of unusually cold weather. Snow was expected by the weekend. On the radio all the talk was of the external financial assistance that Ireland was receiving from Europe and the IMF, the extent of the loss of sovereignty involved and the role that Ireland's finances were playing in the crisis buffeting the euro and the EU. Anger and dismay among the public was such that Fianna Fáil's popularity ratings were falling to levels where its continued existence had become a topic of conversation. Bertie Ahern's place in the history books was going to be very different from the one he had dreamed of.

I pulled in near Enfield, at the new motorway stop on the M4, for a late breakfast and a look through the morning newspapers. When I was getting up to leave I was greeted by a former multi-millionaire publican and hotelier sitting at a nearby table. We'd met down at the courts when his businesses were being put into receivership by the banks. It was a cold day, we agreed, but beautiful too. He was heading to the west.

On the road between Longford and Carrick-on-Shannon I got my first glimpse of boom-time housing estates built on the edges of towns and villages. For some reason a type of ice-cream yellow was the colour of choice. The houses were large, and the estates in the midst of the otherwise monotonous grey-green countryside looked like some alien crop that was threatening to grow out of control. Every now and then I passed a would-be mansion adrift in a field, the site abandoned, the structure half built and open to the rain and the wind.

I'd chosen Carrick-on-Shannon because of what Ruairí Quinn had told me about his surprise at being asked, during a visit there when he was Minister for Finance, whether or not he would grant special tax designation status to the whole county. In the town I met the local estate agent Liam Farrell of DNG Farrell, a brother of Pat Farrell, the chief executive of the Irish Bankers' Federation and former general secretary of Fianna Fáil. We met in Liam's office looking out at the Shannon in a new development alongside the

Landmark Hotel. He remembered the meeting with Quinn and what he said was a more encouraging encounter with the then Taoiseach, John Bruton. What you have to remember, he said, was the economic situation at the time in Co. Leitrim. 'It was appalling.'

The county was a poor backwater known for bachelors and suicide. The only thing going for the county at the time, according to Farrell, was that its young people had the highest per capita involvement in third-level education. 'It was a meal ticket out.' Such organisations as the Irish Farmers' Association, the chambers of commerce and the business community generally felt that Co. Leitrim was being overlooked by the Government and was in need of a fiscal stimulus.

With the change of Government in 1997 the lobbying effort switched to Fianna Fáil. Charlie McCreevy was targeted even as the groups involved feared that they had already missed the boat. Shoppers from Carrick-on-Shannon were going to Sligo, Mullingar and even to Liffey Valley. Designation was granted to Co. Leitrim and other counties in McCreevy's 1998 budget and, according to Farrell, the people who had lobbied for it were ready to put it to full use. 'Some town renewal efforts didn't work. But here there was co-operation, and in 1999 the town took off.' The back end of the town, where the Landmark Hotel and Farrell's offices now stand, had been the 'backside' of Carrick-on-Shannon, an area of swamp looking out on the river. But piles were driven down to the rock below, and developments such as the one we were sitting in were constructed. 'It was very exciting, and there was a trickle out to other towns where it was viable.' It is difficult for outsiders, he said, to understand the psychological effect the arrival of such places as the Landmark Hotel had on the general population—the lift it gave people just to walk into its lobby and know that this was a new, top-class hotel, and in Leitrim. The tax exemptions were 'the most important bit of fiscal legislation for Carrick ever.'

At the end of the period for which the designation had been allotted there was still a bit of work to be done, and a six-month extension was granted. By about 2002 the work had been done, according to Farrell. 'The main players, who got in early and did quality stuff, moved on elsewhere.' He himself, along with a partner, built an award-winning multiplex cinema. An indoor swimming-pool was built which attracted people from miles around. New shops such as Tesco set up in the town. The streetscape was improved beyond measure.

However, the Government continued to extend the scheme. The people who had lobbied for the measure in the first place were not lobbying for these extensions, Farrell said, though obviously some parties were. The incentives began to attract 'a lot of people who did not have experience and who didn't build what was needed.' His firm was involved in selling the vast bulk of what was built, but he felt that 'from 2003 the good had gone out of it.' Yet what was being built continued to sell, and prices continued to rise. After a few years 'you felt like a fool if you said you thought it was going to end now.'

Some questioned who was going to live in the housing that was being built, even though people were not leaving the county like they used to, and even though there was some immigration. The US credit card company, MBNA, set up a service centre in the town employing a thousand people—something that would not have happened if the housing for its staff members had not existed. The Department of Social Welfare moved some of its administration to the town as part of the decentralisation process.

> It was after 2003 that the development outside the town happened. People pushed the envelope out, to locations that were a bit iffy. Planning permission was granted, and sites were sold on to builders. Builders have different skill sets to developers. They're not the same. Developers tend to do more research. Not all of them are builders. Some builders built in the wrong place. Meanwhile, Ireland kept forging ahead. Credit was so available and property was so in flavour. It was a kind of intoxication.

Now the town has to deal with the fact that it has all collapsed. According to Farrell, getting the people who had built the houses and the office developments to sell at radically reduced prices is not easy. 'People can be very tied up in a scheme emotionally. For many it was an important part of their life, and it is difficult for many of them to adjust to what has happened.'

Even while believing that what occurred was a disaster Farrell retained a kind of optimism. The whole ghost-estate story had been overdone by the media, he said. The houses that were built could be put to some use, but prices needed to fall even more than the 40 to 60 per cent by which they had already dropped—likewise with the glut of hotels built because of the unwise tax incentive scheme for the sector promoted during the boom. When the price for hotels dropped low enough, he said, people would be willing to take them on and run them in a viable way. Commercial property deals in Carrick-on-Shannon sometimes involved a rent-free first year, giving new businesses an opportunity to get off the ground. If dealt with cleverly enough, what had happened could be put to good use and form a basis for increased vitality in the town.

But what will not go away is the low architectural standards and design values that were allowed. Throughout the country the whole phenomenon of tax incentives for property has formed the basis for a huge proportion of the 'built environment', but no effort was made to create something admirable— something that future generations would be able to value and admire. Farrell criticised the Department of the Environment for allowing tax incentives for houses that don't have wooden doors or natural slate. Hand-made brick should be allowed outside Dublin. 'It was a missed opportunity.'

Afterwards I went driving out the road towards Leitrim. As you come close to the village the estates begin to appear. I pulled into one called Cois Abhann, a development of sixteen detached houses, each with exposed brick and yellow plastered walls. The doors and windows are PVC. The four-bedroom houses, a large sign advertises, qualify for section 23 tax relief. I stopped beside one of the few houses with a car outside the door and garden furniture in the garden to the rear. The man who opened the door was renting. He said that about half the houses were empty, that some of them were shells, without proper kitchens or proper flooring. I told him what I was doing. He suggested that I visit an estate on the other side of the road, a few hundred yards closer to the village.

Tax designated announced the large roadside sign indicating the presence of this estate. *Des Foley and Sons proudly presents Dún Carraig Céibh, an estate of three-bedroom townhouses, four-bedroom semi-detached, and four-bedroom luxury detached houses.* The development is off the main road, up a steep, curving entrance that brings you to a small roundabout, the townhouses in an arc facing you, a turn to the left leading straight into grass, the turn to the right leading into the rest of the estate. The roadway continues along the crest of the hill; there are some semi-detached houses on the right, yellow and cream, some exposed brick. The road ends at a metal and wire barrier that traverses it, beyond which there is no tarmacadam, but there are a number of large, detached houses looking down over the land and the small lake below. One of the houses is a distinctive blue. The glass in the windows still had stickers attached. Inside, you could see rolls of yellow insulation on concrete floors, interior doors lying where the workers had laid them. There was even a rusting yellow tipper. It was an on-land version of the *Mary Celeste*. Snowflakes began to fall.

A young woman who lived on the estate pointed me towards two of the houses that were owned by their occupiers, but no-one answered when I knocked. A man out for a smoke at a nearby house was happy to talk. He told me he rented from the man who built the houses, Des Foley, owner of

Gerti's pub in nearby Keshcarrigan. He thought Foley still owned most of the houses, renting out some of them. There were signs offering houses for rent, home-made signs like the ones you might see elsewhere in the countryside offering free-range eggs or strawberries for sale. I decided to head for Keshcarrigan.

To get there you have to drive back towards Carrick-on-Shannon and then take a left. The road is narrow and winding; the land to each side looks unpromisingly soggy and poor. Lakes large and small appeared and disappeared as I travelled along what at times resembled a lane more than a road. The sun had fallen below the horizon, and the sky had turned a mix of black and grey when I crossed a bridge and arrived in the village. Gerti's was almost the first building on the left, just after some tall and weather-beaten hoardings advertising new housing. The village was a short string of houses and shops. I parked by the old stone Garda station and made my way back to the pub.

'You ask, and I'll tell you whatever you like,' said Des Foley when I explained what I was doing. The pub was empty save for an elderly man watching a boxing match on a widescreen television. There was a fire burning and a friendly wooden bar, but the temperature was too low to call the room cosy. I suggested that, instead of my asking questions, he would just tell me his story, where he was from, how he came to build Dún Carraig Céibh.

He agreed. He grew up just outside the village, on a small farm of poor land, though his late parents would not have been happy to hear him say that. 'They fought hard enough for it.' He went to London to work in the 1960s, when he was sixteen years old. It was what young men did. One Christmas thirteen of the fifteen boys who'd been in his class in school were in London. He worked on English building sites for seven years and then came home in 1974 to help his parents, who were growing old. He worked on their thirty acres and did some plastering on the side—any construction work that came his way. After about five years he started a tool hire business with a former school friend, Noel Doherty. They worked together until 1991. Then he bought the pub.

At the time, the Shannon-Erne canal was being developed, and he decided to call the pub Gerti's Canal Stop. One year ten television crews called to the pub, one including Jill Dando. The pub did okay, and in the meantime he was doing some construction work on the side. Not much, because there was no money. By the time the tax designation scheme arrived in 1999 he had some sites and extra farm land, and he and his son built a few one-off houses. Then, in 2001, he built a development of twelve houses in Keshcarrigan, 'a big development then.' The houses were priced at about €65,000 each. One or two were bought by local people, and the rest were bought by investors and people from Dublin who wanted them as holiday homes or to shelter rental income from other property they owned. (People with substantial income tax bills could reduce or erase their bills by buying housing in Co. Leitrim and other designated counties.) One house he sold for about €60,000 was resold for €149,000 about five years later. His next development, again in Keshcarrigan, had twenty-four houses and three commercial units. The units now house a hairdresser's, a restaurant and a solicitor's office.

'People who were passing on the canal saw the houses, the quality, the cost, the nice location. The word spread.' Houses that had cost €65,000 were now worth €100,000, then €150,000. The price of sites and materials went up, and the cost of labour doubled. His next scheme had thirty-six houses in it. At one time he was doing 'two houses a week, and I had fifty lads employed. I had lots of customers. I'd say, I have a new site, and they'd say, Hold one for me.' Some people were buying houses because their tax accountants were telling them to.

The one on the hill—Dún Carraig Céibh—was to be the last of them. He had already had enough of it, and then he heard that the Minister for Finance, Brian Cowen, was extending the scheme once more, for six months. 'We all went mad building because of that,' he said, though he is not trying to shirk responsibility.

> We were all over twenty-one years of age, and we could have known there were too many houses being built. But, as Bertie Ahern would say, if you weren't being positive you were being anti-Irish. The advice from everyone was 'Go at it, yeh boy yeh.'

He wasn't worried. He had promises from prospective customers, people he had dealt with before. They liked houses in Co. Leitrim because of their size, their quality and their price. AIB, his banker, said, 'Go, go, go!' They encouraged him to buy the site, and the money for the development was 'there in a week.' Foley said it was his policy to put his own money into the developments so that the bank was being asked to put up only 50 per cent.

Then, in August 2007, he noticed a change. The showhouse went on view, and people were interested, but then some said they couldn't shift houses they were going to sell before buying his. 'Even at that stage some people were saying it was only a year's blip.' He thought people in Carrick-on-Shannon might buy them, because they were up to €100,000 cheaper than similar houses there. He sold about one-third of the scheme. The rest lies empty still.

It's not a question of what am I going to do with it. It is a question of what will the bank tell me to do with it. I'm one year trying to get an interview with the bank manager.

Foley has used his own resources to fit out and furnish some of the houses, which he has managed to rent. He would like to complete the development. 'When you put thirty or forty years' work into something, you like to see it completed.'

The housing bubble provided manual employment for the local men, many of whom learnt valuable trades. Now many of them have gone away, to Britain or the United States. Some are still at home but are on social welfare. Despair has returned to a region where the suicide rate has at times been among the highest in western Europe. He hears it in the pub, Foley said, people talking about it. He draws a finger across the front of his neck.

Bertie Ahern once came into the pub with a local Fianna Fáil man. 'The two of them stood there with their mouths open. "Right," I said, "the bar's over here. Who's ordering?" And they just left. They bought nothing.'

INDEX